'Nothing can equal Egremont's account of one of the last Nazi atrocities of the war, in January 1945, when 7,000 starving Jewish prisoners on a death march from Konigsberg – the capital of East Prussia – were driven into the frozen Baltic and shot or drowned by SS guards . . . Egremont has written a book that tries to make sense of this history – not as a single, chronological narrative, but as a sequence of short, interconnected essays in which measured reflections, portraits of the leading political and cultural figures and conversations with exiles from this "forgotten land" are interwoven. Egremont's allusive prose style seems to echo these multiple perspectives: changing frontiers, blurred racial identities, shifting allegiances and the mass movement of people – a story for our time.'
New Statesman

'The experience of reading Max Egremont's wonderful evocation of the final years of East Prussia is like watching a film whose images you know will stay with you for years to come.'   *Country Life*

'Max Egremont is an admirable writer: painstaking in his research, elegantly humorous, coolly fair-minded, a man of deep sympathies but with no swagger to his keen intelligence. Egremont will take me into terrain where I have never been.'
Richard Davenport-Hines, *History Today*

'His poetic writing captures the atmosphere of the region, intensified by the voices of those he met. Above all, *Forgotten Land* bursts with life stories, from the landowners of old to those that survived expulsion after the war or have returned since to a land that will never be forgotten.'   *We Love This Book*

'Max Egremont has been fascinated by this lost world and all its contradictions for years and his new book mixes a personal quest with the strange history of the place . . . Represents the very best form of travel writing'   Anthony Beevor, *Mail on Sunday*

'The book's canvas is remarkable . . . Egremont's compelling tale exploits his boundless intellectual curiosity, mastery of German and eye for whimsy as well as tragedy . . . his literary journey through [East Prussia's] past makes fascinating reading.'   *Sunday Times*

FORGOTTEN LAND

MAX EGREMONT was born in 1948 and studied
Modern History at Oxford University. As well as four novels,
he is the author of *The Cousins* and *Balfour: A Life of
Arthur James Balfour*. His acclaimed biography of
Siegfried Sassoon was published in 2005.

MAX EGREMONT

FORGOTTEN LAND

Journeys Among the Ghosts of
East Prussia

PICADOR

First published 2011 by Picador

First published in paperback 2012 by Picador
an imprint of Pan Macmillan, a division of Macmillan Publishers Limited
Pan Macmillan, 20 New Wharf Road, London N1 9RR
Basingstoke and Oxford
Associated companies throughout the world
www.panmacmillan.com

ISBN 978-0-330-45660-9

The publishers gratefully acknowledge Carcanet Press for permission to
reproduce lines from Edmund Blunden's 'Can You Remember' from his *Selected Poems*,
edited by Robyn Marsack 1982, copyright © Edmund Blunden 1982.

A CIP catalogue record for this book is available from
the British Library.

Map by ML Design
Printed and bound by CPI Group (UK) Ltd, Croydon, CR0 4YY

Visit **www.picador.com** to read more about all our books
and to buy them. You will also find features, author interviews and
news of any author events, and you can sign up for e-newsletters
so that you're always first to hear about our new releases.

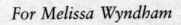

For Melissa Wyndham

Contents

List of Illustrations

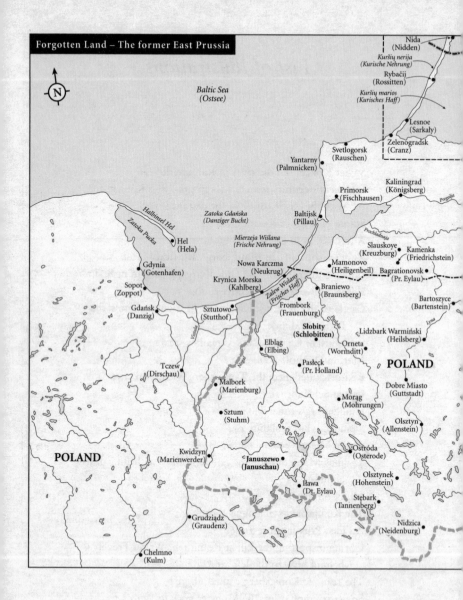

Forgotten Land – The former East Prussia

Introduction

Marjellchen is a restaurant in a street of monolithic apartment blocks off Berlin's Kurfürstendamm. It's a dark place inside, heavily cosy, almost a caricature of a certain antique Germanness. The clutter includes beer tankards and ancient marzipan boxes, armorial shields (one from the old Königsberg, now the Russian Kaliningrad), pictures of deer in the wild, of castles, harbours and twisting medieval streets, of wide lakes and forests. Glinting bottles of central European spirits line the bar, also evoking the old times: the Aquavit Samländer, East Prussian Kartoffel (potato) Schnapps, Pillkaller, Trakehner Blut. 'Marjellchen' means girl in a now rarely spoken dialect from hundreds of miles away, in a land now divided between Russia and Poland – the old East Prussia.

Speaking German, I ask the waiter for a menu. He smiles a little condescendingly, walks across to a desk and brings over one that has been translated into English. The fare is sturdy stuff, appropriate for long, snowy winters. It's hard to choose between Creamed Herrings East Prussian, Smoked Ham of Deer, Fried Cockerel Legs, Grapevine Snails, Fillet of Pork Squire's Style, Masurian Jugged Game, Grandmother's Semolina Blancmange.

Is Marjellchen a gathering place for those with roots in the province that ceased to be German when the Red Army stormed through it in 1945? Later, as I leave, two middle-aged couples are standing outside and I ask why they chose Marjellchen. Were their families originally from what the restaurant owner's East Prussian grandmother called her 'cold' Baltic homeland? The four of them laugh. One of the men says, no, they know nothing about

East Prussia, gesturing with his hand as if to push the place away: nothing at all. It's Marjellchen's food that they like – good sustenance to protect you from the winter wind.

*

East Prussia was on the edge. Perhaps this historic pressure on its people – their anxiety and sense of threat, how they faced these – was partly what drew me there from Britain's island safety. East Prussians used to talk of going into the Reich, particularly during its last years, as if travelling to the mother country from a distant outpost. After the First World War, the province was cut off from the rest of Germany by the Polish Corridor, the thin strip stretching south from the Baltic that had been given to the new Poland in the Treaty of Versailles. Many East Prussians felt the need to stress, before and after their homeland's extinction in 1945, that the place had been German for five centuries. Stalin had brought about the huge population change, seizing their identity. The Germans were expelled and Poles and Russians moved in.

What were these supposedly long-lasting frontiers? Over time, they had changed as the borders of Prussian districts, the frontiers of Poland and (since 1871) those of Germany shifted. After the Treaty of Versailles, East Prussia's western frontier was along the River Vistula, east of Danzig (now Polish Gdańsk). It stretched eastwards along the Baltic shore and south to what was then the new Poland's northern frontier, then north-east, including Königsberg, up through Tilsit (now the Russian Sovetsk), over the River Niemen to the most eastern town of pre-1945 Germany: Memel (today the Lithuanian port of Klaipėda).

Five centuries of continuous German life, it's said – since the Teutonic Knights, a crusading order of chivalry, had set out in the thirteenth century to conquer this remote land for Christendom, converting or killing (like the crusaders in the Middle East) its pagan people. So East Prussia evolved into the German Empire's most eastern redoubt, tramped over by invaders. Immigrants sought refuge there from persecution in the rest of Europe, from anti-Semitic Russian tsars, from French Catholic kings or Austrian archbishops.

This makes nonsense of any claims of racial purity. In January 1945, the eleven-year-old Arno Surminski fled his village in the East Prussian district of Masuria, with most of the inhabitants and his parents. The Red Army caught up with them, they were marched back and the older people deported to the Soviet Union, leaving behind Arno, who never saw his parents again. Later, as a writer in the west, Surminski thought of his lost homeland as an extraordinary mix – a small part of Asia, invaded by Tatars, also the country of the old pagan Prussians, the Lithuanians, the Russians, the Poles, the Ukrainians, the Teutonic Knights, the Germans, the Huguenots from Catholic Europe, the Turks and the Mongol invaders, the Swedes during the Thirty Years War, the French under Napoleon.

In the sixteenth century, with the ending of the Teutonic Knights' control of the region, Duke Albrecht, the Hohenzollern ruler of East Prussia, swore allegiance to the King of Poland, bringing the land into the Polish–Lithuanian Empire. In the seventeenth century it passed by treaty into the lands of the Hohenzollern Elector of Brandenburg whose descendant was crowned King in Prussia in Königsberg in 1701.

Duke Albrecht called on his fellow European rulers – Henry VIII of England, the Holy Roman Emperor Charles V, King Ferdinand of Hungary and Bohemia – to support him against the Turks (the Asiatic hordes) who threatened civilization: a rallying cry of Christendom used five hundred years later by Goebbels against the invading Red Army. In twentieth-century Germany, East Prussia could seem an anachronism, still a bastion of the Junkers, the militarized aristocracy from east of the River Elbe that provided much of the officer corps of the German army. Yet Königsberg was the city of the philosopher Immanuel Kant and, in the eighteenth and early nineteenth centuries, a place of astonishing intellectual discovery. In East Prussia there was tolerance and bigotry; after 1871, in the newly united Germany, it became increasingly fearful and reactionary – against threats real and imagined, in the form of the Poles, the Bolsheviks or economic decay on the edge of the new Reich.

In 1945, the bastion crumbled. The northern part – Königsberg and its ice-free port, an enclave about the size of Northern Ireland – was taken by Stalin for the Soviet Union; the rest joined the new communist Poland. More than most of Europe, East Prussia is strewn with symbols of a turbulent past – in its buildings, its ruins and its graves. Poland has absorbed the southern parts, with a few remaining tensions. In the north, the Russians of the Kaliningrad region find themselves cut off from the rest of Russia since the early 1990s by a Poland and a Lithuania now outside what was the Soviet bloc, places they go to increasingly often. Many Kaliningraders compare their lives not so much to those of other Russians as to those of Poles and Lithuanians in the European Union, and, although dissatisfied, have hopes of change.

For Germans, however, East Prussia is a memory – one that they can shape into myth and regret, fading perhaps but still a reminder of how they once were, in what their forebears thought of as their country's (and civilization's) most eastern redoubt. A place of reconciliation, of fantasy or of hope: perhaps, after its last painful years, this is now East Prussia's destiny.

1: The Whispering Past

I think of a long line of people, walking slowly across an empty winter landscape – victims of what was done to others in their name. Duisburg is on the River Ruhr, in what is still, despite comparative decline, one of the most heavily industrialized parts of Europe. It's a town for manufacturing – cars, machine tools, construction equipment, chemicals – in the post-war Germany of pedestrianized shopping streets, bland medium-rise offices and apartment blocks built mostly after the medieval centre was bombed: not much that is extraordinary here, you might think. But one of the signs outside the railway station points to the Museum of the City of Königsberg, a reminder of a very different place, a lost country thousands of miles to the east.

The route goes through a shopping district, past a piece of public art – a vast brightly painted bird standing on two short fat legs that revolves slowly above a pool of murky water, mostly ignored by passers-by: again nothing strange, just a botched municipal attempt to brighten up the northern winter. To the right of this, down a side-street, is what remains of an older Duisburg: the gothic town hall, a dark Lutheran church, medieval brick walls, the river and the converted warehouse that houses the city museum, opposite one of the largest and oldest enclosed cranes in the world.

It's raining so I walk quickly, glancing at the small boats parked in a marina on the Ruhr. Has a country ever been so patronized, or looked at with such vicarious excitement or ghoulish fascination, as Germany since 1945? The British of my generation (born in 1948) are particularly guilty of this. It's as if they want to revive some old theatrical production, sinking into plush velvet seats to sigh, gasp and (sometimes) laugh at warmly familiar lines. In this drama, bad news is satisfying – gains for extremist parties, skinhead demonstrations, crass remarks by a German minister about Poland or the Jews. Yes, the audience thinks, this is how it should be. They can never escape. Our recent past is good, theirs is terrible; we'll always have this over them.

We want to be shocked in Germany, like children on a fairground ghost train. Years ago, when learning German, I'd sat eavesdropping in Munich cafés, picking through fragments of older people's talk – about holidays in Spain, children, grandchildren, deaths, births, an overvalued Deutschmark – for glimpses of the bad old times. My haul was meagre – only a few words that, creatively scanned, could almost hurt: a brief tirade, for instance, against the smell of Turkish kebab houses. There must have been plenty of veterans available then to deliver monstrous opinions while sitting on geranium-filled balconies, against Alpine views – people only superficially rinsed in post-war bleach – but they avoided me.

Surely it's better to try to reach the fear that lay dark in people's minds – and in the Duisburg museum I start the search. When I ask for the Museum of the City of Königsberg that is somewhere in this building, the woman at the desk suggests I might like a ticket that includes everything. I accept – and go quickly past the art, the pottery shards, the glassware, the seals and the ancient implements up some stairs to a long, wide room where there are no people, not even security guards.

This memorial to Königsberg, once the capital of the German Empire in the east, gets few visitors – but the glass-topped cases and boards of printed text tell much about the drift of modern Europe. For Königsberg, the end started with huge British air raids on two nights in August 1944 before the surrender to the Red Army some eight months later. The display here in Duisburg has a sense that because so much was destroyed, every drop must be squeezed from what survived – early books, drinking tankards,

ornate amber boxes or models of ships, advertisements for businesses in the old city, costumes of the student duelling clubs where
young Prussians proved their courage.

The last case shows ruin – rubble, bullet-holed street signs,
one for the Horst-Wessel Strasse, named after the Nazi hero. The
journey towards this brings back a better past, often through
those who lived in or left their mark on the city – Martin Luther,
Napoleon, Kant and his fellow philosopher J. G. Herder, the artist
Käthe Kollwitz, the last German emperor, William II – before
Hitler and the end in April 1945. Rebirth comes in photographs
of German–Russian reconciliation in Kaliningrad, the Soviet
place that Königsberg became. The Germans were ordered out,
the Soviet commanders reporting to Stalin that the last one had
gone in 1948. What's left of them now is an archipelago of
memory: Marjellchen with its Pork Squire's Style, archives of photographs, accounts of the good old days, recordings of elderly
voices and infrequently visited museums threatened with cuts.

Some months later, I go to Lüneburg – a serene, small town
north-east from the Ruhr region, about twenty miles or so inland
from the Baltic coast, its partly medieval centre immaculate, as if
washed by loving devotees. The place is quiet outside the main
shopping streets: particularly deserted around the East Prussian
Landesmuseum, a new (or newish) structure of brick and glass,
dazzling on a harsh, bright day. This silence seems far from
changing frontiers and disputed identity. At the end of the last
war there were over a million refugees from the old eastern territories in Lower Saxony, in and around Lüneburg, and further
west in Schleswig-Holstein – and many settled here.

The East Prussian Landesmuseum's hall is light and empty,
perhaps because the exhibitions are seldom crowd-pulling with
their displays of restored textiles, traditional rugs, information
about coastal erosion or different types of Baltic fish. Other sec-
tions deal with aspects of the old country; soon the charts, the
boards of information, the blown-up photographs and the stuffed
animals and birds begin to crowd in. Over it all is the landscape:

the Kurische Nehrung (the Curonian or Curland Spit, or Peninsula, that juts into the Baltic); Masuria with its thousand lakes; the
nineteenth-century overland canal; Rominten heath and forest,
south-east of the horse stud at Trakehnen – the hunting land; the
elk woods east of old Königsberg; the bird life at Rositten, on the
Curonian Lagoon. This could be a hard country – where fishermen
were reduced to catching crows in nets for food in winter, biting
into the birds' necks to kill them without damaging the meat.

As in Duisburg, Kant and his time feature strongly – Königsberg's (and East Prussia's) intellectual high point. As in Duisburg,
cases show amber boxes, jewellery, tankards, crucifixes, ancient
knives and examples of the goldsmith's art before the section on
East Prussian culture and artists like Käthe Kollwitz or the writers Agnes Miegel and Johannes Bobrowski, who tried to reconcile
nostalgia with truth. Out from Königsberg are the country districts; most of East Prussia was rural, sending corn and horses and
timber to the rest of the Reich from drained and difficult eastern
lands. The section on the years after 1918 – the creation of the
Polish Corridor that cut East Prussia off from the rest of Germany
– has photographs of people voting in the plebiscites when they
were asked if they wanted to be in the new Poland or the new
Germany (there were massive majorities in favour of staying
German): a reminder also not only of the nationalistic Tannenberg Memorial but that from 1920 until 1932 Prussia was led by
the Königsberg Social Democrat, Otto Braun. Then comes the
end: the British air raids and the Red Army's victory.

The display boards have grim statistics: of the hundred thousand people in Königsberg in April 1945, when the German
commander General Otto Lasch surrendered, only twenty-five
thousand survived to join the German exodus in 1947–8. Two
hundred and forty thousand refugees from East Prussia had
arrived in Denmark as the war was ending. From January to April
1945, some four hundred and fifty-one thousand people were
taken by ship from Pillau, Königsberg's port; between a hundred
and eighty thousand and two hundred thousand crossed the

frozen sea to the Frische Nehrung, or the Vistula Spit, the thin peninsula that reached westwards, the counterpart to the eastward-pointing Kurische Nehrung. Another five hundred thousand reached the peninsula over the ice from points west of Pillau. The refugees suffered strafing and bombing. They were often caught by the Red Army and captured, raped or killed.

One model shows part of the great trek or flight to the west, its mock-up figures wrapped against the cold, walking with horses and a tractor and carts piled with agonizingly chosen possessions: the pain dulled by the belief that, after the peace treaty, they would come back. Those left behind could expect little mercy. In February 1945, the Russians began the forced deportations from the districts outside Königsberg although the city had not yet surrendered. The journeys in goods wagons could last from three to six weeks to often deadly Soviet work camps in the Urals or on the Don.

While I am looking at the section on the Rominten game reserve, an old man pops out from among the stuffed creatures of the wilderness – the lynxes, wolves and fish eagles, the snow owls, buzzards, bison and elk, and the hunting trophies, the formidable stags' heads, some shot before 1914 by the Emperor, one killed in 1943 by Rominten's last master, Hermann Göring. The old man is small, brown-faced with short grey hair and alert eyes. He says that he grew up in a village near the forest, now in Poland, just across the border from the Kaliningrad district of Russia. He doesn't care who knows it but the Poles have turned his old home into shit (*Scheisse*) – he went back ten years ago and was nearly sick.

Can this be a part of the display, I wonder – laid on by the museum? I ask where he lives now. Outside Lüneburg, he says, and he comes here often since he retired. What's gone can never come back. Yes, the place is – and he repeated the word – *Scheisse*; he wanted me to know. Then he clasps my arm, smiles and walks off. If it is a tableau, he won't be overworked. There's no one else nearby.

*

East Prussian survivors often look back to an enfolding sweetness. In the country districts particularly, the routine had a
security of its own. Winter came in November with the fitting of
secondary windows inside the permanent frames, the hanging up
of woollen clothes to rid them of the smell of moth-repellents –
before white sharp days and clear star-filled nights or freezing fog
that burned off quickly in the morning sun. You travelled by
sleigh to a soft flow of bells, wrapping yourself up in sheepskin
rugs, or tobogganed or skated on icy fields where drains had burst
or skied to neighbours or watched the ice-sailing regattas on the
Masurian lakes, cradling hot drinks and eating bratwurst. Christmas meant marzipan, carp and goose and a tree with white
candles followed by a ritual on Boxing Day evening when a man
on a hobby horse and others dressed as goats (carrying goats'
heads) or storks entered the house to bring fun. In summer you
might go to the Baltic, to a seaside resort. On the Curonian Peninsula – the Kurische Nehrung – the fishermen spoke a strange
dialect and women in black tended long lines of smoked fish over
juniper-wood fires. The wearing of black had begun, it was said,
because death had been so frequent under the shifting dunes. In
those days (the old days) the peninsula's lagoon and the sea were
clean and pure. You had a choice for swimming – the smooth
inner water or the strong Baltic waves.

For those expelled from East Prussia after 1945, a new land
took shape, in parallel to their new life – that of the past, a huge
monument beside which everything else seemed small. The past
may be distorted any way you want; to think or to write about it
can be to hide the present or the future behind beautiful brocade.
So exile can mean conservatism or self-pity or comfort in the
company of the dead who are buried in that lost land.

The land: *das Land*, *Bernsteinland* (the land of amber), *Land
der dunklen Wäldern und kristallnen Seen* (the land of dark
woods and crystal lakes), *Menschen, Pferde, weites Land* (people,
horses, distant land). This word, on its own or added to another
– as in *Landschaft* (landscape) – can resonate with anger, joy or

regret. One of the most famous lines in German poetry is from Goethe's novel *Wilhelm Meister*, when the strange creature Mignon longs for the south, for the land of lemons and oranges, of myrtle and the bay tree, a lost place of happiness and of love:

> 'Kennst du das Land wo die Zitronen blühn?' ('Do you know the land where the lemon-trees flower?')

It's partly consoling; the land, at least, remains where it was: your other country – although lived upon by others. The poet Agnes Miegel, forced out of East Prussia in 1945, liked to think that Russians and Poles would soon work the same fields so that someone could enjoy them. Meanwhile, in exile, she could do what she wanted with the memory.

Nostalgia permeates a catalogue of books about East Prussia sent out some sixty-five years after the province's end: *Our Beautiful Samland*; *East Prussia – My Fate*; *Anecdotes from East Prussia*; *The Last Summer of Mauritten*; *Childhood on the Pregel*; *School Memories from East Prussia*; the 1941 postal directory of Königsberg; *Last Days in East Prussia*; recipes from an East Prussian kitchen (a short book); photographs of old castles and manor houses; memories of flight in 1944 and 1945; DVDs of films – from 'before the bombs fell' – of the towns like Elbing, Memel, Thorn and Marienburg, of Königsberg's *Schloss*. In the films you see a calm country – either in summer sunlight or covered in bright snow; trains leaving Königsberg's *Nordbahnhof* for the Samland coastal resorts, for Labiau and for the Curonian Spit, the Kurische Nehrung; then shots of what happened later under the post-war Polish communist or Soviet rule. A lighter note comes with a CD called *The Happy East Prussian*: 'cheerful stories and songs in the East Prussian dialect'; and another of East Prussia swinging between the wars – 'The Cheerful Tilsiters', 'The Masowian Trio', 'The Königsberg Musicians', 'The Elbing Sparrows'.

East Prussia was Germany's (some claimed western Europe's) eastern redoubt. People remarked on its neat towns and villages, its cultivated fields – the order imposed upon broad lakes, poor soil and apparently illimitable forests. There was a sense still of colonization, though much of it had been controlled by Germans since the fourteenth century. Asia began at these frontiers, it was said. System against chaos, a threatened civilization, a hard place to be – these formed the land's myth.

*

If you go east, from Lüneburg and Duisburg, away from the past, back to Kaliningrad (the old Königsberg) there's competition, more than six decades after the expulsions, to be the last German – someone now to be cherished rather than expelled or killed. I see this when I meet the farmer Johann van der Decken on a bright late-autumn day. We are near the Russian town of Gusev, until 1945 the German Gumbinnen, twenty or so miles from Kaliningrad. Aged about fifty-five, bearded, his face tanned below the line of his cap, Johann has been here for twelve years. He really is, he says, the last German working this land; true, there'd been a group near Chernyakhovsk (the old German Insterburg) but most of them were leaving. As for Stahl, an old man who'd been born in East Prussia and then came back – he just keeps a few cows and pigs: not proper farming.

Johann's farm – some two thousand acres of wheat, barley, oil-seed rape and dairy cows, employing thirty-four people – is big, different to those of Stahl and the Chernyakhovsk Germans in another way; Johann has no links at all with the province. He grew up near Hamburg and before coming here he worked in agriculture in Africa, where he met his Russian wife. Is he like the Germans who had come east to develop the land centuries earlier, following the Teutonic Knights? First Africa, then Kaliningrad – Johann is a pioneer. He's building (or rebuilding) the place. Kalin-ingrad agriculture had collapsed in the 1990s, after the closure of the huge Soviet collective farms.

Johann van der Decken had come from outside to what had been East Prussia, not like Klaus Lunau, who lives in the neatest wooden house in his street in the pretty Baltic sea-side resort of Zelenogradsk (once the German Cranz). As I walk with Klaus Lunau through Zelenogradsk, past the hideous glass and brick house built for Boris Yeltsin (who never spent a night in it), he says that he really is the last German from the old Königsberg in the Kaliningrad Oblast (or district), having retired here from intelligence work for the German army and police. But what about Gerda Preuss, I ask – the old lady who had lived since the 1945 Soviet take-over in Königsberg with her Russian partner, Maria? What about Rudolf Jacquemien, the communist poet? Klaus says that Gerda Preuss and Rudolf Jacquemien are dead. Only he remains.

All of them, Johann van der Decken, Gerda Preuss and Klaus Lunau, feel or felt secure in Kaliningrad because they married or lived with Russians; Rudolf Jacquemien came there in the 1950s, an idealistic Marxist, so was different: not a survivor but an immigrant. The larger part of the old East Prussia, its southern bit, from the Russian frontier to the Vistula or Weichsel River, went to Poland after the last war. Here there are more Germans, several thousand, many from the large Polish minority that had lived for centuries under German rule. If you want greater evidence of the old German east, it's in the churches and castles and civic buildings or on the faded headstones of the graves scattered across this forgotten land.

*

In a Hamburg bookshop, I find a large section on the former German eastern territories – Silesia, Pomerania and East Prussia. Among the books are a history of the great neo-classical Dönhoff house at Friedrichstein, with photographs taken before its destruction in 1945; an illustrated account of the journalist Marion Dönhoff's flight west ahead of the Red Army; and her own memoirs of childhood and escape, written after she'd become one of the most admired women in post-war Germany. The shelf also has a novel, later filmed, by one of Marion's young relations about the trek west, a neat European romance between a young German aristocrat and French prisoner of war. There are also collections of sun-filled photographs. One is called *Beautiful East Prussia, Pearl of the East*.

Several post-1945 survivors of the East Prussian landowning families – or Junkers (from Jung Herr or Young Lord) – wrote their memoirs; from these we know about the Dönhoffs of Friedrichstein, the Lehndorffs of Steinort and the Dohnas of Schlobitten. The books tell of a still partly feudal society, a world (apparently) of obligation and trust. Marion Dönhoff depicts a frugal innocence in the huge pre-war Friedrichstein that is almost bleakly dutiful. One of the estate workers at Schlobitten, the Dohna property, told Alexander Dohna's startled young wife that everyone in the place looked upon her as their mother. Hans von Lehndorff, the last heir to Steinort, evokes the place's beauty and worthwhile life. All these seem to say: is it so wrong to regret the passing of this world?

It's near the end of winter so Hamburg is cold, its wealth dulled by a leaden twilight. I think of my meeting with Marion Dönhoff some eighteen years ago, how in one of her books she describes hearing at night in her house in the Hamburg suburbs the distant shutting of a car door, a break in a silence that had brought back her earlier life in a much more remote place. Before the war, Hamburg and Königsberg had both been rich trading cities; in 1944 and 1945 both suffered terrible destruction. Then came the two kinds of rebirth – the Soviet and that of capitalist western Europe. When I mentioned to Marion Dönhoff the immense difference between rich Hamburg and poor Kaliningrad, she hadn't responded; perhaps it was too obvious.

This day in Hamburg I have lunch with two German friends and we talk about the millions of refugees who had come after the war to the new Germany from the old eastern territories. In the communist zone, they were controlled by the Soviet occupiers but in the democratic west these people formed a large and active group. Konrad Adenauer, the Chancellor of the new Federal

Republic, feared an island of anger and reaction. They were given money and, in places like the Duisburg and Lüneburg museums, memorialization of their former lives.

This didn't put an end to resentment and demands for a return of what had gone; although my friends don't say so, I think that the absorption of so many is an extraordinary achievement. We talked about the leader of the Bund der Vertriebenen (the largest organization of the expelled), Erika Steinbach – how she infuriates the Poles, particularly those who now live in what was, until 1945, the southern part of East Prussia. Should this be worrying? No, because her latest campaign is for a memorial in Berlin to the expelled people – not about property or frontiers. Frau Steinbach had wanted the memorial for the Germans whereas others, particularly in Poland, say victims throughout Europe should be commemorated. Much more important points had been settled at the time of reunification, when the German Chancellor Helmut Kohl accepted the post-1945 frontiers. The legal challenges brought by a few Germans who had left Poland in the communist time and now wished to reclaim land weren't important. I remembered what a Polish politician said to me – how you could play on German guilt. Perhaps this could last for ever – an infinity of darkness.

When I first went there in 1992, Kaliningrad had also seemed darkly shocking. I got off the train into a parody of Soviet planning with cracked concrete, cratered streets, people bent against the cold and wet and a sleek German tour coach gliding past belching Ladas and dirty, dented trams. Rumours went round – that Helmut Kohl wanted to buy the place back for the newly reunited Germany: that the Germans, Poles, Lithuanians and Russians might run the enclave (now cut off from the rest of Russia) together. In a broken-down hotel that was patrolled by prostitutes and drug dealers, I asked two Russian students what they thought should happen. One said that the name must be changed; Mikhail Kalinin, Stalin's henchman, represented the bad years (it jolted me to think that there had been a worse time). Now the place should

Soviet housing on the river in Kaliningrad.

be called Kantgrad, to show that Russia's most western land was now part of a new Europe.

Those who write or talk about the city still stress its horror. It has 'bad karma', I was told – this hideous, failed Kaliningrad, forever doomed, stifled by a confused and bloody past, riddled with AIDS and drugs and smuggling and crime. Is it worse than many other Russian cities blighted by Soviet planning? I don't think so. Kaliningrad *does* have its own inhuman centre, as if a great scoop had lifted up a whole quarter, replacing it with wide avenues and chipped concrete walkways, potholed highways and bridges over the slow dark river, often seen through a haze of pollution, across memorials, heroic statues and models of weapons commemorating the Great Patriotic War. On the trams, obviously over-burdened people make you feel ashamed to be rich and happy. But beyond this is a layered history, the sense of stones beneath concrete, of streets and houses of a foreign past not yet dissolved into a new identity. The Russian poet Joseph Brodsky, when he came to Kaliningrad in the 1960s, wrote of the trees whispering in German.

In spite of Soviet destruction, the past can come suddenly back, like the quick lifting of a blanket. You see it in the neat pre-war German railway stations – resembling giant parts of an ancient train set – the paint not thick enough to hide the old names: Rominten, for instance, in black gothic lettering at the stop for the old imperial hunting lodge, once the preserve of the German emperors and that passionate slaughterer of all game, Hermann Göring. The tomb of Immanuel Kant survived the bombs and the changes, to become a sacred place where newly married Russian couples are photographed, the bride's white dress brilliant against the memorial's pale-pink stone and the cathedral's dark-red Prussian brick. The students I first met in 1992 have done well, mostly through links to the west; Eduard and Olga look outwards from Kaliningrad, working for foreign companies or for the European Union. To them, it's inconceivable that the place can be anything other than Russian. But they know that Königsberg is what makes this Russian place different.

Probably the German city had never been beautiful – idiosyncratic perhaps, with its mysterious corners, self-conscious medievalism, crooked streets, gothic towers and dark blocks of warehouses along a slow, oily river. The former Chancellor Helmut Schmidt – who passed through Königsberg on his way to the eastern front – remembers a very provincial place. Most of the buildings – even the famous red-brick fortifications around it that guarded western civilization – were nineteenth century, making, at best, a place of character and memory, enfolding its people in a limited, comfortable world. The centre – the castle, cathedral and university district – was what the Soviets and the bombing changed most. After 1945, they blew up some of the churches; now the Juditterkirche, the oldest church in East Prussia, is a place of Russian Orthodox worship, with the old German cemetery next to it. German money has paid for much of what has been done since 1991, often – as with the cathedral and its stiflingly inoffensive civic interior – alongside Russian government funds.

In this post-Soviet age, black limousines and dark-suited bodyguards, former members of the special forces, wait outside the Kaliningrad clubs, restaurants and hotels; the show of money mocks any idea of communism. Most of the city government's plans for tourism seem to leap over the Soviet years and, as you walk round, you sense their brevity. Across from the concrete are the sugary early twentieth-century baroque of the former courthouse (now the headquarters of the Russian Baltic Fleet), the red brick of the nineteenth-century copies of the medieval gates and the Dohna tower (now the Amber Museum). German or Prussian gothic is still a powerful presence, mostly nineteenth century, except in the outside of the restored cathedral, one of the largest brick gothic buildings in Europe. A lake, dark green and pungent in summer, stretches from where the castle once was before the Soviet triumph of the building of the high, still empty and asbestos-ridden old Communist Party headquarters. More recent buildings can seem stagey, crudely imitative, Königsberg in caricature; they are certainly not Soviet.

The tourists are mostly German. When Kaliningrad first opened to the world in 1991, many of those who had lived there before 1945 came back for the first time since the expulsions. It's said that several, standing perhaps where the castle once was, or in Victory Square (formerly Kochplatz, named after himself by the last National Socialist Gauleiter, Erich Koch) or what had been the main business street, the old Steindamm, or the former Lindenstrasse – where the former Jewish orphanage still stands – were overwhelmed, bursting into tears at the memory of terror or of loss.

The street names are now changing back; Gorky Street has become Hoffmann Street again. Tour guides point out other obvious survivors – the neo-classical old stock exchange or the theatre, given a new pillared façade by the Soviets, with the statue of Friedrich Schiller in front of it, surviving 1945 apparently

Eighteenth-century warehouses in pre-1945 Königsberg,
with the castle tower in the distance.

because a soldier chalked on it that this was a great poet. Near
the nineteenth-century university buildings, the guides lead their
groups down into the bunker where the last German commander,
General Lasch, directed the drawn-out defence of Königsberg;
then perhaps they go to the Oceanographic Museum (a Soviet
addition, with whole ships and submarines docked on the Pregel)
or to the zoo, a tired place where slow-breathing animals lie
beside murky pools. The zoo is the place for Hans's story: how
astonishing care was lavished upon one hippopotamus during the
horrific human suffering after the siege's end. More than forty bits
of shell and bullets were pulled from Hans's armoured skin and a
Red Army vet slept alongside him, tending the wounds or mas-
saging the hippopotamus's heaving stomach as it endured chronic
indigestion. What could be done? Eventually, after massive infu-
sions of vodka, Hans walked, or staggered, again.

*

In 2007, fifteen years after my first visit, I call on the German Consul in Kaliningrad in the bright, newly built villa where he has his office. Guido Herz explains how uninterested he was previously in this part of the world, anxious perhaps to block out any imagined plot of a surreptitious German retaking of Königsberg. Short, dark-haired, tanned and dapper, quick in speech and gesture, he is, he says, a Roman Catholic from Heidelberg: not a Prussian or with any emotional attachment to the old East Prussia or the eastern former German lands – none at all. His face shows distaste, as if these places give him pain.

He looks at me sharply. He and Berlin accept completely that this region is Russian – and he sees the city as divided into two parts: the Russian present and the German (or Prussian) past. Did I know that Kaliningrad is booming – booming, booming, booming, he repeats, breaking briefly into English? There is 10 per cent growth per annum and very low unemployment. Which German firms are here, I ask? The Consul is sensitive perhaps to the charge of commercial imperialism. He says only that there are several: one that makes children's goods. The BMW assembly plant is nothing to do with Germany and is a Russian company. It also assembles KIA cars from Korea.

Booming, booming, booming – a volley of triumph. This may be true of the city. But out in the country I remember the pools of green-brown water on fields where the old drainage systems have broken down; the old woman in the stained headscarf who had offered me shrivelled grapes from her garden in a near-derelict house by a red-brick former Lutheran church; then, in Kaliningrad, at the furthest end of the old castle pond (past the two memorials to the Soviet submarine captain who had sunk the German liner the *Wilhelm Gustloff* in 1945, with the loss of thousands of civilian lives) the lighted windows of dilapidated industrial buildings at night, as if people work or live there.

Guido Herz says it's true that the Russians had not wanted a consul – but he's the second and they have welcomed him. When I ask about the groups in Germany that are pressing for recognition of what they or their expelled ancestors lost or suffered, he explains that East Prussia is not so strongly represented among these as the Sudeten Germans or Silesians. Had I heard of Erika Steinbach, their leader? Guido Herz smiles. She has little influence now, he thinks, in Germany. It suits the Poles to use her – and again he breaks into English – as a bogeywoman. I think also that it suits those who move among the ghosts to remember that Chancellor Helmut Kohl, just before German reunification, had told the *Vertriebene* (expelled people) that they had been treated very unjustly.

One must get things into perspective, Herz says. The former East Prussia makes up only 0.4 per cent of Russian territory. The Russians have no fear of the Germans. Why should they? It's the Czechs and the Poles who are anxious. Kaliningrad is a place of victims, he thinks: victims of the air raids, of Hitler, of the Red Army, of Stalin, of environmental disaster, of poor urban planning, of isolation or of neglect. Even more victims have been sent here, from the Chernobyl explosion, from the Armenian earthquakes; others came from all over the old Soviet Union, from choice or pressure. The problem has been in forming an identity. They need the German past, shown now in Königsberg and Ostmark beer, the number plates with 'Königsberg' written on them: the historic symbols – the restored cathedral, the medieval gates, Kant's tomb. I think that Kaliningrad is old enough now to assert itself. From almost everywhere in the city you can see those two symbols of Russia: the huge new Orthodox cathedral and the empty concrete tower that was built to be the Communist Party headquarters.

Guido Herz has been sent on a mission of reconciliation. Germany is the closest foreign country for those who live here, he thinks – closer than neighbouring Poland, Lithuania or Belarus. Evidence of it is all around – in the streets, the parks, the squares, the graves, the statue of Schiller, the plaque on Agnes Miegel's house, the way the Soviet centre blends at its edges into the pre-war suburbs, the gliding tourist buses. Outside the city, it's harder, he admits. You can rent land but speculative buyers, taking advantage of tax concessions brought in to lure people to the region, often do nothing with what they have bought. Collective farms, abandoned after the demise of the Soviet Union, had replaced skilled German farmers; and much of the drainage was destroyed in the war. The land needs to be cherished. Once it produced some 20 per cent of the wheat in Germany.

What's happened since 1992 is a letting in of light and money, a break from the military: the arrival of shopping and nightlife, the demolition of some of the bleaker post-war housing, a discovery of the past. In one of the tourist brochures, there's a photograph of an elderly long-haired man unravelling a napkin, facing two tall silver-gilt candelabra and tiered dishes of fruit, sea food and caviar; the caption says, 'It takes time to choose – Mr Benetton, the owner of the clothes brand, in a Kaliningrad restaurant.'

Alexei, a businessman in his early fifties, would have been impossible twenty years ago. In his first career, he was an army officer, reaching the rank of colonel, reputedly in the KGB. Now he lives with his family in Kaliningrad in a smart house from the German time. His father, also a professional soldier, came from Leningrad (the name given to St Petersburg from 1924) to the city in the 1950s, having served in Poland, among other places. Alexei's two daughters were educated here. One now works in Moscow.

In his jeans and open-necked shirt, Alexei is fluent. One of his tasks, at the request of the region's Governor, Georgy Boos, a rich businessman put in by Putin, is to promote Kaliningrad. He has studied the history of the region and sees it as Russian but with a European focus. He has read Kant and can easily identify with both the Russian and the German periods – why shouldn't he? Alexei's eyes flit impatiently towards the window. This is Europe, he says, and he's a European. But his office is only partly furnished; one feels that he may want to move on. The name Kaliningrad is bad, Alexei says. Obviously Königsberg isn't possible but the region is not German or Soviet – and I know what's coming next. Something with Kant in it would be suitable, he thinks. After all, Kant was briefly a Russian citizen.

Alexei runs a regional development agency, with funding from local and national government. One of his projects is a joint Russian–Brazilian venture involving frozen food, importing this from Brazil, but they hope within four to five years to get the raw materials – poultry and cattle – from farms in Kaliningrad. It's not so profitable now for businessmen to go into agriculture as into cars, logistics or trade. The special economic zone means that there are no customs duties and very low taxes on profit or property. This encourages firms to set up in Kaliningrad but also aids importers. Much of the food comes in from Lithuania or Poland, in addition to Alexei's Brazilian frozen meat.

Alexei says the resources here are limited – not enough workable land, a shortage of skilled labour. So workers come in from Turkey, Kazakhstan and Ukraine. Russians are starting to enjoy the place – it's relaxed, a good environment, cheaper living, friendly. People from Moscow or St Petersburg have property here for weekends or summer homes on the coast. Young people are staying instead of moving off to bigger places.

There is isolation. If you fly out to the rest of Russia it's quick, but to go overland across Poland or Lithuania still involves getting an expensive visa that unblocks the way to any country in the European Union, apart from Britain and Ireland which did not sign the Schengen Agreement. So if you reach Poland or Lithuania you can go on to Paris or Rome. Alexei knows Poland. He thinks that relations between what he calls ordinary Russians and Poles and Lithuanians are good. But it's not popular to speak Russian in Poland.

Those were the boom times, in 2007. Governor Boos boasted that here the Russians, whom he thought 'the most flexible people in the world', had made the transition from the stifling Soviet era to the new capitalism. They had joined the west, while remaining Russian. For instance, they would welcome missiles to the region as a patriotic response to the missile-defence system planned by George W. Bush for the Czech Republic or Poland. Low taxes brought more businesses. Tourist plans included a series of giant casinos and a replica of Disneyland; 'for the visitor every day must be packed', the Governor declared. Some of the atmosphere of old Königsberg would return – in the rebuilt castle or in new buildings along the river.

Isolation is no longer possible. The global financial crisis has hit Kaliningrad, mocking Boos's hubris. Unemployment has risen, more than in most Russian cities. Prices have gone up; new building has either slowed or halted; the electronics sector (the assembling of products like television screens for foreign companies) has been virtually wiped out. The demonstrations that broke out across Russia in March 2010 were particularly well supported in Kaliningrad, with people carrying mandarin oranges as symbols of the tanned, small, round Governor. Putin moved; Boos was sacked. The problem is that many in the Kaliningrad region, cut off from the rest of Russia by Poland and Lithuania, compare it to another Europe, to the new life of Poles and Lithuanians within the European Union where young Kaliningraders often travel. The western dimension has come back to this forgotten land.

*

None of this resembles the great build-up of hatred that marked the end of East Prussia. It came even to a comparatively serene Britain when the future of the German eastern territories was raised in the House of Commons by the Prime Minister Winston Churchill on 15 December 1944. The debate was about what form post-war Poland might take. The plans were still hypothetical; Allied troops might be inside western Germany and the Red Army pouring across the eastern German frontiers, but the enemy was still fighting hard.

Churchill's oratory rose, evoking a strange country, far from Westminster – 'the most desolate' Pripet Marshes; Danzig, 'one of the most magnificent cities and harbours in the whole of the world' – as he spoke of Polish concessions to the Soviet Union in the east in return for conquered territory in the west. Germany would lose East Prussia, with its capital of Königsberg, coronation city of the Prussian kings. What would happen to the Germans? Expulsion was, the British Prime Minister said, the best answer: the shifting of millions of people – 'a clean sweep' – as had happened after 1918 when the frontiers between Greece and Turkey had been redrawn.

Why shouldn't there be room in a new Germany for the expelled East Prussians, Silesians, Pomeranians and the rest? Six to seven million Germans had been killed in a war 'into which they did not hesitate, for a second time in a generation, to plunge all Europe and the world'. Ten or twelve million prisoners of war and slave labourers taken to Germany from previously conquered territories would be sent back to their own countries.

There was some sympathy at Westminster that December for the German victims. One member of parliament was shocked at the idea of '5,000,000 Germans again forced from their homes and transferred to western Germany'; another declared that 'The Poles do not want East Prussia as a compensation. It is the same as if you took away East Anglia from Britain and gave it to Germany, and offered us Normandy instead. It is a monstrous suggestion.' But the Conservative Robert Boothby claimed that the province was 'to-day what it has been for the last two centuries, the focal point of the infection of Prussian militarism . . . The German population of East Prussia should be, as the Prime Minister said, expelled. It is rough but, by God, they deserve it.'

Outside parliament, a campaign began against the expulsions; British churchmen condemned them and George Orwell wrote of 'this enormous crime'. The Polish poet Czesław Miłosz told an English friend he couldn't understand such sentimentality, which was apparently founded on the unrealistic belief that the hatred elsewhere in Europe could be stopped. Appalling destruction had already hit East Prussia when the Red Army crossed its borders in

October 1944. Two months earlier, in August, the RAF had bombed Königsberg, smashing the city's historic centre. After the raids, fires burnt for days. Smoke, loosened timber, rubble and the stench of corpses had formed a cordon around what had once been thought of as one of the last redoubts of western European civilization.

Its tight streets, wooden buildings, packed warehouses and winds from the Baltic had always made Königsberg prone to fires which, centuries before, had terrified its most famous citizen. The dying philosopher Immanuel Kant often fell asleep while reading, and one night his head nodded into some nearby candles that set fire to his cotton night cap. Already nightmares plagued him; old street songs heard in childhood and ghostly murderers became fearful torments; when his servant answered his cries, Kant thought the man had come to kill him. In daylight, the philosopher wrote, 'No surrender now to panics of darkness.' Until then he had insisted on a silent bedroom, without light: not even a glimpse of the moon through a shutter's crack. Now, in the new dark terror, he brought in a lamp and a clock whose tick and striking of the hours helped towards peace.

Kant did much to give his home city its identity, not only as part of an intellectual revolution that rocked Europe but as an outpost of civilization. Hadn't this 'civilizing' impulse been the essence of the land since the thirteenth century and its conquest for Christianity by the Teutonic Knights? To the Russian novelist Alexander Solzhenitsyn, East Prussia meant something else, especially in comparison with his Soviet homeland: material progress and efficiency. Ever since arriving there with the Red Army at the end of the war, Solzhenitsyn had never lost his astonishment at those neat farms, villages and towns where he had tried to control his men in the terrifying riot of looting and violence:

> 'Tiles, tiles – and see the towers,
> All the turrets and the spires,
> And houses built of solid brick'

Before:
– 'Our columns pour ahead like lava
– With wild cries, whistling, headlights' glare
Klein Goslau, Gross Goslau –
Every village – is now a fire!'

It was the huge Soviet offensive of June 1944 that began the last months of German East Prussia. Previously the province had been spared the worst of the fighting, although the wounded had passed through Königsberg and those with sons or husbands on the eastern front would have heard about the change from advance to retreat. Many imagined a short Russian occupation, quickly followed by liberation, as in 1914, or a negotiated peace and return of their land. This time, however, the spirit and power of the invaders was different. In October 1944, Soviet troops were on German soil, near Gumbinnen, between Stallupönen and Rominten Heath. The small town of Nemmersdorf was captured, then retaken by the Germans – but not until the Red Army had unleashed terror on an unimaginable scale.

Goebbels and the Nazi propaganda machine thundered against the 'fury of the Soviet beasts', evoking the ancient ghosts of the Asiatic hordes. Now, however, there could be no help from the rest of Christendom. The German occupation of the western Soviet Union had been horrifically cruel – Communist Party members hanged instantly, Jews either shot or sent to extermination camps, women raped, men carted off to the Reich to work as slaves, 'the fascists' laughing as they burnt their victims' corpses. More than three million Soviet prisoners of war died in German camps in a regime of terror and starvation. The Wehrmacht shot or hanged innocent people in villages suspected of harbouring Russian partisans; the requisitioning of food led to widespread famine. Nearly seven and a half million Soviet civilians are thought to have been killed under German occupation. The Germans had found local collaborators, particularly in Ukraine or on the Baltic, who had suffered under Stalin; but

Teutonic contempt, made worse by Nazi racism, prevented more extensive help.

In July 1944, the Red Army entered the first extermination camp to be liberated, at Majdenek, near Lublin and the Polish–Soviet border. The thousands of victims were Jews and also Russians and Poles. Soviet anti-Semitism notwithstanding, propaganda made the most of Majdenek, emphasizing the message that accompanied the massive Red Army offensives in the last year of the war. The Germans were beasts; Soviet rage and revenge were just. Even intellectuals and admirers of western European culture shared these feelings. The writer Lev Kopelev (a Red Army officer at the time who later settled in Germany) ordered his men to get out of their jeeps and relieve themselves on the hated German soil after they had crossed the border into East Prussia.

In the middle of November, the front fell silent, with the Red Army on Rominten Heath. The offensive seemed to have faltered; Christmas and New Year were calm. On 13 January 1945, the surge began again. Captain Alexander Solzhenitsyn, an officer in the Soviet artillery, received a bundle of leaflets bearing Marshal Rokossovsky's message to the troops – that this was the last great offensive and 'Germany lies before us'. Earlier, Stalin's decision had been revealed to the troops by political commissars – that moral scruples should be cast aside in a campaign of revenge, looting and terror. Repelled, Solzhenitsyn told his men that they should represent 'a proud magnanimous Russia'. Once the advance began it proved to be impossible to enforce this. The writer was horrified by the violence inflicted on the orderly land yet even he couldn't resist taking some Russian books that were banned in the Soviet Union, and, from a German post office, piles of fine paper, handfuls of German pencils, paper clips, labels, folders and bottles of ink. He also seized, from the house of a German miller – who had fled – illustrations from a book on the First World War, photographs of the Russian Emperor Nicholas II and the generals of both sides who had once fought here, on the eastern front: the Germans Ludendorff and Hindenburg, the Russians Samsonov and Brusilov. Captain Solzhenitsyn walked through the devastated towns – Neidenburg in flames, Allenstein where trains of German refugees were still arriving. It was in Wormditt (now the Polish Orneta) on 9 February that he took the fatal telephone call – an order to report to brigade headquarters, where he was arrested for having made jokes about Stalin in a letter to a friend. Solzhenitsyn's time in the Gulag had begun.

*

As I read about the ghosts that I'd found on my East Prussian journeys, their experiences often seemed oddly symbolic. The young Martin Bergau, marching before the war with the Hitler Youth near the Baltic, glimpsed an elk loping away as if in mockery of their intrusion into its wilderness. In July 1944, Heinrich von Lehndorff, whose ancestors had come east some four centuries before, fled the German police through his own woods. In 1945, Johannes Jänicke's wife opened the door of their rectory in a Baltic seaside village to confront Red Army soldiers in search of loot and women. In the autumn of 1944, the forester Walter Frevert killed his last stag in Rominten forest, the rifle shot mingling with the sound of the approaching Soviet guns. In Königsberg, the nineteen-year-old Michael Wieck, from a cultured family of musicians, tossed bodies into bomb craters that served as graves, many of the dead having killed themselves rather than face the Red Army. All these dead Germans, perhaps once proudly Aryan, overwhelmed him with the miracle of his own survival, as a Jew.

Four years later, the last Germans were shipped out. The Wieck family bribed a Soviet official before being told to report to the train station with hand luggage and enough food for seven days. A thousand Germans were loaded on to freight cars and the chaste, shy Michael found himself lying next to women and girls who giggled at his confusion. Very slowly they moved across Poland, let out at intervals for exercise, the weather warm at last in Soviet-occupied Germany where, in a quarantine camp, the Wiecks decided to try for freedom in the west.

Friends and relations got them out but to adapt was hard. Taken to a film at the British Information Centre in Berlin, Michael found it depressingly trivial after what he had seen. He settled in West Berlin, enrolled at the Berlin Conservatory of Music and was joined by his mother, his parents having separated. Shyness and anxiety and thoughts about the past plagued him. In 1950 he married Hildegard, from a Prussian gentile family, becoming aware that people wanted him, as a Jew, to absolve them of responsibility. Weren't the bombing of the German cities and the Red Army's brutality just as bad, they asked?

He thought of emigration and went alone to Israel but felt the country would be difficult for his gentile wife. By now he was a violinist in an orchestra, still having nightmares, frightened that his cries would wake his colleagues in hotels when they were on tour. He recalled how in a camp outside Königsberg he had sworn to God that he would always be easily satisfied, never greedy for things. Why was happiness so hard to find? What and when should he forgive and forget? Even now Michael Wieck's heart jumps when he hears talk of 'the Jews'.

In post-war Berlin, the world couldn't quite be re-ordered. The Wiecks made friends with a man who revealed he had been in the army in the Lichterfeld barracks, an SS headquarters; a cousin, the actress Dorothea Wieck, told of banal conversations with Hitler, how charming he was; Michael's father-in-law said scornfully that the Jewish scientists had saved themselves by emigrating early. Michael thought that his wife's family weren't pleased that she had married a Jew.

Perhaps emigration would be better – and they chose New Zealand, a lovely land he'd seen while on a tour with the Berlin Chamber Orchestra. Michael Wieck encountered anti-Semitism there and missed German culture so much that, after seven years, he, his wife and their four children came back. Everyone had, he thought, a potential for hatred and timidity, for obsequiousness and cruelty – and the past was inescapable. On a concert tour in the Soviet Union, he and the orchestra flew over the Baltic coast and the Curonian Spit and he trembled, felt feverish; then they were above Königsberg where he had lived in joy and terror, a contrast now to his much calmer life. After he had moved to Stuttgart, to join its Radio Symphony Orchestra, he was on tour in Jerusalem. At the Wailing Wall, a small boy, resembling the young Michael, recited the Torah, with a rabbi and the boy's family. Taken back to his own youthful faith and innocence, Michael wept, engulfed by joy and pain. Were the tears a warning not to forget? Were they an apprehension of God?

Statue of Kant in Kaliningrad.

In Berlin, Michael Wieck had yearned for a particular landscape, for the Baltic; he was, he thought, still an East Prussian. He had seen the dramatic changes – how when the Red Army came, the Nazis turned into grovelling creatures, how liberated Poles became bullies. His Jewishness – so vital in the Hitler years – was forgotten under the Russians when the Germans helped him. He thinks now that persecution often comes out of a search for identity. It's enough, he thinks, to be a human among other humans; to be an outsider in a community is to be intellectually independent. Perhaps real security and peace come only after death. It's hard to see this coming soon to the spry eighty-three-year-old who welcomes me to his Stuttgart house.

2: A Frontier Land

On 12 September 1911, Lieutenant Colonel Alfred Knox, the British Military Attaché in St Petersburg, put his bicycle on to a train bound for Warsaw in Russian Poland. Knox had written to the Russian general staff about his wish to study the Napoleonic campaigns of 1807 and 1812. This ostensibly innocent enthusiasm for military history would allow him to go on a spying mission into the potential battlefields of the German and Russian border lands, to report on what he saw there to the British War Office. The colonel had no doubt that war was coming, having a distrust of German intentions which he thought were not taken seriously enough by the politicians in London. Britain should, he believed, officially join the alliance of France and Russia against the German and Austro-Hungarian empires. Knox thought also that the next war would be decided as much in the east as in the west.

Alfred Knox – large, forthright, dark-haired with a moustache – was proud to be a 'simple solder'. Born in 1870 – the son of an army officer – he claimed that his family had been in Ireland for about two hundred and seventy years. But this Ireland was Ulster, the Protestant enclave in the north; originally from Presbyterian Scotland, the Knoxes had been part of a migration from mainland Britain that came to dominate the whole country. Like most conquerors, they thought their civilization was superior to the one they had conquered.

Before Russia, it was British imperial India that shaped Alfred Knox. As ADC to the viceroy, Lord Curzon, from 1899 to 1900, and as an officer on the turbulent north-west frontier, he knew how tenuous British control of the sub-continent was: how dependent on prestige. Often he lived in what he saw as extreme isolation: five months, for instance, in an outpost surrounded by barbed wire, 'without a single white man near.' Any hint of weak imperial government would, he thought, be exploited, by agitators or revolutionaries. Knox was a gifted linguist, learning Pushtu at Peshawar and, in 1906, Russian while on language leave in Moscow. From 1908 he was at the War Office, working in the Russian sub-section; in 1911, he became military attaché in St Petersburg.

Russia was the great mystery: the oppressor of Poland, an affront to liberals – a vast land of revolutionaries, secret police, backward peasants, rapid industrialization, untold natural resources, an absolutist monarchy and potentially the largest army in Europe. Knox knew that the defeats of 1905, when Japan had humiliated Russia, need not have been so catastrophic. When the Tsar and his ministers, fearful of the political cost at home, asked for peace, Russian forces, after early disaster, were fighting well. He knew also the German fear of this great empire. 'A bold raid into East Prussia' and an attack on Königsberg, coronation city of the Prussian kings, would have an effect upon Germany which Prussia had dominated since German unification in 1871. 'Prussian territory', Knox wrote, 'has not been invaded for nearly one hundred years.'

This ostensibly secure state had in fact been often invaded, by the Poles, Swedes, French and Russians. Since its defeat by Napoleon, however, Prussia had risen again. In the early nineteenth century, the Prussian Reform movement overhauled the education system (already the most advanced in Europe), abolished serfdom, promoted free trade, introduced compulsory military service and, in 1812, made full citizens of the Jews. At the Congress of Vienna in 1815, Prussia, as one of the victorious powers, had its territory extended westwards. It now had the Rhineland, Westphalia and what became the centre of German industry, the Ruhr. Prussia dominated the German customs union,

Alfred Knox in ceremonial uniform.

the Zollverein, founded in 1834 – an arrangement which the Austro-Hungarian Empire did not join. The climax of all this was the post-1871 domination of the new German Empire.

The eastern part of the country partly benefited from this ascent yet also stayed its poorest region. In Königsberg, trade with Russia boomed. But in East Prussia's country districts, particularly the wild, poor lands of Masuria, the scene was different. Agricultural reforms and the abolition of serfdom undermined the sense of responsibility that some large landlords felt towards their dependants, leaving small farmers and tenants unprotected from low prices, cattle disease, failed harvests and a harsh climate. The decade from 1840 to 1850 brought misery – deaths from starvation, typhus and cholera. Emigration became a flood; from 1850 to 1870 almost one and a half million people travelled westwards from East Prussia in search of work.

For the Jews, however, the place seemed a refuge – and many
fled there from the Russian pogroms. Between 1817 and 1861 the
Jewish population of Königsberg increased from 953 to 2,572
amid a liberal atmosphere. Even in the rural parts of East Prussia
tolerance lingered until the rise of nationalism that followed
German unification in 1871. In 1825 the Philiponnen, a sect
persecuted by the Russians, settled among the Masurians; their
descendants still live near the town of Johannisburg (now the
Polish Pisz). A large Polish minority, mostly in Masuria, saw
the King of Prussia as their protector. Their Prussian patriotism
created an atmosphere different from the tensions and violence
that beset the British in Ireland, Alfred Knox's home.

To the rest of Europe, Prussia's identity, since the mid-
eighteenth-century expansionist times of Frederick the Great,
was rooted in efficiency, military power and absolutism. The
imposition of reform – which aimed to achieve equality, an uncor-
rupt bureaucracy and educational improvement – could seem
high-handed. The pitiless, brilliant Frederick brought greatness,
yet also a confused identity behind the remarkable victories.
The East Prussian critics of the Enlightenment – J. G. Herder and
J. G. Hamann – were in part rebelling against a French intellectual domination that was shown by the King's friendship with
Voltaire and his contempt for the German language and culture.
East Prussia he saw as a wild, barbaric place with a vile climate –
much too hot and insect-ridden in summer, freezing in winter,
better for bears than for human beings.

Frederick's absolutism couldn't last, even with its overtones of
enlightenment, and in 1848, revolutionary protest forced King
Frederick William IV to make Prussia a constitutional state. But
the new constitution, with a powerful upper house appointed by
the king, entrenched the power of the conservative Junkers, a
bulwark of the ruling Hohenzollern family, particularly east of
the Elbe. An odd fact about the East Prussian aristocracy is how
long its significance lasted. The 1848 upheavals raised other questions of identity. Polish cultural nationalism, suppressed by the

Russians and calmed by Prussian tolerance, stirred among East Prussian Poles. Yet many of them still looked to the king as their protector; and King Frederick William IV was cheered on his visits to Masuria.

King William I, Frederick William IV's brother and successor, appointed Otto von Bismarck as his prime minister. Bismarck, who came from a Pomeranian Junker family, was sympathetic to the landowning class in the east. He distrusted democracy, loathed liberalism, and, like Louis XIV and Napoleon, used military force to make his country into the greatest power in continental Europe. Three wars – against Denmark in 1864, Austria in 1866 and France in 1870 – created first a dominant Prussia and then, in 1871, the colossus of a German empire.

Bismarck, who became the empire's first chancellor, moved swiftly to make peace – but the anxiety created throughout Europe by this quick, brutal display of military power lasted until 1914. The army stayed outside democratic control and the many uniforms in the streets, particularly in Berlin, seemed to show the basis of imperial Germany's strength. With this came a new nationalism, as if to solidify the young empire. Bismarck's so-called *Kulturkampf* directed against the Roman Catholic Church; disapproval of the use of the Polish and Lithuanian languages; a renaming of Polish-named towns; the new red-brick schools (the same colour as the castles of the Teutonic Knights): all these showed an increasing intolerance of minorities. A myth took hold – that the eastern territories needed a form of colonial rule to civilize their drunken, lazy Slavs. The public pronouncements of the new Emperor William II – who dismissed Bismarck in 1890 – reflected this. East Prussia sought refuge in this new aggressive assertion of identity. In the elections of 1907, only Königsberg voted liberal.

In Bismarck's time, Germany had been in alliance with Russia. But, after the 'Iron Chancellor's' dismissal by William II, the latest version of this alliance known as the Three Emperors' League – of Austria-Hungary, Germany and Russia – broke up, largely over the Balkans where Russia, champion of the Slavs, opposed Austro-Hungarian attempts at greater domination. The French, smarting from their 1870 defeat, seized their chance, making a full alliance with Russia in 1894. Both countries now saw the new Germany as the threat. Britain, joined in a loose entente with France since 1904, began to take a more sympathetic view of the autocratic Tsarist regime.

This was the land that the Englishman Alfred Knox entered in September 1911: a country of vast estates, struggling small farms and poor agricultural workers sometimes not much better off than when they had been serfs: an anxious region of Europe, apparently threatened by a resurgent Russia, a land – with its red-brick castles and Lutheran churches – where isolation fuelled identity yet in whose capital city of Königsberg traces of the liberalism of its greatest citizen, Immanuel Kant, could still be found. What interested Knox was what might happen in a war between the Central Powers (Germany and Austria-Hungary) and the Dual Alliance (Russia and France). He had heard that Germany would leave at most five corps on the eastern frontier, delegating to Austria the task of fighting Russia 'while she deals with France'. Knox thought that the Russian cavalry would launch raids across the border into East Prussia. The psychological effect on Germany of any invasion would be immense.

In Warsaw Knox was told he should carry a revolver while bicycling in Poland but he felt safe on reaching the law-abiding atmosphere of Germany. At Neidenburg (now the Polish Nidzica), in the shadow of the rectangular fortress of the Teutonic Knights, he took his bicycle off the train. He asked 'a street loafer' how to get to Hohenstein (now Olsztynek), to be asked, in his turn, where he came from. One can sense the hauteur in the response – 'I told him that I was an Englishman'. This was either not enough or too much. A policeman came and took Knox to the local courthouse where an official questioned him for two hours, going through his papers which included a French map of Eylau, where General von Bennigsen had fought Napoleon. The German said he was sure there were British agents in the region, studying the new system of fortification.

Knox believed he knew what had attracted attention – his bicycle. 'A British machine,' he wrote, always fascinated foreigners 'owing to its superior make'. Crowds collected round it – so much so that henceforth he took the bicycle up to his hotel room to prevent further hysteria. He had, he thought, learnt another lesson – 'that it was better to enquire from women: they were more obliging and less inquisitive than men.' Back in Russian Poland, he had a more threatening encounter; after coming down from a hill where Napoleon had once stood above the River Nieman, he found four secret policemen and a gendarme who had beaten up his cab driver for having let a foreigner roam across these places of possible future military significance.

Knox's report describes this frontier land. The Russian position seemed to be weakened by the disaffection of what he called 'subject' races: Lithuanians, Poles and Jews. The Lithuanians were, he thought, 'fairly contented'; the Poles had been crushed; and the third 'subject' race, the Jews, had endured vicious pogroms under the tsars. Knox felt, not surprisingly, that 'neither Pole nor Jew can be depended upon as loyal Russians'. Things were more harmonious in East Prussia. In German Masuria, on the frontier, the languages were Polish and Lithuanian but the people were 'Lutherans' and 'good Germans', and (the Edwardian anti-Semite Knox noted) 'there are fewer Jews.' The landowners created a rural conservative atmosphere; the large towns, however, were 'socialistic'. Like Solzhenitsyn later, Knox was amazed by the contrast; in Russia the population was decreasing, the settlements 'invariably filthy', with bedraggled horses and broken-down carts trundling along wretched roads, whereas the German towns and villages were neatly ordered. The extensive East Prussian railway network ran with startling efficiency compared to the primitive, meagre Russian system. Trade also showed German organization, admittedly counter-balanced by the impressive Russian potential. The port of Königsberg, for instance, worked well yet depended on its grain export trade, two-thirds of which came from Russia's western provinces.

Knox considered that the greatest obstacles to a Russian invasion were the lakes, generally frozen from the start of January until the end of March. The huge woodlands – the forests on either side of the River Nieman, the Kaiser's hunting domain at Rominten, the Johannisburg forest where Bennigsen had hidden his advance from Napoleon – were crossed by railways and metalled roads on the German side. But large, dense areas remained practically impenetrable, particularly for cavalry; in Russia these were wilder although during the snowy, freezing winter even the best metalled highway became useless.

The Colonel's report conveys the sense that beyond Germany's eastern frontier lay chaos. Indeed Knox's journey was, to a certain extent, one of exploration for few people in western Europe knew much about the region that, for many, seemed to exist on the continent's most distant ramparts. In 1913, the introduction to Karl Baedeker's guide to Germany gave the places most likely to interest visitors. 'Eastern Germany', the book says, 'lies outside the range of the ordinary tourist' although Danzig had interesting brick churches and some baroque buildings – and the castle at Marienburg was 'the noblest secular building in medieval Germany'. Königsberg, however, the capital of East Prussia, had 'little to offer the sightseer'.

Baedeker printed only a few details of this city of 246,000 people (a figure which included a garrison of 9,500). It was, contemporary sources declared, a trading centre for grain and timber where barges carried cargo along the River Pregel that was linked by a canal to Pillau, an ice-free port on to the Baltic. Königsberg had become one of the largest centres for the import of tea (into Russia and Poland) and peas and linseed, eaten as cheap food, again principally in Russia and Poland. Industry took the form mostly of sawmills or iron-foundries, linked to the region's agriculture. Two buildings dominated the city: the castle and the cathedral. A gothic tower of the castle stretched upwards from a structure much changed since the sixteenth century yet still possessing an air of dark, solid medievalism; the last nationally important event there had been the coronation in 1861 of the Prussian King William I – later emperor of a united Germany – although (Baedeker said) the present Emperor William II stayed in the royal apartments on visits to his eastern capital. Within sight of the castle, the red-brick cathedral was on an island in the River Pregel that had some of the city's oldest buildings. Begun in 1325, during the Teutonic Knights' crusade to bring Christianity to the Baltic, not completed until the middle of the fifteenth century and restored in the years 1901–7, it still had its western tower unfinished. Inside were mural paintings of the fourteenth and sixteenth centuries. Among the monuments and graves of the Grand Masters of the Teutonic Order was a memorial to Duke Albrecht, Königsberg's sixteenth-century ruler, the founder of the university and a follower of Luther.

Königsberg was a city of memorials. Those to the first Emperor William I and the Prussian King Frederick I were outside the palace, as was Duke Albrecht's; a bronze statue of Bismarck loomed in the Kaiser Wilhelm Platz; the beautiful Queen Luise, who had pleaded with Napoleon for her country, had a memorial in the castle. Opposite the theatre was Schiller, who could have known little of Königsberg; also in the Kaiser Wilhelm Platz was the tomb of Hans Luther, the son of Martin. On one of the city's brick gateways, the Königstor, the statues showed a mix of national and local: King Ottokar of Bohemia (a thirteenth-century leader of the northern crusade after whom Königsberg had been named) and (again) Duke Albrecht and King Frederick I. There were busts or statues of Kant in the Parade-Platz (near Schiller) and in the senate hall of the university, and there were printed or written reminiscences and mementoes of him in the museum. Next to the cathedral was his grave with a further bust, and carved words from the *Critique of Practical Reason*: 'the starry heavens above me and the moral law within me.'

What of the town's pleasures? Among these in 1913 were

the zoo, the Botanical Gardens, the pictures in the municipal museums (including works by Caspar David Friedrich, Lovis Corinth, Frans Hals), the parks and open-air concerts in summer; the ceremony on the castle's tower when a choir sang at sunset; and the sea, not far by road or rail: Rauschen, Cranz and Palmnicken on the Samland coast and the Kurische Nehrung, or Spit, with its high, dangerous dunes. Cranz was the most popular seaside resort. Russian and Polish Jews came there, feeling safe in the more tolerant East Prussia. Although generally welcome, they tended to avoid the fashionable beach-side promenade where they might receive cool glances but rarely anything worse.

*

Lorenz Grimoni, curator of the Königsberg Museum in Duisburg, recalls his old homeland of East Prussia. What remains, he asks? Is it just photographs and memories, poems about dark woods and crystal lakes and exile?

I think of him as Lorenz although I've never called him this because we stick to the German formality of Herr Grimoni and Herr Egremont – which may give more structure to our talks. Lorenz reveals his memories, of his childhood at the end of the war, on East Prussia's western edge, of the best Christmas ever, in 1944 before the flight west in a slow train trying to dodge the Red Army. 'It went like this,' he says of the journey. I watch as he draws quick, deep lines, almost tearing the paper. Later in our talk, he does it again – 'Like this,' the pen going deeper, as if to make a more secure trench. His own story is quite typical, he thinks – he was born in 1939, near Hindenburg's old home at Neudeck, yet untypical perhaps in that he was baptized in the old castle chapel in Königsberg because his grandparents lived in the city. His father was a schoolteacher and joined the wartime Luftwaffe, ending up in a British prison camp in Schleswig-Holstein. The young Lorenz had been ill with tuberculosis; now he is thin and straight, eyes bright behind glasses, missing nothing. Again he speaks of the flight – to Danzig on that slow train, by rail again to Saxony, across the Elbe, to Magdeburg: then post-war life in Düsseldorf where his father taught again, before Lorenz was ordained as a Lutheran priest. What he wants is to see that history isn't forgotten.

I sense that Lorenz knows how British moral self-righteousness rises if Germans hint at any entitlement to pity. He has already headed this off by reminding me, in the most courteous possible way, of the RAF's destruction of the medieval centre of Königsberg, and the slaughter of many of its people. What he wants is recognition for East Prussia's beauty, its history and its genius. Kant taught at the University of Königsberg where Herder and Hamann studied. In Frauenburg (now the Polish Frombork), some thirty miles west along the Baltic coast – from whose cathedral tower you can see Kaliningrad – Copernicus revolutionized science.

Lorenz's stories often cross frontiers. Kant spent several years as a subject of the Russian Tsarina Elizabeth when the Russians occupied Königsberg; Herder believed the Teutonic Knights' campaign of conversion and conquest was an affront to the native culture and therefore wrong; there's doubt about whether Copernicus was Polish or German. And whose country is East Prussia? Are people still frightened of who might want it? When looking at one of the land's ruined Prussian manor houses, symbols of conquest, I was chased across a field by its Polish owner who was wielding a shovel and shouting perhaps one of the few German words he knew: 'Nein! Nein!'

Ruins – even a few bricks or stones or an overgrown grave – show that history is hard to destroy. At Slobity in Poland (formerly Schlobitten in East Prussia) on an outside wall of the church there's a war memorial – a stone tablet set into the brick – that lists several members of the Dohna family, who owned the big house nearby. In the 1920s, the last Dohna to live at Schlobitten, terrified of revolution, stored arms behind the church's organ. Now when I mention the Dohnas to some of the present inhabitants, only a few hundred yards from the big house's ruins, these Poles look at me as if I am mad. Who knows or cares now about these ancient Grafs or Fürsts, even if they had once attended Kant's lectures in Königsberg and been friends of Frederick the Great, the Emperor William II and Reichsmarschall Hermann Göring?

The Junkers – the landowners east of the Elbe – were looked on as a people apart. The Emperor William II's friend Philipp von Eulenburg, whose disgrace after a homosexual scandal had threatened to engulf the throne, inherited property in East Prussia before 1914. Eulenburg liked to compare his family's three estates: one near the Dutch border at Cleves in what is now North-Rhine-Westphalia; another in Brandenburg, not far from Berlin; and the third in East Prussia. The Cleves property, he thought, was in character and culture two hundred years ahead of the one in Brandenburg, because of its proximity to progressive Holland; but he put his East Prussian estate two hundred years behind Brandenburg which meant a four-hundred-year gap with Cleves. This was as much time as separates the twentieth century from the still partly medieval society before the Thirty Years War.

Eulenburg was bitter after the scandal, when many of his relations and friends had deserted him. In his memoirs he looks coolly at the east, particularly at his cousins the Dohna family. He admires the local patriotism of East Prussians and the landscape's beauty, calling it a paradise for horses and people, and traces the history back to the Teutonic Knights and the early settlers – pioneers, he thinks, like the colonizers in the Americas or Africa. He thought the nearness to Russia had made the people different, like Russian or Slavs, implying a primitive feel to the place. The Germans, Eulenburg believed, had no talent for colonization, and had dealt badly with the Polish and other minorities, exploiting them instead of offering consistency and security. The grand East Prussian families often inter-married, creating the idea of a caste apart, an isolated world – and with this went that other colonial characteristic: opportunism, exemplified, Eulenburg thought, by Duke Albrecht's sixteenth-century decision to turn his duchy into a vassal state of the King of Poland. They were out for themselves – this was the only allegiance these rich East Prussians knew; such ruthlessness darkened their behaviour. Had it really been necessary for his Dohna cousins to put a perfectly sane uncle into a lunatic asylum because he had publicly questioned their supposedly distinguished ancestry?

There were, a German friend told me, three landowning families that, before 1945, were among the richest and most important in East Prussia: the Dönhoffs, the Lehndorffs and the Dohnas. Each had territorial power and possessions, symbolized by their houses: the Dönhoff neo-classical castle Friedrichstein, the Lehndorff 'great wilderness' at Steinort and, west from this – some miles south-east of Elblag (formerly the German Elbing) and north-east of Pasłęk (once Preussisch Holland) – Schlobitten, the Dohna mansion. Schlobitten is a ruin with jagged walls and crumbling outbuildings, more destroyed than Steinort but not completely lost like Friedrichstein.

There's a photograph in his memoirs of the last Dohna owner of this place, Fürst (Prince) Alexander zu Dohna-Schlobitten, revisiting his old estates in 1974. The Fürst is talking, and apparently giving advice, to the Polish director of the Słobity collective farm, Mr Konarzewski who is neat in a suit and tie (perhaps put on especially for the Prince's visit) while a jacketless, shirt-sleeved Alexander Dohna wears Wellington boots, as if ready for work in the fields; only his large, angular head and height seem appropriate to a Fürst of the old German Empire. By 1974, any hope of return had gone; it was Mr Konarzewski who controlled the Słobity woods – where the last Emperor and Hermann Göring had once hunted – and it was a Polish Roman Catholic priest who listened to the requests that the Fürst might be allowed to pay for the restoration of the family graves in what had once been the village of Schlobitten's Lutheran church.

In the museum in Duisburg, the display ends with a case of rubble and photographs of Russians and Germans together; for Königsberg, only the past remains. Enjoying Lorenz Grimoni's commentary, his patience, the sandwiches he has brought for our lunch, his references to his life as a Lutheran pastor when he worked briefly in Kaliningrad – I want our talks to go on for weeks. Even then, there would be more to learn.

'You use the word "atmosphere" [*Stimmung*] a lot,' Lorenz Grimoni says, suddenly irritated. I say that the atmosphere of the place as it had been before the cataclysm of 1945 is what interested me. It was something I'd glimpsed years before when, while learning German, I stayed with a schoolmaster and his family in Lower Saxony, not far from what was then the border with the communist East German state. When I spoke of East Germany (Ost Deutschland) my host put me right. The German Democratic Republic, or the DDR, wasn't east but middle Germany. East Germany is further east, in what is now northern Poland and the Russian province of Kaliningrad, in the old Silesia, Pomerania and East Prussia. This wasn't nationalistic dreams, he said, but fact. I wasn't encouraged to raise the point again.

The island British don't understand borders, Lorenz Grimoni says: how in central and eastern Europe there was a frequent crossing of these. People mixed, yet they feared another country that was just over a fence. His own name must originally have been Italian although the family had been in East Prussia for centuries. He points at a huge map that shows the spread of the Teutonic Order. In the Middle Ages, its churches and castles were scattered through what are now Hungary, Italy, Alsace, northern Spain, south to Sicily, east to the Baltic. He mentions the start of modern Europe with Charlemagne ruling from Aachen. Before that – and here he smiles – the conquering Anglo-Saxons came to Britain from Germany. Europeans share much, he says: not least, I am left thinking, this long German reach.

In the borderlands, most of the landlords and the middle class on the Russian side were Germans or Poles or Jews. The Tsarist state accepted the Baltic Germans as property owners and administrators of the expanding empire: Sergei Witte was Nicholas II's Prime Minister; Bennigsen, a Hanoverian, led the Russians against Napoleon; Count Karl Nesselrode was the non-Russian-speaking Foreign Minister from 1815 to 1856; General von Rennenkampf invaded East Prussia in August 1914. Of the sixteen most prominent Russian generals at the start of the First World War, seven had German names.

One must remember its treasures, its images of tolerance and culture – the silver-bound books made for Duke Albrecht, a prince of the Reformation; the castle and the university libraries; the Wallenrod books given in the seventeenth century; the cathedral tombs of the Polish Radziwiłłs. Now those who had lived in Königsberg are dying and their children are in the new Germany, soothed by its prosperity. But the history of the old east is not only German but European history; Copernicus, with his Polish and German roots, shows the need to think in European terms, to remember weak frontiers.

On 7 July 2009, a manuscript came up for sale in London – a part of Duke Albrecht's own copy of a treatise on warfare, dated around 1555 and originally in Königsberg. Three-hundred-and-eighty-one pages long, illustrated in full colour, heightened occasionally by liquid gold, and bound in eighteenth-century calf, it shows the change from soldiering based on feudal duty to the modern professional army. Albrecht is depicted as the supreme commander, with an escort of colourfully attired foot-soldiers. He makes a magnificent figure in heavily jointed armour decorated with gold stripes, a broad black hat rimmed by frothing feathers, the distinctive full beard beneath a wide-eyed imposing face, similar to the statue of him outside Kaliningrad cathedral, near the tomb of Kant. In the treatise, the enemy is the Turks (the Asiatic hordes) who threaten the monarchs of the west – Henry VIII of England, the Holy Roman Emperor Charles V, King Ferdinand of Hungary and Bohemia – and civilization. It is Duke Albrecht and his Prussians, on Europe's eastern edge, who guard the frontier.

The libraries of Königsberg, of the university and the castle, were strong in music, manuscripts from the time of the Teutonic Order and the history of the Baltic; the first book printed in

Lithuanian came out of Königsberg. At the end, as the frontier crumbled, books, manuscripts and records of four hundred years were taken west on lorries, ships and trains – a symbolic reversal of the northern crusades – to escape the Red Army. Others were burned in the raids of August 1944 or looted or taken into the victors' collections. Among the treasures was Duke Albrecht's silver library – twenty opulently bound volumes – thought at least partly to reflect the taste of Albrecht's second wife, Anna Maria – showing the brilliance of the goldsmith's and silversmith's art in the age of the Reformation; some had been made by Königsberg craftsmen, others at Nuremberg.

Are the silver books beautiful, or are the decorated surfaces and heavy bronze clasps a crude show of luxury and power? You can see some of them in the University Library of Toruń (formerly Thorn). The bindings have that low light of old silver; their decoration – elaborate patterns of foliage or images like that of the Virtues or biblical scenes such as the Creation, Abraham's sacrifice or Jacob's dream – is still fresh. In the centre rondel of one is Duke Albrecht himself, in armour, holding up his sword, the other hand resting just below his breast plate; another rondel shows his wife Anna Maria, some forty years younger than he: her hands clasped across her fur-lined cape, a flat brimmed hat above her large-eyed face. Albrecht was a prince of the Reformation; Luther came to Königsberg. Within their bindings and heavy wooden boards, the texts, printed in Wittenberg or Nuremberg, are contemporary Protestant devotional works: not rare. It is the outward show that Albrecht and his wife were seeking. The bindings are a sign of the ambition and confidence of these rulers of a small Baltic state.

During the Second World War, books from German-occupied Polish, Lithuanian, Latvian, Ukrainian and Russian libraries were taken to Königsberg as part of the programme of cultural imperialism – or so-called 'rescue' of culture from the Slavs. The Nazis were particularly interested in German book collections in the east – in the libraries in towns like Breslau, Danzig and Königsberg – seeing them as bastions of German civilization. In 1944, as the Red Army approached, this arrogance crumbled. From March of that year, the Königsberg librarian, Carl Diesch, reported on plans for evacuation. Some manuscripts and early printed books were put in a bunker and other rare items were dispersed to large houses in the province.

In August, Diesch and two of his most important assistants were sent on military duties to Lithuania. He returned to Königsberg after two months, frantically arranging for the evacuation west of historic material, which is now in the Prussian State Archives at Berlin or at the University of Göttingen. On 6 April 1945, the librarian was on the last ship to leave Pillau, accompanied by seven chests of books and manuscripts, most of which were lost during the chaotic journey. After the war Diesch went to Leipzig where again he became a librarian and continued his research into the romantic period in German literature. He showed National Socialism's pervasive stain, when an anti-Semitic passage he had written during the war about the poet Heinrich Heine resurfaced. Diesch claimed that such sentiments had been expected then of all who held state office. But the piece darkened his last years. His death in 1957 was marked by a stiflingly discreet obituary in a university journal.

When he fled from Königsberg, Carl Diesch left behind some hundred and forty thousand books and manuscripts that had been distributed among various large houses throughout the province. The silver library was at Schloss Karwinden (now the Polish Karwiny), near what was then Elbing (now Elbląg). When the Poles moved into what had been the south-western part of the old East Prussia, the books from Karwinden and other hiding places were brought together at Pasłęk (formerly the German Preussisch Holland). In 1947 some twenty thousand of these were chosen for the library of the new university at Toruń where the pre-war Wilno University was to be re-established. The new Poland had moved westwards. In the changed borders, the formerly Polish Wilno had become the new Lithuanian (or, until

Kant's tomb outside Königsberg cathedral.

1990, Soviet) Vilnius. In the two years since the war's end, the collection at Karwinden had shrunk, through theft and loss. The silver library had been reduced from twenty books to some fourteen or fifteen. Now one, without its printed text, is in the Polish National Library in Warsaw, another (again the binding alone) in the castle at Kraków, one in the Masurian museum in Olsztyn (the former Allenstein – not to be confused with the very much smaller Olstynek to the south-west, the German Hohenstein) and the rest in Toruń.

Friendship or familiarity with a place's history can beat hatred, Lorenz Grimoni thinks. He has an example of this; Yuri Ivanov, the Russian writer who moved to Kaliningrad after the war, had once felt such loathing for everything German that when he came to Königsberg with the Red Army he had helped to cut the sculpted heads off one of the city gates. But later, in the 1960s,

after years in Kaliningrad during which he became increasingly
fascinated by its past, Ivanov campaigned against the blowing up
of what was left of the castle. He had come to Duisburg with a
Russian delegation and Lorenz's mother, also full of hatred (in her
case for the Russians), was reluctant to meet him when, guided by
Lorenz, he toured the town's Königsberg museum. But Ivanov, a
big jolly man, had charmed her so much that she gave him some
of her dead husband's East Prussian books.

Lorenz drives me back to where I'm staying and when I ask
how many people come to the museum each year he is reluctant
to say. Who pays for it, I wonder? The city of Duisburg gives the
room, the heating, the light and a cleaner; the German federal and
state governments help, and supporters raise the rest. You can't
judge the success of a museum by attendance figures, Lorenz
says; visits to German museums in general are down but they had
a Kant exhibition recently that drew in thirty thousand people.
We pass through the centre of Duisburg. Lorenz reminds me
that 80 per cent of the city had been destroyed in the war by
the British bombing.

*

Lorenz Grimoni thinks the Teutonic Knights brought civilization
to the east. The poet Johannes Bobrowski, born in East Prussia in
1917, believed the opposite – that Germans should feel guilty not
only about the recent horrors on the eastern front, which he had
seen as a soldier in the Wehrmacht, but also about the earlier conquest – with its extinction of the pagan Prussians and destruction
of Baltic–Slav civilizations in what is now Poland, Russia and
Lithuania. The land in Bobrowski's poetry is still unconquered –
a region of great rivers, of the Vistula, the Memel and the
Nieman, of the Masurian lakes and forests, of coastal lagoons
and havens, of beautiful myths of heroes and of gods. This was
what the Teutonic Knights – the German order of chivalry –
entered when they launched a northern crusade with papal
blessing in the thirteenth century. It was to be an equivalent to

the campaign against the Muslims in the Holy Land but aimed principally at the pagan Prussians who lived on the south-eastern edge of the Baltic.

In September 1991, the Professor of Slavic Studies at Princeton wrote to the *New York Times* to correct the 'common error' of calling the original Prussians Slavs; they were, Professor Charles E. Townsend stated, 'a Baltic tribe, akin to the modern Lithuanians or Latvians'. In medieval Europe, the Wends, the so-called 'west Slavs', lived to the west of these old Prussians, between the rivers Elbe and Oder. There must have been movement of people, spurred by trade along the Baltic coast, in fur, fish and amber. Then, after the conquest of the old Prussians by the Teutonic Knights, Slavic Poles moved into the newly Christianized lands, chiefly into Masuria, the south-eastern part of what became East Prussia.

Racial identities quickly became blurred yet provided reason enough for conflict. The eleventh-century German chronicler Adam of Bremen described areas of tension that were still being fought over by Poles, Germans and Russians in the twentieth century. In his history of Königsberg, Fritz Gause, director of the city's archives and museums at the end of the war, says that Slav settlements came under the early influence of German or Goth culture from the land by the River Vistula or further south; Gause's use of the word *Kultur* – the opposite of barbarity – is surely significant. Heinrich Himmler, an amateur archaeologist, came to the East Prussian estate of the Dohna family in the 1930s to examine some remains nearby, hoping for evidence of original Germanic settlement.

To Fritz Gause, the Teutonic Knights' campaign was heroic. But to Poles and Russians it could seem a precursor of the German forces of 1939 and 1941 that had the black cross of the Knights on their planes and tanks. The Knights – the Warrior Monks – combined force with self-denial. The crusade was brutal – but not more brutal than those in the Holy Land. It attracted knights from throughout Christendom, including the future King

Henry IV of England. The English kings Edward I and Edward III contributed to its costs. Chaucer's 'verray parfit gentil knyght' went on a northern campaign or 'Reise'.

The northern crusaders needed extraordinary toughness, for the Baltic's south-eastern edge was an inhospitable wilderness – a country of elk, bears and wolves, of long icy winters and intense short summers – a place, Frederick the Great thought later, unfit for humans. Red-brick castles began to appear, evidence of conquest; bishoprics were established at Marienwerder in 1243 and at Königsberg in 1255, the city that was named after King Ottokar of Bohemia (who had joined a crusade in 1254). Much of what became East Prussia was under the Knights' control by the end of the thirteenth century and they pressed further east. In 1386 the baptism of the Lithuanian Prince Jagiełło, who also became King of Poland, began the conversion of Lithuania, the last pagan state in Europe.

By 1409 there was conflict between the Polish-Lithuanians and the Teutonic Knights and, in 1410, at Grunwald, the Order was defeated and its grand master, Ulrich von Jungingen, killed. The 1410 battle became a symbol either of national triumph or of shame. It was fought near two villages, one called Grunwald, the other called Tannenberg. To the Poles and Lithuanians it became the victory of Grunwald; the Germans, however, took the other village's name for what to them had been a defeat at the hands of the Slavs – Tannenberg. Five centuries later, in August 1914, when a German army defeated a Russian one near the site, the Germans called this the second battle of Tannenberg, as if to wipe the 1410 Slav victory of Grunwald off the map.

The power of the Orders was waning when in 1511 Albrecht of Brandenburg-Anspach, from the Franconian family of Hohenzollern, with a Jagiełłon mother and King Zygmunt I Stary of Poland for an uncle, became Grand Master of the Teutonic Knights. Nineteenth-century Polish nationalists saw Albrecht's public homage to his uncle the Polish King as a triumph; in fact, it freed Albrecht from the theocratic Orders and began the ascent of Königsberg, his capital city. Albrecht held power for fifty-seven years, first as grand master, then as Duke of Prussia. His lands became the first evangelical state, with a Lutheran University founded in Königsberg in 1544. The two faiths – Polish Roman Catholicism and Prussian Lutheranism – tolerated one another; unlike in England, remarkably little destruction of Church property occurred as a result of the Reformation. Polish and German were spoken throughout East Prussia, after Polish overlordship ended in 1656. In 1618, with the end of Albrecht's direct line, Brandenburg and Prussia were united under the Hohenzollern Elector of Brandenburg.

Settlers came to East Prussia from the west and the accumulation of large estates began. The Lehndorffs arrived in the fifteenth century, the Dohnas and the Dönhoffs at about the same time. In the eighteenth century, there was more immigration: Protestants thrown out by the Archbishop of Salzburg in 1732, Mennonites from less tolerant parts of Germany, Huguenots from France. Königsberg became an international port, with traders from all over Europe. But the land was always hard, devastated by plagues, needing to be drained and reclaimed. Its precarious security was shown in 1656 when Tatars stormed into Masuria, perpetrating massacres still used in the twentieth century to evoke terror of what might come from across the eastern frontier.

Königsberg was chosen for the coronation of the King of Prussia in 1701 because, unlike Berlin, it was outside the boundaries of the Holy Roman Empire, thus freeing the new king from having to acknowledge the Habsburg Emperor in Vienna as his overlord. In 1713 Frederick I was succeeded by Frederick William I, who doted on his regiment of tall soldiers and forced his oldest son Frederick (later 'the Great') to watch the execution of Frederick's best friend, Katte, who had been involved in a failed attempt by the boy to flee from Prussia and parental tyranny. Frederick William I consolidated an absolutist state, sound finances and a powerful army and encouraged immigration, particularly into his eastern domains. Tax increases hit the smaller farmers but the nobility flourished and built many of the large East Prussian houses. The ascent of Prussia as a great power began in 1740 when King Frederick II, 'the Great', inherited from his terrible father the strong state that made an adventurous policy possible. With such coups as the conquest of Silesia in 1740 and the First Partition of Poland in 1772, Frederick turned Prussia into a European power, and the perception of a cold, militarized kingdom began. By 1786 it was the thirteenth-largest European state by population but with the third largest army: with a population of 5.8 million, Prussia had an army of 195,000, or a soldier for every twenty-nine subjects.

Frederick's foreign adventures were no more cynical or brutal than those of Louis XIV or Napoleon or the later imperial expansion of Britain and France. Also they were not always successful. They gained territory for Prussia – Silesia, Roman Catholic Warmia in the first Polish partition (Danzig and Thorn came later) – but also brought about defeat when Königsberg came under Russian rule from 1758 until 1762. Kant wrote a letter of homage to his new monarch, the Tsarina Elizabeth.

Prussia, shown to be fragile by Frederick II's defeats, was overwhelmed by Napoleon. The Prussian court fled from Berlin to Königsberg in December 1806, then further north-east to Memel in January 1807. After the battle of Eylau, in February 1807, Napoleon ruled his empire from the East Prussian castle of Finckenstein for ten weeks, while having a liaison with the Polish Countess Marie Walewska, before winning a decisive victory in June at Friedland. The Teutonic Knights had built fortifications at Friedland some four hundred and fifty years before.

The humiliation of the Prussian King, Frederick William III, was demonstrated by the King's presence as a mere observer at the meeting on 25 June 1807 between Tsar Alexander I and Napoleon on a raft on the River Niemen at Tilsit. Queen Luise's approach to Napoleon on 6 July in the town, when she pleaded for her defeated country, was appropriated by manufacturers of commemorative plates as a beautiful romance, although the effect on the Emperor was minimal. Memorials to the Russian dead were put up later by the Prussians on the battlefields of Friedland and Eylau.

In 1807, the French Emperor seemed invincible. On 10 July, after the meetings at Tilsit, he entered Königsberg, to flowers and the pealing of bells, to take up residence in the castle until the 13th. The French occupied the city for thirty-nine days. The people of Königsberg – unlike Berliners under a similar occupation – were said to have been 'meritorious' and 'reserved' and the conquerors kept, on the whole, good discipline; Königsbergers were surprised to find so many German Rhinelanders in French uniform. The city suffered from the plunder of war, the French taking from the castle all the amber in the royal apartments and turning the old weapons into scrap metal. The buyers of this loot, Fritz Gause, the last director of the town's archives and museums, notes in his history of the city, were 'Jewish merchants'. The invasion brought missed harvests, forced requisitions and plundering. The trade of the port was closed to enemies of the French. Huge bonfires of English goods blazed by the Königstor, the city's main gate.

Forced into an alliance with Napoleon, Prussia, particularly its eastern territories, seemed to have only a great past and a future at best as a French or Russian satellite. The King and Queen came to Königsberg from Memel in January 1808 and stayed until December 1809. At that time of apparent humiliation, the administrators responsible for the reforms that revolutionized Prussia again gathered in Königsberg: Stein, Gneisenau, Humboldt. But first, in 1812, the city – and its surrounding region – was forced to help equip what was now its French ally for the invasion of Russia; the teeming herds of oxen needed by the Grand Army showed the extent of Napoleon's empire, coming as they did from Lombardy, the Low Countries and what is now Croatia.

It was reported that the French had taken Moscow. By the end of November very different rumours were confirmed by the first refugees. In December, columns of frost-bitten, ragged troops accompanied by skeletal horses trudged westwards, ridiculed by the people of East Prussia. Taking advantage of French disarray, the Prussians, at the Convention of Taurrogen that month, abandoned the alliance with Napoleon in favour of neutrality. Now the Russians were their liberators and Tsar Alexander I was greeted at Lyck, on Prussia's eastern frontier, by a priest and a joyful crowd.

*

Colonel Alfred Knox's risky East Prussian journey of 1911 had irritated his superiors but by March 1914 he was back in favour after an important dispatch on the Russian army.

Knox wrote that Russia was the only great European power to have had recent experience of modern warfare: in Manchuria in 1904 and 1905 when, in spite of dreadful tactical errors, the army had been remarkably brave. He stated that 'owing to the rigour of the climate and the lower general civilisation, all ranks are more fitted than the men of central Europe to stand privation and nerve strain'. Another asset was 'the simple, almost fanatical, faith of the Russian soldier in God and the Emperor.' What they needed was more time – the men, 'grandsons of serfs', lacked initiative and too many reserve officers came from the 'unpatriotic' intelligentsia but by April 1917 the Russians could have over two million men under arms. At the War Office in London, General Sir Henry Wilson wrote on the dispatch, 'It is easy to understand now why Germany is anxious about the future & why she may think that it is a case of "now or never".'

Five months later that anxiety boiled over. In June 1914, Knox took his leave, planning to return to St Petersburg at the end of July. In Berlin, on his way to Britain, he read of the murder in Sarajevo of the Archduke Franz Ferdinand and his wife: then reports came of Austria's ultimatum to Serbia. Knox thought that the European tension would soon slacken, as it had in 1908 and 1912, but on 27 July, at breakfast in his home in Ulster, he received a telegram ordering him back to St Petersburg. After a morning on the golf course, he crossed that night from Belfast. The talk on the ferry and later in London was about the possible coercion of Ulster into a new Ireland under Home Rule, which he strongly opposed.

At Berlin, on the train, Knox read of Russia's partial mobilization. Further east, the railway bridge at Marienburg, beside the huge castle of the Teutonic Knights, was guarded by troops, some in the combat uniform of field grey. Deeper into East Prussia, the atmosphere became more tense – and not until they were across the frontier, into their homeland, did the Russian passengers speak of their hatred for Germany. The train reached St Petersburg on 31 July; the following day, at 6 p.m., Germany declared war on Russia. With patriotism bursting out all around him, Knox felt isolated until 4 August when Britain, after the German violation of Belgian neutrality, entered the war alongside the Russians and the French.

To Alfred Knox, that time seemed 'wonderful' – the start of a 'great adventure'. The innocent enthusiasm of August 1914 is part of the myth of the old world; and when Fritz Gause, the historian of Königsberg, wrote of his own memories of that time, he showed nostalgia for a patriotic unity as yet untainted by Nuremberg rallies or racial hatred. Even French restaurants, Gause noted, changed their names to German, attesting to the proud Germanness of these descendants of Huguenot immigrants. It was known that East Prussia was at risk. No one knew what might come across the Russian frontier – and the war revived the sense of a land on the edge.

To the Junkers – the landowners – patriotism was essential. They ranged from those struggling on a few sandy or boggy acres to families with vast estates such as the Dohnas or the Dönhoffs. Prominent supporters of the Hohenzollerns in the old Prussia, admirers of Bismarck in the new German Reich (although doubtful about his liberal social welfare reforms), they saw themselves as pioneers, living and working on a tough if beautiful land. In a country still fumbling for a national identity their position was of symbolic importance, as representatives of the historic mission in the east. Through the Emperor and the army, where their families filled the officer corps, the East Prussian landlords could influence these two powerful extra-parliamentary parts of the German state. In August 1914 one of their leaders in the Reichstag was the extraordinary figure of Elard von Oldenburg-Januschau.

Through inheritance, marriage and purchase, Januschau had collected estates in the east (south of Königsberg) and west of the region (centred on the village of Januschau where he lived when not attending parliament in Berlin). A loud and forceful campaigner against lower food tariffs (which would give cheaper food to workers in the new industrial Germany), he believed passionately in agricultural protection – the only way, he thought, that the German east could survive. There was an imperial edge as well; the Poles in Germany, in his view, resembled the Irish in the United Kingdom (to whom he felt the British were being too indulgent in offering Home Rule) and they must accept German domination or leave.

Januschau had fought duels in his youth, recalling these with pride although he had been briefly imprisoned for one of them. He had been eight years in the army – the best time, he thought, of his life. Large, bluff, with a small goatee beard and pock-marked skin, ready to use his fists at election meetings, he loathed democracy. Should Germany be ruled from above or below, he asked? To him the voice of the people was like the lowing of cattle; the Emperor, Januschau said in a famous parliamentary speech, should be able to disband the Reichstag with a lieutenant and ten men. When another member feared for Germany's future, Januschau struck the table and said that the country was secure as long as it had a large army. In 1908, when Germany supported Austria-Hungary's annexation of Bosnia against the protests of other European powers, he wanted a preventive war against France. He was sure that neither Britain nor Russia was prepared. Three million German soldiers could take Paris within days.

Junker leader: Elard von Oldenburg-Januschau in Berlin.

With this public belligerence went an amiable manner and a bantering charm. Januschau was close to General Paul von Hindenburg, who shared his origins in eastern Germany; less predictable were his friendly relations with opponents like the Social Democratic leader August Bebel, the Jewish businessman and politician Walther Rathenau and, later, Joseph Goebbels. In August 1914, he was helping with the harvest at Januschau, the estate with its manor house where he lived, near Deutsch Eylau (now the Polish Iława). Although almost sixty, he wanted to fight but, as a reserve officer, was called to join the staff of the Emperor's eldest son, the Crown Prince. Januschau had no doubt of a quick German victory.

*

When Januschau's grandson came to the manor house, in the winter of 1945, the battles that had begun in August 1914 were long over. Hans von Lehndorff, a surgeon in Königsberg during the city's last days, had escaped and was now depending for his survival on working as a doctor for the new Russian and Polish rulers of East Prussia. Amid the danger and suffering, he felt consoled, even partly protected, by the sense of the land's power, of its possession of him – quite different to the idea of ownership and control that had been so strong in his grandfather. Lehndorff's feeling was outside time, beyond the world's reach.

He sensed this timelessness on a moonlit winter journey, through the Finckenstein forest and the woods of the Januschau lands, full of memories that were so strong that they seemed like a companion beside him. The manor's lodge had been burned down; the graves were still there but had been ransacked. When Lehndorff reached the park and saw the house with a lamp on the veranda and lights inside, he watched from a distance and heard doors slamming, the noise of the Russians. He met a wagon with some muffled workers on their way to the fields who gave him the news: last winter's trek to escape the Red Army had reached no further than Stuhm, some twenty-five miles away, where Lehndorff's mother and brother had been shot by the Russians. A man in the village might shelter him, the locals said, but he should watch out, for the place was guarded. Ten minutes later he was taken in by the German who had been recommended to him. It was now 30 degrees below zero but his excitement and anxiety were so great that, even in his thin clothing, Lehndorff did not feel the cold.

A year earlier, the trek with his mother and brother had left Januschau. At Stuhm they sent a cyclist to Marienburg to see if there was any chance of getting over the River Nogat; the man returned saying that the large crowds there made it doubtful. So they stayed at a farm, waiting for the Russians – who came on the evening of 25 January 1945. There was a fracas, involving assaults on women. Hans's brother was wounded by a knife, and his mother bandaged him up. The Russians left, then came back to ask who they were – and then shot the two Lehndorffs, mother and son. Another sixteen people were shot or burned alive; the women were raped and the young men carried off; others walked back to Januschau and to captivity. Lehndorff was relieved to hear that the end had been quick, as his family's imagined fate had haunted him.

The land had been turned into a collective farm by the Russians, whose commander seemed affable – and hundreds of Germans were still in the area. Food was a mixture of sugar-beet peelings, potatoes and corn left over from the last harvest. The German survivors had developed an uneasy understanding with the Russians and they urged Hans von Lehndorff to tell the commander that he was a doctor, to demonstrate his worth. Over the wooden gate to the courtyard, near the manor house at Januschau, hung a portrait of Stalin. The fat, elderly commander agreed that Lehndorff should live with an old estate ranger and tend the sick. Januschau was changing as the Junkers' world went up in flames, many of its rituals already in ashes. The Russians fired two thousand cartridges to kill one red deer and a wild boar and fished the lake by using explosives.

Tending his family's graves became Lehndorff's way of restoring some kind of order to his shattered life. He recalled his youngest brother, who had been killed in France, a delightful humorous boy; his body had been brought back to Januschau (although this was not allowed) by another brother. The next brother had died six weeks later after a brain haemorrhage; another brother had been killed on the eastern front – someone, Hans von Lehndorff felt, who had found his true self as a soldier. Absent were his mother and his eldest brother – the inheritor of Januschau, also a wartime soldier – both of them thrown into a mass grave after being shot on the trek. He thought of his strong mother, of how her occasionally wounding power had been mixed with healing, of how depressed she had been after her children's deaths.

Many of the local Germans now called themselves Masuren to stress their new Polishness – and gradually the district was handed over to the Poles. In July, in the scorching heat, Hans von Lehndorff fell ill, with a high fever and a sense that he was losing his mind. Recovering enough to move to the nearby town of Rosenberg and work in a hospital there, he found a place in ruins. It was now called Susz by the Poles who were arriving by train and lorry from parts of the old Poland that had been taken by the Soviet Union, undecided about where to settle. The luckiest were the first-comers, immediately behind the Red Army, because they found the best houses. Already, there was a priest, a doctor, a mayor, a lady dentist, a solicitor, a forester, a postmaster, a station-master, a chimney sweep, a hairdresser, a shoemaker, a tailor, a butcher, a baker, an inn-keeper.

In the course of visiting the sick, Lehndorff passed Neudeck and Langenau, the two Hindenburg estates, once owned by the man who had symbolized revival and reassurance as a victorious field marshal in the First World War and then as President of Germany; both houses had been burned down while Neudeck village lay damaged among uncultivated fields. The Poles were kind to him when he attended them or delivered their children – and, going to mass in the Catholic church, he felt shame that they seemed already prepared to forgive the Germans. In October, he and a German nurse walked in the Januschau forest and he spoke to her about his grandfather, feeling joy in talking about the past; how this old man was always with him when he made a moral decision. The place brought back childhood memories of Hindenburg, how the whole village had welcomed the victor of Tannenberg, coming up to the house to see the giant, ponderous figure sitting in the dining room.

By December the snow was back. Lehndorff was sent to the hospital in Marienburg to help cope with the aftermath of a train crash, to find the wrecked skeleton of the castle. At Christmas he visited the graves at Januschau again. Some strange normality had come to the place, with dinner parties, even games of bridge, and the Russians moving out which made things more difficult for the Germans under the Poles. Not until May did the transports leave for the west, and Lehndorff was allowed to take very little luggage. The journey into the new Germany was often terrible for the dispossessed East Prussians, with harassment, starvation, overcrowding, many deaths and long, long delays.

Lehndorff was lucky. He went by train, passing three days in a camp on the way where he was quite well fed although the refugees were reminded by the commandant of what the Germans had done to the Poles. The train trundled on, thirty people in each goods wagon, through Thorn, Bromberg and Posen, across neglected fields and bombed-out towns. After two days, it reached Kohlfurt, going slowly over a narrow river – and at the next stop they were in Germany. At a camp in Hoyerswerda, Lehndorff worked in a makeshift hospital, feeling as if he were back in Königsberg, before, a few days later, he left for Berlin, anxious to tell everyone what had been happening in the east.

3: 'Talent is a Duty'

In the museums in Duisburg and Lüneburg, you see photographs of pre-First World War calm – those evocations of a gentle, bourgeois, dressed-up world. In fact there was turmoil and pioneering energy. In August 1914, Germany had the world's largest socialist party and its industry, science and welfare and education systems were powering ahead of the rest of Europe. But what other nations saw and heard in Germany – the Emperor's outbursts, the military strength and naval expansion, the demand for colonies, an adventurous foreign policy – seemed to point to international conflict. Militarism was identified with Prussia; it was what had turned the country into a great power. In the east of the country, it flourished in men like the Junker Elard von Oldenburg-Januschau with his distrust of democracy and the sense that, ultimately, only force and subsidy could protect his land.

Radicalism still had its place in Königsberg where two representatives of the Socialist Party, Hugo Haase, a Jewish lawyer, and Otto Braun, a former printer, represented the city in the Reichstag. Both were sons of cobblers, both had opposed Austria's provocative ultimatum to Serbia after the assassination of the Archduke Franz Ferdinand, both feared the Russian Empire. Haase opposed the war, Braun unenthusiastically supported war credits, stirred by the idea of a preventive war against Russia. That August, a couple who agreed with Haase and Braun were staying at one of the city's hotels. Käthe Kollwitz, an artist whose portrayals of an underclass – victims of Germany's rapid industrialization – had infuriated the Emperor, was with her husband

Karl, who worked as a doctor in Prenzlauerberg, a poor district of Berlin. They were on their way back to the capital after a holiday in their birthplace when they heard soldiers singing in the street. Karl ran out to see what was happening; it was war. Back in the room, she 'wept and wept and wept'.

Years later, after the catastrophe, as she stood in her son Peter's room, Käthe Kollwitz remembered how the boy had run with his elder brother by the Baltic at Rauschen, as if chasing after what he could become – a feeling or a dream – saying, 'I want to be wild.' Surely this will and urge must linger with those who had seen it; perhaps it was why he still seemed to be here among his possessions, like the cupboard with the glass door behind which you could see, among other things, a plaster cast of the head of Narcissus, brought back from Peter's travels in Tuscany. On the wall was a silhouette of her son's profile; a pair of skis stood in one corner and a guitar. Above the iron bed, he had hung a picture of the Rodin sculpture of a couple kissing.

A wooden table and a chair stood in the room's centre; the books lining the shelves on another wall showed a modern young man's collection – Nietzsche's *Thus Spake Zarathustra*, Zola's *Germinal*, Oscar Wilde, Wedekind's *Spring Awakening*; there were also sketch books and drawings and, by the window, an easel. Like his mother, he had been an artist. Peter had seemed, Käthe Kollwitz thought, to be making a series of discoveries about what he could be: a billiard-playing dandy, a wanderer in a pure wild country, an idealist who sought knowledge and beauty and change, a yearning adolescent who felt world-weariness, a patriotic German thrilled by Italy or the Swiss Alps, a solitary dreamer with many friends.

A balcony looked out on to this impoverished part of Berlin where the Kollwitzes lived: a view of a brick water tower, a fountain in the square, a brewery in the distance, grey apartment blocks, some partly derelict houses. Swallows flitted through the summer; Käthe Kollwitz remembered also how the night sky had fascinated Peter with the feeling it induced of life's smallness. Also over the iron bed was a page from a calendar with Kant's words, 'Two things fill the mind, with ever new and increasing wonder and awe, the more often and the more seriously reflection concentrates upon them: the starry heavens above me and the moral law within me.'

In 1867, the year Käthe Kollwitz was born there, Königsberg was a city of a hundred and fifteen thousand people, overwhelmingly evangelical (or Protestant) with about three thousand Jews and two thousand Roman Catholics, many of whom were Poles. The medieval centre was darkened by tall buildings, warehouses near the river and apartment blocks or houses. Seven stone and wooden bridges crossed the River Pregel. New warehouses were built for wheat and rye and other crops but also for textiles, glass and porcelain, tobacco and the amber from the mines on the coast.

Born Käthe Schmidt in 1867, the fourth child of Carl Schmidt, she grew up in a house near the Pregel, next to the yard of her father's building business. It was her mother's family – the Rupps – that displayed obvious rebellion. Frau Schmidt's father, Julius Rupp, had been a teacher in Königsberg and an evangelical clergyman before he was disciplined for his unorthodox views. In 1846, he founded the Free Evangelical church which welcomed like-minded Roman Catholics and was keen to accommodate secular philosophy, taking the side of the radicals in the revolution of 1848. Rupp remained its leader until his death in 1884 when his son-in-law Carl, Käthe Kollwitz's father, succeeded him.

The dark, northern city seeped into the young Käthe. Wandering with her brothers and sister through its narrow streets and yards, down to the river, where they once found a corpse washed up on the bank, she watched its life – the barges, the high warehouses, the waterside pubs, the fishermen, the dock workers and the sailors. She began to draw this world, which to her seemed more beautiful than the grace or refinement of prosperity; she wasn't attracted to these people through social commitment, she said later, but because of their beauty. Königsberg was where

she first saw the poor, the dark side of Germany's booming industrialization, and she began to depict them with romantic pity. Not
surprisingly, religious imagery occurs often in Käthe Kollwitz's
work, an echo of the Rupp piety. With this came a preoccupation
with suffering, a horror at what people could inflict on others, at
how painful so-called progress could be.

Having been barred from the civil service because of his radicalism, Carl Schmidt had started a successful building business.
He educated his daughter privately, because women were often
ignored in the state system, and even paid for his son Konrad to
travel to England to meet Frederick Engels. Käthe was a nervous
child, a victim of stomach cramps and tantrums. Two of her
brothers died in childhood, her mother seemed like a loved and
revered Madonna; and she remembered wanting to die, to escape
pain and loss. She disliked school but read Goethe and Schiller
at home in her father's library and became absorbed by the
engravings of Hogarth that he had in the house. The high point
of the year was the summer holiday in a fisherman's cottage on
the Baltic at Rauschen that the Schmidts had bought – but the
creed of her grandfather Rupp and his circle dominated her childhood. She never forgot its idealism and sense of obligation, the
belief that 'Talent is a duty'.

Käthe went to study art in Berlin. Etching began to interest
her more than any other medium, partly through the skill at it of
her early teachers, and also because of its power not only as social
comment, without the potential prettification of colour, but as
a way of reaching more people. Studying in Berlin, Munich
and Königsberg made her see that the eastern city's years as a
lively intellectual and artistic centre were past. Her work stayed
essentially traditional but the naturalism of the etchings and
lithographs was sharp with contemporary themes, avoiding rural
life as a subject, with its inevitable nostalgia. An early self-portrait
shows her laughing (a mood never drawn by her again), the joy
perhaps coming from the discovery of her gifts. For her first narrative series, she went to literature – to the poverty and violence

in Zola's novel of working-class life, *Germinal*, using as a background the riverside bars of Königsberg with their dark interiors, narrow benches and blackened walls of a romantic underworld.

Karl Kollwitz, an orphan and a socialist (and with the same evangelical background), was training to be a doctor in Berlin where he met a fellow medical student, Konrad Schmidt, who introduced him to his sister Käthe. Her father wanted her talent to be nurtured outside marriage – and also thought her too unattractive to find a husband – so he sent her away to study in Munich. When she and Karl did marry in 1891, at the end of a seven-year engagement, Herr Schmidt, moved by his concept of duty, urged her to give up art or she would not have time to be a good wife. For once, she ignored him – and Karl took her to Berlin, the imperial capital, to the working-class district of Prenzlauerberg. Here she felt liberated enough from the austere Schmidt household to let more emotion into her work.

Their home at 25 Wörther Strasse, on the corner of what was then Wörther Platz – where they lived for fifty years – and Karl's practice as a doctor became the background to her life. Dr Kollwitz's surgery and his wife's studio were on the second floor, over the premises of a watchmaker, with the family's rooms another floor up. A visitor would find the door opened by a maid who stayed with the Kollwitzes for years; a narrow, dark passage led into the living room where there was a broad green sofa and an oval table, a writing desk by the window and, in the corner, a large tiled stove. The family gathered at the oval table with their friends during the turbulent and exciting years before 1914. The Prenzlauerberg house was tidy, not bohemian: a place of order and work.

In this new world she abandoned the *Germinal* cycle for another naturalistic subject: a series of lithographs and etchings based on Gerhart Hauptmann's *The Weavers*, about a workers' revolt in Silesia in 1844. The play had been banned because of its contradiction of the official optimism of the time and the Emperor objected to Käthe's inclusion on a prize's shortlist.

Käthe Kollwitz in a reflective mood.

Perhaps he recognized, and feared, her work's powerful aesthetic beauty and romanticism, as in *From Many Wounds You Bleed O People*, with which she had wanted to end the *Weavers'* cycle – a corpse of Christ with two naked women instead of the thieves, or the 1900 Holbein-like *Downtrodden*, which depicted a poor family. She shows the influence of Ibsen, Gorky, Zola and Hauptmann, of Goya and Hogarth, of Munch, and, as with the symbolists, frequent use of a figurative Death. It is the art of the gothic north, very emotional, expressionist in its reach into feeling.

Käthe Kollwitz used the younger of her two sons, Peter, as a model. She held him for hours while working on the 1903 etching *Woman with Dead Child*, and when he complained of exhaustion, he said, 'Don't worry, Mother, it will be very beautiful.' Hans, the elder boy, was more difficult: moody yet imaginative. She thought that Hans was like her and she found Peter easier. While not demonstrative, she spoke freely to her children and, in this time of Freud, talked about sexual feelings and early love, far beyond what had been discussed during her own Königsberg childhood.

Her reputation grew with her technical skill in etching, drawing, lithograph and aquatint. On two trips to Paris, the art capital of the world, without Karl and the children, she met Rodin, visited museums, cafés and galleries and found the dance halls of Montmartre quite different to Rupp or Schmidt austerity or to industrial Berlin. Prenzlauerberg could give rise to a feeling of entrapment, with everyone dependent on her, but Käthe Kollwitz's art was rooted irretrievably there or in her north-eastern origins – not in the bright colours and blurred boundaries between abstraction and realism that she found in Paris. In 1908 she followed the *Weavers* cycle with *The Peasants' War*, inspired by a sixteenth-century revolution, where scenes of unforgiving darkness show human beings in beast-like conditions. Black Anna, leader of the revolutionaries, seems to lead her forces out of the earth in a great wave, doom and death etched into their raw, skull-like faces. Only the victims are shown, not the perpetrators of injustice. *Battlefield* has a peasant finding her dead son – for which the child Peter modelled, his mother weeping as she drew him.

It is a dark view. In *Carmagnole*, inspired by Dickens's *Tale of Two Cities*, French revolutionaries dance against what looks like the tall, dense buildings of medieval Königsberg; *Woman with Dead Child* has its black and white heightened with gold wash, the mother apparently devouring her child; in 1903 Hans had nearly died of diphtheria. *Female Nude from the Back* of 1903 is one of her few uses of colour, the green shawl an unashamedly aesthetic touch.

Käthe Kollwitz's diary has glimpses of the remembered Paris of 1904 and 1907, of a later love affair with the Jewish Viennese publisher Hugo Heller and of her secret erotic drawings inspired by this. More freedom came through her winning of the Villa Romana Prize in 1907 which meant the use of a villa in Florence for a year. She was mostly on her own in Florence for Karl was too busy to come, Hans could not interrupt his studies and Peter (aged eleven) visited only occasionally. At first she thought the city decadent but the light and life and the work of artists like Donatello began to move her. On a trip to Rome with an English friend she saw Michelangelo's *Pietà*, and was overcome by his depiction of maternal love and the sanctity of suffering. The frescoes in the Italian churches seemed astonishingly bright in contrast to the urban poverty of industrial Berlin.

But Berlin, or the part where she and Karl lived, was her theme – the violence, the drunkenness and the suffering, the burdens put upon the wives of victims which she thought she had a duty to show. Käthe Kollwitz believed more in Rupp's ideas of universal brotherhood than in political socialism – but duty was vital. When Heller's wife died in 1909, Käthe could have left Karl for him, but she stayed, dreaming of her lover, telling a friend that when Karl and the boys no longer needed her she would return to Paris and to freedom. Her work, in fact, has few traces of what was new in Paris – and in 1911, with other artists, she signed a letter of protest against German museums buying French works of the avant-garde. Typical of her style, completely different to what she thought of as abstract art's confusing obscurity, was the 1909 etching *Unemployed* – of a man in a room with his children, the tone dark and hopeless. The caption reads 'If they didn't need soldiers they would also put a tax on children.'

In the summer, the Kollwitzes went east, to Königsberg and the coast, to Rauschen and the Spit – the Kurische Nehrung. In 1909 Käthe's mother, who had moved to Berlin after her husband's death, was with them; and the gathering of Rupp and Schmidt cousins seemed shrouded in remembrance, in her own sense of getting old and in Karl's irritation, especially during a big family lunch on a trip to Memel. The family was in Königsberg for the dedication of the memorial to her grandfather Julius

Rupp, on the centenary of his birth – a portrait relief of him by Käthe herself, her first exhibited piece of sculpture. She had been afraid that it was 'kitsch'; in fact she thought the head adequate and was moved by the hymn-singing of the members of the Free Church. The inscription on the memorial expressed Rupp's ideals: 'Who does not live according to the truth that he recognizes, is himself the most dangerous enemy of truth.'

Her work showed the harsh world of her husband's patients but it also conveyed yearning and fear, as in a scene depicting a child and the smiling figure of Death fighting over a woman. She dreamed of having another baby, the sweetness of an infant in her bed; the urge clashed now with a sense of age, a dread of working too mechanically, like a grazing cow. Was she already out of her time, already lost in this new world where imagination seemed to be much more important than technique? On the anniversary of their engagement, Karl told her that only during her affair with Heller had he doubted their marriage – and she felt both happy and oppressed. She had known no one who could love so much but sometimes his love tortured her. She wanted to be free again, as with Heller or in Paris or in Italy.

This feeling of missed experience, of routine's net, must have grown when her sister Lise, who saw promiscuity as a weapon against stifling bourgeois ideals, began a love affair. Peter had become fascinated by Wilde's *Ballad of Reading Gaol* and *Portrait of Dorian Gray*. He talked freely with his mother about homosexuality and sexual desire. Had Hans and Peter discussed such matters often with each other, she wondered? Peter was a rebellious idealist, bored with conventional education, enthralled by the romanticism of the Wandervogel movement, whose members hiked through the mountains and hills or camped under starlit skies, having mock battles that tested their courage. Her love for Peter – partly a wish to hold on to a relentlessly passing life – could seem unbearable. In October 1912, when he left to work on a farm before resuming his art studies, she wept in the night; to be near him was happiness, even an erotic delight. Käthe wondered how she would take it if he was homosexual, but the idea did not frighten her. In November 1913 her uncle Theodore Rupp hanged himself in his house at Rauschen. A month later, on New Year's Eve, she wrote of a good and constant burning love for Karl but without ecstasy. The prophecies of war filled her with dread.

In April 1914, by one of the lakes near Berlin in beautiful spring weather, Hans and Peter and Käthe Kollwitz discussed the philosopher J. G. Fichte's *Speech to the German Nation*, the boys speaking of a rebirth of German youth in a new patriotism. She saw how influenced they were by this, much more than she had imagined. Hans had even brought together a group of friends who thought it inspiring. Peter spoke of his wish to combine his art studies with some manual work to help others. Käthe thought of a line of descent from her grandfather Rupp's idealism to that of her own sons. Another memory came to her: how they had slept when young – Hans on his back, with his arms folded over his breast; Peter's body curved, arms stretched away from him. When her mother left in June to go to the East Prussian coast, Käthe thought again of the modesty of the Rupps, of their gentle example and sense of duty.

In July, there was a further death – another of Käthe's uncles – and the family gathered for a cremation in Berlin – a dark contrast to Peter's romantic hope. Sometimes in photographs he seems earnest, especially in one taken with his brother Hans (whose face is longer, more calm) where Peter stares through rimless spectacles at the camera, lips slack in adolescent uncertainty. Then, a year later, in uniform, he is more sure, the lips tighter, slightly smiling, calm as Hans had seemed the year before, still thin, a large nose beneath the soft military cap, large buttons and belt buckle bright against the dark tunic. What looks like a cigarette is held between his second and third fingers.

Peter celebrated the summer solstice with three friends by a lake south-east of Berlin, all wearing flowers in their hair, a foretaste of the 1960s in this last summer of peace. They planned a

trip to Norway, to an empty land fashionable among the Wandervogel; some days after this came the assassination at Sarajevo.
In the middle of July the group went north. Years later, in 1994,
Hans Koch, a survivor, spoke of the Norwegian journey in the
calmness of old age, showing what Peter could have become – a
serene observer of the world's mistakes, disillusioned with socialism, the founder of a successful business, ready now for death. In
the northern wilderness they heard of mobilization, followed by
the declaration of war. All wanted to enlist and peace ended with
a journey back from Bergen to Oslo by train during which the
four German friends met some friendly English and French travellers who were now their enemies. The group took the ferry to
Rügen, then the train to Berlin, their faces burned by the sun,
talking excitedly about their new identity as fighters, lit up by sen-
suality and the thrill of imagined battle.

Hans Kollwitz went into barracks on 5 August. His mother,
moved by her elder son's tranquillity, tried to prepare herself for
loss. Her grandfather Rupp's words came back – that God never
took without having given more than he had taken. On 8 August
she was sitting at the table in the living room when she heard
Peter's quick footsteps in the passage. That evening, the three –
Käthe, Karl and their younger son – talked into the night; and two
days later the argument began that haunted the rest of her life.
Peter wanted to volunteer and because he was under age he had
to have his father's written permission. Karl said that the boy's
year hadn't been called up yet so the country had no need of them
to which Peter answered that Germany might not need those of
his age but it needed him. The talk swung to and fro; the son
looked at his mother and pleaded that he was ready. She stood
and he followed her to the door where they kissed and she
pleaded with Karl to let him go. It should be the boy's decision,
she believed, so Karl signed the paper and Peter departed for the
barracks, leaving his parents alone, 'weeping, weeping, weeping'.

The boys came home often during the short army training.
Sometimes they all sang together and once Käthe and Peter read

the history of the Prussian wars of liberation of a century before. Käthe might rebel against the public view of women's dutiful, even joyful, sacrifice, yet like most German Social Democrats, she and Karl supported the war, believing in the need to fight encircling enemies – autocratic Russia, decadent and vengeful France, jealous Britain. They enjoyed the idealistic unity and the early success. News on 21 August of victories at Brussels and Metz brought flags on to the streets, although Karl read the next day that the Governor of Königsberg had told old people and children to leave the city. There were stabs of pain. Peter, the more delicate of her sons, the more sensitive, must be spared to see the world's beauty so that he could say, like Goethe, 'I saw the world with eyes filled with love . . .'

After the invasion of Belgium and France, rumour came of a ceasefire in the west. Käthe Kollwitz hoped that the boys might never have to fight but 'Russia remains' and reports reached her of her childhood's country under threat: Insterburg surrounded, battles near Königsberg, Tilsit in flames. In the first week of September, Sedan Day, commemorating the 1870 victory of the Prussians over the French, brought the flags out again with joyful crowds and captured guns from the western and eastern fronts. News came of the French President's flight from Paris and of a great triumph in East Prussia, at Tannenberg.

4: A Polished Helmet

On the evening of 13 August 1914, Alfred Knox arrived at Peter-hof, near St Petersburg, to join the train of the Grand Duke Nicholas, the Russian Commander-in-Chief. They set off slowly westwards, the Grand Duke discoursing on how he hoped to go to England for some shooting soon; how the German Empire should be broken up into little states; how extraordinary it was that the German Ambassador's wife had thought that revolution-aries would blow up the Winter Palace. The meals on the train were good: three courses for lunch and dinner, accompanied by a choice of vodka, claret, Madeira or Cognac. On 16 August, they reached Baranovich, to hear news of the Russian invasion of Germany.

In East Prussia, euphoria turned to anxiety. Refugees from the frontier areas crowded into Königsberg, others poured west, by boat or by train, terrified by rumours that the province was to be abandoned to the Russian hordes. On 17 August, the Russian First Army under General Rennenkampf crossed the frontier; on the 20th it drove the Germans back from Gumbinnen. On 21 August, General Samsonov and the Russian Second Army entered East Prussia from the south, taking the German towns of Willenberg, Ortelsburg and Neidenburg a day later.

Knox went north, towards the German front and the con-quered towns. He thought about the two Russian generals – Samsonov and Rennenkampf – who were said to hate each other, even to have come to blows on a station platform during the war with Japan, although probably this was a myth. He had met Sam-sonov a year earlier, at manoeuvres south-east of Samarkand, and had found him 'as so many Russians are, of a simple and kindly nature'. The Englishman knew little of Rennenkampf, who came from a Baltic German family. Neither officer had commanded more than a division of cavalry against the Japanese.

General von Prittwitz, commander of the German Eighth Army in the east, panicked and wanted to retire westwards as far as the River Vistula, abandoning Königsberg and great swathes of territory. Prittwitz was dismissed and on 22 August the German Commander-in-Chief, Moltke, appointed Erich Ludendorff, hero of the capture of Liège, to be chief of staff to the man brought out of retirement to take the eastern command: Paul von Hindenburg. Myth soon appropriated these men, both Prussians: Hindenburg – heavy, imperturbable, a master of silence – in particular becoming the symbol of two pivotal moments: Tannenberg in August 1914 and Berlin in January 1933 when, as President of Germany, he asked Hitler to be chancellor.

Born in 1847 into a Prussian military family in Posen, where his father was stationed, Hindenburg had roots further east, at the estate of Neudeck, near Rosenberg; at least two of his ancestors had fought with the Teutonic Knights. Every summer the family gathered at Neudeck, his parents moving there permanently in 1863, after his father's retirement. The fragility of the place, its position on an invasion route, was shown in stories of the French under Napoleon on their way to, and back from, Moscow.

After a mediocre record as a schoolboy, Hindenburg went to a Berlin Cadet School where he rose to the highest class and attended Heinrich von Treitschke's nationalistic lectures. As a young officer, he fought in the war of 1866 against Austria – when a bullet grazed his head – and in the Franco-Prussian War of 1870, representing his regiment at Versailles in 1871 for the declaration of the German Empire. It was to the new Germany, henceforth, rather than to the old Prussia, that Hindenburg was loyal and the protection of German unity became his creed. In 1903, the climax of his pre-First World War life, he became commander of an army corps at Magdeburg and was later considered, but not chosen, for higher posts. Magdeburg showed his political talents, not least the gift of knowing when to speak and when to stay silent. Other characteristics were his ability to delegate and to relax, a consciousness of the effect he could have on people and a deep interest in his own reputation. On his retirement in March 1911, he was disappointed not to have risen higher.

It might have been expected that Hindenburg would pass his last years in eastern Germany where he was proud to have his roots. Instead he and his wife, the daughter of a Prussian general, went to Hanover where he had a circle of cronies, did some shooting and read the Bible every day and military history and the newspapers, breaking this routine once to go on his only foreign journey for pleasure rather than military conquest: to Rome, Florence and Naples. When war broke out in August 1914 there seemed to be nothing for the pensioner in Hanover. It was humiliating – 'I sit like an old woman behind the oven.' Then Prittwitz panicked.

On the western front, the startling success had been Ludendorff – hero of the capture of Liège, the first German soldier in the war to be decorated by the Emperor with the Pour le Mérite, the highest imperial award for military achievement. But he was neurotic and moody, also (at forty-nine) too young to command an army, so someone had to be put in above him – a calm presence, a steadying hand of symbolic solidity, not a military genius but 'a polished helmet'. Hindenburg's terse answer to the telegram of appointment became part of the legend: 'I am ready.' When a special train drew into Hanover station on the morning of 23 August at 4.00 a.m. – an hour late – with Ludendorff on it, Hindenburg was waiting in his uniform of Prussian blue, not having had time to obtain the field grey of active service. They had never met before and on the journey eastwards, Hindenburg demonstrated his special skill; he spoke to Ludendorff, agreed with his subordinate's plans (which included keeping the Eighth Army east of the Vistula), then went to sleep.

They arrived at the new headquarters at Marienburg, in the shadow of the castle of the Teutonic Knights. To some officers, the new commander seemed to be much aged: huge, stiff-limbed, like a miraculously half-animated corpse. The next day Hindenburg and his staff drove off on roads crowded with refugees and troops going up to the front. Eventually they reached the cause of a clarion-like passage in his ghost-written memoirs – the East Prussian village whose name the Germans had given to the battle of Grunwald: the place where King Władisław II Jagiełło's Polish–Lithuanian force had defeated the Teutonic Knights in 1410, halting the Order's apparently relentless move east: 'Tannenberg! A word pregnant with painful recollection for German chivalry, a Slav cry of triumph, a name that is fresh in our memories after more than five hundred years of history.' On arriving at Marienburg, however, he had written more prosaically to his wife, 'I believe your old man may become famous . . .'

Rennenkampf slowed his advance, fearing the garrison in Königsberg on his right. He wanted to give Samsonov time to get through the forests and lakes in the south-east to crush the Germans, who were thought still to be retreating. The belief grew that this must end with Cossacks in the Reichstag and the palaces of Potsdam. But there was chaos on both sides. As Samsonov's Second Army entered East Prussia, it was hampered by shortage of supplies, bad discipline, late arrival of orders, exhaustion in the heat, lack of telephones and a poor communications system whose wireless messages were easily intercepted. 'We had an ally,' the German Staff Officer Colonel Hoffmann said later of the Russians' radio traffic. 'It was the enemy. We knew all his plans.' Rennenkampf and Samsonov had been cavalry leaders, not familiar with the slow movement of vast armies, and they were up against men who knew the ground; flat, empty East Prussia had been one of the main pre-war training areas of the German army. The extensive German railway system and good roads allowed quick movement whereas the Russian roads, as Knox had found

in 1911, were in bad condition, ostensibly to delay invasion, and the few railway lines soon became congested.

The Russians hoped that the East Prussian Poles would welcome their fellow Slavs. Knox reported that as the Russians advanced into Masuria many Germans left but the Poles stayed. He liked the Poles and was moved by their tragedy, hoping that a Russian victory would lead, as had been promised, to a united Poland under Russian protection rather than a country divided between Austria, Germany and Russia. In another display of Edwardian anti-Semitism, Knox was much less sympathetic to the Jews, commenting on their determination to be on the winning side and their unctuous manner, claiming not to have known that a Jewish corpse was dead until it failed to salute him. The kindness of the Russians to their prisoners was, he thought, wonderful; he heard stories of German brutality – officers stealing from Polish houses, committing gratuitous damage, setting fire to haystacks, violating women. Later he watched Russian soldiers burn down a Polish manor house, to punish the young owner who had an elder brother serving in the Austrian army and had been harbouring enemy troops.

At its start, in August 1914, the First World War was a war of movement – the French invading Alsace, the Germans sweeping into Belgium and northern France: colossal armies on the march. Not until September did the long stalemate of trench warfare in the west begin, after the German advance had been checked outside Paris, at the battle of the Marne. On the eastern front, however, these great movements remained a feature of the campaigns, with armies retreating or advancing over wild flat country. That August the Russian invasion revived nightmares in East Prussia of earlier devastation: of Gustavus Adolphus's Swedes during the Thirty Years War, of the Tatars and the Asian hordes. Was this to be the final defeat of the northern crusades?

By 25 August Knox was with Samsonov in Neidenburg. He found the town much changed since his visit in 1911, its main square scarred by burned or damaged houses. The fighting devastated the eastern part of East Prussia; fields were churned up, houses wrecked, a harvest either left to rot or seized for troops and much damage caused by German and Russian artillery. More than a hundred thousand East Prussian families lost everything; thirty-nine towns and nineteen hundred villages were more than 50 per cent destroyed; forty thousand buildings were left in ruins; farms suffered devastating losses of livestock. Over half a million people from the country districts took refuge in Königsberg; in August 1914 some twelve thousand of these fled west by sea to Danzig, Pomerania or Brandenburg. Civilians suspected of spying were shot by the Russians; thousands were sent over the frontier as prisoners, often to Siberia, from where many never returned. The Cossacks ransacked parts of the country.

One effect of all this was to draw the remote east closer to the rest of the Reich. Cities like Frankfurt, Cologne and Leipzig began twinning arrangements with districts or towns in the invaded province, there were collections of clothing and money; and the threat brought East Prussian ethnic groups like the Protestant Poles closer to their German neighbours, particularly if they had property to lose. Yet the first great twentieth-century war in the east seems quite gentle compared to what was to come. In Gumbinnen, General Rennenkampf appointed a German schoolteacher to be governor of the town, and in Insterburg a German doctor was put in charge of civilian administration. When the Germans re-took Neidenburg on 28 August, the wounded who had stayed there said how well the Russians had treated them.

When the war began, Tilsit, a border town in northern East Prussia, was calm. Reports brought good news from the west, allowing people to forget that 'a violent enemy' was forming up on the other side of the River Niemen. Then refugees started to arrive; it was even suggested that the famous Queen Luise Bridge over the Niemen should be blown up to slow the Russian invasion. A hotel proprietor, Paul Lesch, engaged in his own act of defiance, changing his establishment's name from the Hôtel de Russie to the Königlicher Hof.

On 25 August, while Alfred Knox was with Samsonov's Second Army in Neidenburg, the first Russians, presumably from Rennenkampf's First Army, entered Tilsit. The officer of the mounted Cossack patrol asked for the mayor. On hearing that there were no German troops in the town, the Cossacks left – but more Russians came the next day: a company of infantry and a squadron of Cossacks with a train of wagons, Paul Lesch noticing their poor equipment. The Russians took over the city barracks, the post office and the railway station, posting sentries on the bridges and the main thoroughfares, imposing a curfew on civilians between nine in the evening and six in the morning. Lesch knew some of the Russian officers from before the war when they had come to his hotel, shocking the German by wanting to stay overnight with women.

On 30 August an infantry division arrived in the city, commanded by the Finn General von Holmsen, an 'educated' man with good German, probably from a Baltic family of German origin. The Russians lived in tents on the edge of the city, the sale of alcohol was forbidden and all restaurants and bars were closed, except for Lesch's hotel, which was kept open for the officers. Tilsit was occupied for three weeks, shut off from the rest of the world. Lesch was summoned with eleven other prominent citizens to the town hall, where General von Holmsen told them that the town must make a contribution of 40,000 marks and they were to be taken to Russia, with only twenty-four hours to put their affairs in order.

The next day the general came to Lesch's hotel, ordered a bottle of Mosel and was fascinated by the eminent Russian names in the guest book: Grand Duke Cyril, Count Lieven, General Rennenkampf and 'my dear friend' Hilmar von der Goltz, a German officer who had been training the Turkish army when von Holmsen was the Russian Military Attaché in Constantinople. Lesch seized his chance. Wouldn't it be better, he asked, to leave the twelve hostages in Tilsit so that they could use their influence to keep order? Holmsen said he would ask his commanding officer, the Grand Duke Nicholas, who was in Insterburg.

The following morning, at six o'clock, Lesch said goodbye to his wife and children and joined the other hostages who were waiting in the town hall with suitcases, thick boots and provisions. The General opened the meeting by saying that the 40,000-mark contribution must stand but that after speaking to his high command he had decided to let the hostages stay in the city. Holmsen was in Tilsit until 4 September, coming every day to Lesch's hotel, where he enjoyed himself so much that he gave its proprietor a written commendation, although the occupiers ordered that the name should be changed back to the Hôtel de Russie.

Just before midday on 12 September, the people of Tilsit heard shooting. German patrols were on the edge of the city and after about two hours of fighting the Russians left across the Queen Luise Bridge before more German troops came from Memel, taking six thousand Russian prisoners, including General von Holmsen. Lesch changed the hotel's name again, to the Königlicher Hof. Now, he wrote, 'Tilsit was free.' It was only then that its people heard of what had happened at Tannenberg.

*

The essence of the German plan of battle for Tannenberg was to concentrate the entire force of what was now Hindenburg and Ludendorff's Eighth Army on Samsonov's Second Army. For this to succeed it was vital that Rennenkampf's First Army did not move south fast enough to come to Samsonov's aid. Tannenberg became a battle of encirclement, with Samsonov's position made worse by slow movement, poor communications, a chaotic supply system and Rennenkampf's inertia.

It was decided that the battle should be fought in the area of Osterode and Hohenstein, to the west of Allenstein, with the Masurian lakes as protection on one side. The staff officer

Colonel Hoffmann suggested that General von François and his I Corps, who were facing Rennenkampf, be moved south-west by rail to meet Samsonov. On 22 August, German aviators reported that Rennenkampf's First Army had stopped; the next day only one German cavalry division faced him, all the other units having moved south where Samsonov's Second Army had been lured on by what seemed like success. A delay in attack by François, ignoring previous orders, let the Russians stumble further into the noose, changing what Ludendorff had conceived as a mere containment of the Russian advance into a massive defeat.

On 27 August the Russians were in Allenstein, the largest town in that part of East Prussia, some of them thinking that it was Berlin. Leaving Neidenburg, Knox, still disconnected from the battle which had started, heard rumours that the German cavalry was moving into the outskirts of the town; in Mlava, on the other side of the frontier, people spoke of an imminent German attack and Knox's night at Mlava was disturbed by convoys of the wounded rumbling over the cobblestones. The next day he was back in Neidenburg, hearing that Samsonov was some miles north-east of the town. Not until the night of 28 August, two days after the start of the battle, did Gilinsky, the Russian commander, order Rennenkampf to go to the help of the Second Army.

Knox saw the warning signs – the difficult wild country, the poor communications, the slow Russian pace, the inability to read captured German documents, chaotic arrangements for the wounded, bad map reading. The roads were thick with stragglers and lost units – and eventually he found the Russian commander sitting on the ground looking at maps, surrounded by his staff. Samsonov stood suddenly, ordering the Cossacks with Knox to give up their horses. Knox started to move away but Samsonov motioned him to stay. The Russian said that he must tell his ally that 'the position was very critical'. Samsonov must remain with the army but Knox should go back to make his report. The General emphasized to the Englishman that 'even if the worst happened, it would not affect the ultimate result of the war.'

Knox felt that the presence of a foreigner could only increase 'the nerve strain' so he said goodbye to Samsonov and his officers who rode off north-west on the Cossack horses, towards the changing front line. 'The enemy has luck one day,' they said to the Colonel. 'We will have luck another.' After an eighteen-hour car journey, Knox, accompanied by eight or ten Russian officers, crossed the frontier, reaching Ostrolenka, where he caught an early train to Warsaw, putting up at the luxurious Bristol Hotel, which was full of rumours of huge German losses.

The next day, 30 August, brought the truth: the Russians had been defeated. The battle was devastating, not least because at the start of the campaign Rennenkampf and Samsonov had had a great numerical advantage: two armies of thirty infantry and eight cavalry divisions against one German army of eleven infantry divisions and one cavalry, a difference made greater by the larger Russian divisions and the fact that the crack German forces were mostly in the west. Because contact was so bad between the Russian armies – and their progress so slow – the Germans could take on one of them (Samsonov's Second Army) in isolation. There had remained the possibility, terrifying to the highly strung Ludendorff, that Rennenkampf might suddenly swing south to come to his colleague's rescue.

The image of Hindenburg and Ludendorff directing victory came to include the winter campaigns of the next year, and remained powerful not only through the war but during the years of humiliation afterwards. In one imagined scene, Hindenburg stands in the snow, a Prussian spiked helmet on his head, binoculars in one hand, the other clutching his ceremonial sword. A ruined house and staff officers behind him, he wears a long grey-blue coat with red facings – an ornamental yet solid figure – and to his right, representing action alongside calm, Ludendorff looks through a two-pronged periscope. In the background, smoke rises from the destruction let loose by the barbarous, defeated invader.

Another image has survived, near what was then the German town of Hohenstein and is now the Polish Olsztynek – a chivalrous reminder of General Samsonov stumbling through the forest, tripping over branches and undergrowth, breathless from asthma, having told his Cossack escort to look after themselves. In the autumn of 1915, his body was found enveloped in a Cossack overcoat, buried in the dry sandy ground, the face framed by a long beard. He had shot himself rather than face humiliation. The Germans put the remains of their old enemy on a train, with military honours, and he was taken back through neutral Denmark and Sweden for burial in the Samsonov family mausoleum in southern Russia. In the silent Masurian woods, however, a small stone pyramid still stands, with an inscription in German: 'General Samsonov, der Gegner Hindenburgs, gefallen in der Schlacht bei Tannenberg, 30 August 1914' – General Samsonov, the opponent of Hindenburg, fallen in the battle of Tannenberg, 30 August 1914.

Tannenberg seemed to be a miracle – a symbol of deliverance. Even the name given to the battle – by Hoffmann or Ludendorff or Hindenburg, each of whom claimed to have chosen it – has a mythical dimension (this time of revenge) for it was from the East Prussian village of Tannenberg (now the Polish Stębark) that the German Orders had marched to fight the Polish–Lithuanian forces at Grunwald. In 1914, little fighting took place there but the name resonated after 1918 as a reminder of the victories in the east. The Russians claimed that the invasion of East Prussia had been a great act of altruism, to relieve the pressure on their French and British allies in the west. It is, as Knox observed, ridiculous to imagine that they set out to sacrifice so many troops and guns. But German anxiety led to reinforcements being sent from the western front before Hindenburg and Ludendorff arrived in the east – two army corps and a cavalry division that depleted the German invasion force in northern France which soon stalled on the Marne.

Could the Germans have taken Paris and won the war in under two months if these reinforcements had stayed in the west? It's impossible to prove because the scenario – of a quick victory or quick defeat in France – is based on hypothesis and illusion. But what's certain is that Tannenberg *was* a decisive victory, an immense propaganda triumph, taking attention from the western stalemate. Some fifty thousand Russians were killed, almost a hundred thousand taken prisoner, against German losses of some twenty thousand. Russian morale began its decline into despair that German tactical and technical superiority could ever be beaten. To Solzhenitsyn, the defeat was one of the 'nodal points' of history, through the German withdrawal of troops from the west (preventing the defeat of the French and the British), the enormous boost to morale that led to German hubristic certainty of a final victory and a quickening of the slide towards the 1917 revolution.

The battle made Hindenburg and Ludendorff. Seen as the saviours of the nation, they went on to become effectively military dictators in wartime Germany, pushing the Emperor and democratic politicians aside. Hindenburg in particular became totemic, a tribal symbol, with wooden statues of him put up throughout the country, people buying nails to hammer into them as contributions to the war effort. His face and his size – the immobile features, the hair *en brosse* in Prussian military style, the thick moustache curling up at its corners as if in defiance, the small, steady eyes, the solidity – comforted many anxious hearts.

After Tannenberg, the Germans hoped for another quick victory, this time against Rennenkampf's First Army – but a stalemate in September at the battle of the Masurian Lakes let Rennenkampf retreat over the frontier. Later that month the Russians counter-attacked, pushing the Germans back to their defensive positions on the River Angerap and the wide, natural barrier of the Masurian lakeland. But East Prussia now seemed safe. The refugees began to return from the west.

5: The Grieving Parents

The symbolic has profound importance in this land. The red-brick fortress at Malbork (until 1945 the German Marienburg) once represented the power of the Teutonic Knights and is now enfolded with its history into the new Poland after brilliant post-war restoration. Further east, the nineteenth-century Prussian forts – symbolically reassuring rather than tactically useful – encircle the cracked, stained concrete of Kaliningrad's attempted Soviet utopia.

The train going east from Gdańsk goes past the Malbork fortress, by the River Nogat. German voices come from the corridor outside the compartment where I'm sitting and I can hear five people – two women and three men – probably in their late twenties, obviously on holiday, using the old German names, as if on trains here fifty years ago: Marienburg, Marienwerder, Allenstein, Frauenburg, Elbing, Danzig, Königsberg. Will they drop the big one, say something shocking? I think that this would fit some deep idea of how things should be.

They enter the compartment and sit down, still talking to each other, a man nodding at me. One of the women says that she came here last year with a friend and rode on hired bicycles from Marienwerder to the flat land by the river where on the other bank you can see the castle at Mewe (the Polish Gniew). The Poles had turned it into a hotel, she thinks (the others laugh), but you could see how strategic a site the place was. A man says the Knights wanted these places to be seen, like the crusader castles in Palestine; and as for that red brick, you can't miss it. Red for danger, I think. They get out at what they call Mohrungen (the Polish Morąg), where the philosopher Herder was born.

In June 1902, William II, the last German Emperor, spoke at Marienburg about domination, evoking, in spite of his four million Polish subjects ('our Poles'), the sword of the Orders in the strong fist to strike out at the Poles, to lash their insolence, to exterminate them. This odd but typical speech prompts images of men in white coats striding up to the rostrum to lead the frenzied monarch away to a waiting van. But that year, and in 1910, the Poles held nationalistic celebrations at Grunwald to commemorate the defeat of the Teutonic Knights in 1410. In Kraków, in July 1910, in Austrian Poland, which was more relaxed towards the nationalities than the German or Russian parts, a Grunwald memorial, paid for by the concert pianist Paderewski, was unveiled in front of a huge crowd. The Nazi invaders knocked it down in November 1939; since 1976, a copy, rebuilt with some of the original stone, has stood in its place.

In 1960, during the post-war communist years, a Polish film of Henryk Sienkiewicz's nationalistic historical novel *Knight of the Cross* was released. A story of opposition to the Teutonic Knights and strongly anti-German (and therefore welcomed by the Soviets), it was seen by millions. The brutal German occupation of Poland during the Second World War, of which this film could seem symbolic, is deep in Polish national memory but the hatred has faded. In 1999 Poland joined NATO; in 2004 it became a member of the European Union, of which Germany is the largest and richest state. The country now sees itself as part of the west; flights to Germany are full, German tourists are welcome, especially in the poor north-east – the old East Prussia – although perhaps among the old a slight unease remains.

Perhaps the role of these red-brick castles and churches and civic buildings now is to be memorials to a dead past, increasingly stately and harmless. Still overwhelmingly powerful, however, is a memorial made by an East Prussian that stands hundreds of miles to the west in what seems, compared to northern Poland,

Castle of the Teutonic Knights at Marienburg,
now the Polish Malbork.

a prosperous Belgian Flanders: Käthe Kollwitz's sculpture *The Grieving Parents*, put up near where her son Peter fell in September 1914.

I've been to Ypres, or the Belgian Ieper, several times, always in winter – for sunlight and a country in leaf and flower seem wrong in what should be a place of enduring darkness. Certain landscapes are overshadowed by what happened or even by what was conceived there: Hitler's beloved Bavarian Alps; the still empty centre of Kaliningrad; the death camps – Auschwitz, Birkenau, Treblinka; the forests of Belarus, eastern Poland and Ukraine where the Soviets and the Germans killed millions; the Wolf's Lair near Kętrzyn (Rastenburg) in the old East Prussia, the Führer's command post.

Ypres – and the land that stretches down through northern France, encompassing Arras, Lille and Amiens, the towns of the Somme – is also permanently marked, particularly for the British who seem at times to be occupying it. The town itself has advertisements for 'Over the Top' trench tours, there's a Big Ben pub, English menus outside the cafés and restaurants and a British Grenadier English bookshop that sells books on the war and trench maps reprinted from the originals. Cars with British plates are parked in the square and move slowly along the tourist routes that take in the many Commonwealth war graves. The war in Ypres is the First World War – for in 1940 Belgium was quickly overrun by the Germans, with far less loss of life than twenty-six years before. Winston Churchill even suggested, soon after 1918, that Ypres should become British and left in ruins as a memorial to what Great Britain had sacrificed for it: an eccentric idea when the immediate reason for taking up arms in 1914 had been the defence of Belgium's territorial integrity.

The town is a neat, symmetrical place that was rebuilt in the 1920s after its almost total destruction, retaining its medieval street pattern and large square in the centre, dominated by the great cloth hall. Tourism is important to the local economy. Previously a centre for textile manufacturing, Ypres now struggles against competition from the Far East and agriculture employs fewer people each year although you can still see the large, almost deformedly muscled, pale Belgian Blue beef cattle in the flat fields near the cemeteries. House prices are among the lowest in Belgium.

What draws the British back? Very many Germans were killed here yet only 2.5 per cent of the visitors to the In Flanders Fields Museum in Ypres are German. Partly this is because, for the Germans and the French, worse tragedies happened elsewhere, in Alsace or Lorraine or at Verdun, in eastern France: places that have now become sites for ceremonies of symbolic Franco-German reconciliation. For the British, Ypres has the two or three battles that bear its name and, only twenty minutes away, the worst slaughter of all, Passchendaele. Only the Somme rivals it as a place of their dead.

Usually they come in groups – often in coach tours – whereas

Germans tend to arrive on their own or in couples or with their families, not more than two families together. Piet Chielens of the In Flanders Fields Museum says that there have been a few signs of hostility to Germans, from Belgians or British, but not many. Ypres is quieter than Arras or Amiens, more given over to memory of the First World War than those larger cities. At night in winter, when you walk through its streets of gabled grey stone buildings, a cough sounds as sharp as a rifle shot, the silence allowing the memory of innocence lost or killed, of British history transformed.

The Belgians have recognized this by letting the British build St George's Church, just off the main square, and the New Menin Gate at one of the entrances to the old city – where the Last Post is sounded every evening at sunset. Both were designed between the wars by the architect Reginald Blomfield – the church primly classical, a little dull, reminiscent of a quiet suburb; the Gate more grandiose, also classical, with an air of conquest. The poet Siegfried Sassoon loathed the pomposity of the New Menin Gate but Hitler admired it. Blomfield's work survived the German occupation of Belgium in the Second World War.

The cemeteries also suffered little damage while the Germans controlled the area from 1940 until 1945. The difference in their national atmospheres is very great, partly a contrast between defeat and victory. There is a calm nostalgia in the way that the British remember their dead – an evocation of tranquil country landscapes or a garden from which anything harsh has been removed. The neat lines of headstones – usually with a tall stone cross on the edge or sometimes among the graves – surround or stretch out from a pavilion of stone or brick that contains a book of remembrance. In the larger cemeteries there may be a colon-nade similar to a cloister, appropriate for contemplation or contained grief. All this gives a sense of quiet, justifiable sacrifice, without anger.

There are many British cemeteries, some vast, others with only a few graves. The dead French were often repatriated; the

Germans did not encourage this for their own dead (although some rich families brought theirs home after the war), but the British insisted that all should be buried near where they had fallen. It is this that makes the huge cemetery at Tyn Cot, near the battlefield of Passchendaele, such a devastating witness to the slaughter of the late summer and autumn of 1917. Even here, though, there's little sense of the despair and the endless loss and suffering revealed in Käthe Kollwitz's extraordinary sculptures, *The Grieving Parents*.

The British war graves are usually in open country, as if in unashamed possession – whereas the Germans occupy more enclosed spaces, tucked away. The British cemeteries let in sunlight; the German ones are thickly planted with oaks, sometimes with rhododendrons or pollarded limes, as at Langemarck, the scene in October 1914 of many young deaths. German nostalgia was not pastoral but focused on the romanticism of heroic deeds and victories that had made a recently unified nation. At Langemarck, a line of secular verse by Heinrich Lersch has been carved over the squat red-stone pavilion:

'Germany must live
And so we must die.'

Hans and Peter Kollwitz were serious crusaders. The hardest time would come afterwards, they thought, because war offered purification and the chance of a new Germany whereas peace brought the task (or duty) of shaping great change. In August 1914, with all the good news from the west, Peter spoke of German troops reaching London soon.

In late September, Käthe Kollwitz read Heinrich von Kleist's patriotic drama *The Prince of Homburg* with Hans – and Peter had ten days' leave because of a bad knee. The boys were at home again, during some beautiful days before Peter went back to barracks in Wünsdorf, near enough for his parents to see him. His mother felt moved by the keen yet devout faces of the young soldiers; she would have liked to kiss them. On 2 October, his cousin took a photograph of Peter – a thin boy, rather dreamy with lips slightly parted, buttons and belt buckle bright on the grey uniform, his body frail against the sky. Eight days later, on hearing of the fall of Antwerp, the Kollwitzes hung the black, white and red imperial German flag from the window of Peter's room, for their sons and for victory.

On 12 October, Peter's and Hans's unit, the 207th Infantry Regiment, was sent to the western front after scarcely two months' training. Before the regiment left, Käthe Kollwitz walked at night with Peter near the barracks where he pointed out the stars and together they heard soldiers returning through the woods, singing songs of the Fatherland. They said farewell at the station, with a lengthy embrace, some words of love and an avowal of his certainty that he would return. On reaching Belgium, the boys marched the last few miles to the front, Peter with Goethe's *Faust* in his knapsack, a last present from his mother. They were in flat terrain – with some tall trees, gaunt poplars – the sound of artillery quite near. Transport went by with munitions, pioneers, senior officers and ambulances with the wounded. The new arrivals went past more marching troops, shrapnel bursting over them as they saw the fires of bivouacs and felt the tension of knowing that they must soon come under fire.

The first card from Peter came to Prenzlauerberg on 14 October, sent on the journey west, from Hanover. Seven days later Käthe wrote of hearing no more news and on 24 October a letter arrived, saying he could hear the thunder of artillery. That evening, in their living room, Käthe and Karl and some friends talked, Käthe thinking of Peter – where is he, is he hungry, is he in danger? On 27 October she wrote in her diary that he had been gone for fourteen days. There was little news, apart from reports of hard fighting at Ypres, Nieuport and Diksmuide.

The Germans hoped to break out of the long front line that ran near the villages of Diksmuide and Langemarck. They wanted to reach the Channel ports and Paris, reviving the war of movement that had ceased in September on the Marne. More reserves had been called up, including Peter and other young boys, so the myth began of a massacre of the innocents – or the heroes of Langemarck. Peter's regiment was positioned around Diksmuide; other units were further south at Langemarck; all were involved in what would become one of the battles of Ypres. The untried troops were up against experienced British, French and Belgian riflemen. Almost one hundred thousand Germans were lost there between 21 October and 14 November 1914.

The road from Diksmuide to Ostend passes near the village of Beerst. This was no man's land in 1914; now it's a country of potato fields and cattle where poplars rise from the edge of crops of sugar beet or groups of farm buildings near the River Yser. In October 1914 this was crossed with trenches and strewn with the dead. 'It is ugly here, very ugly,' one of Peter's comrades wrote although he felt glad that the tension of waiting was over. Peter Kollwitz and his detachment were put into trenches a little over a mile east of the Yser. Peter himself was killed instantly by a bullet on the night of 22 October, the first of his regiment to die, shot by a Belgian defending his country. His comrades buried him near the trench. Eight days later, the official letter arrived in Prenzlauerberg: 'Your son has fallen.'

On 11 November, some dozen miles to the south of Diksmuide and Beerst, around the village of Langemarck, in an area defended by British regular troops, another group of young, untried Germans went into battle singing 'Deutschland über Alles'. The young Austrian Adolf Hitler, a volunteer in a Bavarian infantry regiment, was there and vowed revenge; others, however, felt a deep bitterness about the crude patriotism promoted by incompetent leaders. 'All a fraud,' Hans Koch, the friend of Peter's who was at Langemarck, wrote of the subsequent myth, sharing Käthe Kollwitz's anger at idealism betrayed.

Another friend of Peter's, Eric Krems, declared that people shouldn't believe speeches about the army's glorious spirit, for many soldiers felt a hatred of war that would soon become hatred of the government. He quoted a Prussian officer who said that four people had made the war – the Tsar, the German Emperor, the French President and 'the English fellow' (presumably the Prime Minister, Herbert Asquith); everyone else had been fooled. The Prussian foresaw a time when there was no German or Russian Emperor but a republic of all the people. Eric Krems, killed at Verdun, aged twenty, in March 1916, never saw this. Hans Koch survived (although twice wounded) and returned to Berlin, where he took part in the revolution in 1918 and 1919. He died in 1995, aged ninety-eight, believing that humanity had a greater capacity for error than for progress.

6: Ober-Ost

Symbols of the East Prussian Junkers have survived on their old lands – and among these is a ruined mansion on the edge of a village in northern Poland. Satellite dishes sprout from the roofs of some newish houses in the main street, firewood is stacked beside rickety wooden huts, stork nests fluff out from the top of telegraph poles and red-brick barns – some used as garages or for storage – show the Prussian past, as do the ruins of the large brick and stone house that once dominated the village. A post-1945 identity is shown in a long low set of stables for what look like race horses, certainly thoroughbreds. Here the mild human disorder glides into elegance; meadows stretch away from the stables, immaculately fenced with white-painted rails like Newmarket or Kentucky, until they become farmland. You can see the green leaves of a potato crop and other fields sown with wheat or barley or rye, before what seems like a woodland wilderness that surrounds this settlement. This is the place where Elard von Oldenburg-Januschau, once a leader of the conservatives and spokesman for the Junkers in the Reichstag, once lived and ruled, where he fought election crowds with his fists and entertained his neighbour Hindenburg – and where I'm chased away by the Polish owner of Januschau's ruined house who wields a spade while shouting, 'Nein! Nein!'

Prussian reforms of the early nineteenth century left the Junkers remarkably unscathed – still important as producers of food and loyal supporters of the Hohenzollerns. Even the abolition of serfdom and the after-shock of the 1848 revolution, when the nobility lost more of its feudal privileges, didn't cripple their powerful role or their domination of the officer corps. Bismarck attacked aspects of the feudalism that gave the Junkers such power. They turned against him for this, many also disapproving of his campaign against the Catholics, perhaps because they valued the cheap Polish labour on their estates. There were anti-Semitic complaints about the influence of Bismarck's Jewish banker Gerson von Bleichröder and the new capitalism that seemed to be seeking privileges at least equal to those of land-owners and farmers. Bismarck, who saw himself as a Pomeranian farmer, felt betrayed. But skilful farming meant that profits from land remained good and the size of properties increased.

The fall in agricultural prices that began in the 1870s with the import of corn from North America and Russia was a threat. In the years from 1883 to 1885 Elard von Oldenburg-Januschau saw the price of his rye almost halved, although a growing income came from the distillation of spirits from potatoes. Once again the privileged status of the Junkers became clear; Bismarck intro-duced tariffs against imported grain, small at first but rising over the years, and so won back his popularity among this powerful class. By 1894, the novelist Theodore Fontane, chronicler of the Junkers, was writing of their 'unbearable demands': how 'they only know themselves and their advantage, and the sooner they are disposed of the better.' In most European countries the nobil-ity grew closer to the bourgeoisie; in Prussia its privileged position seemed to be more entrenched, more exclusive.

The Junkers felt threatened – by cheap imports from across the border in Russia, by a potentially rebellious Polish minority and by the bankers and businessmen whose new commercial power might overwhelm the landed interest. Tariffs, which Januschau thought essential to his survival, meant high food prices; liberal politicians complained also that the Junkers paid badly, took advantage of cheap immigrant labour from Russian Poland, and offered use of land rather than wages (the 'cashless society' later recalled nostalgically by Marion Dönhoff), which bound workers even more tightly to them. The treatment of seasonal labour could be brutal. The landlords knew that there was a plentiful supply from across the border.

Elard von Oldenburg-Januschau's fear of democracy grew during the First World War. By 1917, he had concluded that the unreliable Reichstag not only wished for a republic but threatened the army 'from the rear' by its feeble requests for peace talks. Three years before, back in his beloved army, he had celebrated his sixtieth birthday under Hindenburg's command in the east, before going west, to the Somme, then back east again, to report to Hindenburg in April 1916 and to see action with an infantry regiment, winning the Iron Cross, first class. Januschau considered that commanding men in battle was perfectly natural – like running his estates. In November 1917, with still no sign of victory in spite of the U-boat campaign and the huge advances into Russia, he returned home to concern himself with the vital production of food. Despising Bethmann-Hollweg, the Chancellor, Januschau conspired to replace him with a stronger man, perhaps Admiral von Tirpitz who had built up the German fleet before 1914. When neither Hindenburg nor the Crown Prince nor the Emperor responded, he blamed democracy.

The ageing Junker traced the decline: the departure of Bismarck, whose successors allowed a hostile ring – France and Russia and Britain – to tighten round Germany; mediocre, civilian leadership; the rise of the Social Democrats; the power of the Reichstag; the threat to the institution he revered most, the monarchy. To Januschau, Hindenburg's and Ludendorff's victories in the east should have been leading to a permanent extension of German rule not only over the conquered Russian part of Poland but over a new and dependent state of Ukraine as well.

In February 1915, the Germans launched another offensive across the Russian frontier, amid violent snow storms and sudden thaws that turned the roads into morasses of mud. The Russian retreat became disastrous; the generals – Sievers and Budberg, both of German extraction – were replaced: and Knox, still a frequent visitor to the front, wrote of 'the worst thing since

Tannenberg'. Russian losses, even up to 13 January 1915 – the first five months of the war – were grim: 13,899 officers, 482,162 men, 319 officials. The superiority of German equipment was overwhelming. From May 1915, the Germans advanced further eastwards; by 18 July they were threatening Riga. On 16 July, Knox left Warsaw, imagining during a last walk in the Łazienki Gardens how the city would be under German occupation; on the night of 4 August, Warsaw was abandoned. By the end of September the Germans were east of Wilno (now Vilnius), several hundred miles into Russia. Knox saw the chaos of the retreat as long lines of Poles fled from the invaders along roads blocked with carts and children driving geese, cows or pigs. The rumour was that the Germans took everything, that it was safer inside Russia's borders, wherever these might now be.

On 5 September, the Tsar took command of the Russian forces, making him even more closely identified with failure. Knox, shocked by the corruption and inefficiency he had found, wrote to the War Office on 19 September 1915, 'If ever there has been a Government that richly deserved a revolution, it is the present one in Russia.' By the end of the month, just short of Riga, the German advance in the north stopped as troops were sent west to Serbia or to France. The eastern front was still a war of movement, in contrast to the stalemate in the trenches in the west. By the autumn of 1915, the Germans were in Lithuania, having taken some 65,500 square miles of new territory which came under the control of their generals, principally Ludendorff, in a colonial entity called Ober-Ost. In January 1916 the Russian general Brusilov had startling successes against the mostly Austro-Hungarian forces, advancing into Galicia – but in 1917, amid revolutionary turmoil in Russia, the Germans reached further east.

The conquerors were shocked and fascinated by this land's filth and disorder, its primitive poor people, the unending forests, the tumbledown settlements, the deep silence and the strangeness. The Russians had left a terrible devastation, destroying much in their retreat. To cleanse all this seemed worthy of the heirs of the Teutonic Knights and a wholehearted programme of improvement began. Bavarian foresters tackled the wild eastern woodlands, surveyors and engineers set to work, roads were cut through the wilderness and by the end of 1915 there had been a transformation, an ostensible triumph of German technical ingenuity over Baltic stone-worshippers. Ludendorff hoped to make a wall of German settlements, under military protection, simultaneously enriching the Reich and defending civilization. There was nothing civilized, however, about the conditions of the work gangs or the complaints of rape and brutality; it was as if a moral frontier had been crossed once the troops and administrators left East Prussia, the last German outpost.

Above all this, an occasional lofty visitor to it, was Hindenburg, whose favourite play – *Wallenstein's Camp* by Schiller – was most appropriate. To many he seemed the reincarnation of the mighty general of the Thirty Years War, and his troops the equivalent of the freebooting *Landsknechte* who had terrified central Europe. The discussion of the possibilities of the east received intellectual foundations in 1916 when the Institut für Ostdeutsche Wirtschaft opened in Königsberg, becoming part of the university there in 1918. Not everyone liked what they saw in Ober-Ost. The writer Arnold Zweig worked in its administration and his anti-war novel, later burned by the Nazis, *The Case of Sergeant Grischa*, describes Ludendorff (called Schieffenzahn in the book) contemplating his sprawling domain: 'It was for them to obey, to follow and bow down. If they did not, they must be trodden underfoot. From a great height, as though from a captive balloon poised far above them, he looked down upon his realm, his towns, his forests, fields, and scattered herds of men and saw – nothing': a vision of arrogance and contempt.

*

Hans Koch, Peter's friend, came to see Käthe Kollwitz in November 1914 to tell her about Peter's last days – how her son had played with the children in the Belgian house where he had been billeted, how he had made friends with and protected a retarded old man who said, on hearing of the boy's death, that he wanted to be with Peter in his grave.

She sat often in her son's room and it became a shrine: 'My boy, I am with you in your room, at your table,' she wrote in her diary on 12 November. The print *Waiting (Anxiety)* was published just after Peter had been killed – a depiction of a woman alone weighed down by what might happen – and at the start of December, after a sleepless night, she thought of a memorial: Peter's body lying with his eyes open to the sky, with his father at its head and his mother at the foot, to be put up in Berlin, in Havelberg, above the river: a memorial not only to her son but to all volunteers. It might be dedicated on a summer's day in a ceremony with schoolchildren singing the patriotic hymn, 'No finer death in the world than to be slain by the enemy.' In her lithograph of 1914, in memory of Ludwig Frank, a Social Democrat politician who, like Peter, had volunteered and been killed, mourners touch each other as they kneel, brought together by Frank's ideals.

She felt alone, torn between anger and pride. In her diary on the last day of 1914 she declared her wish to be 'faithful' to Peter's love of his country, to the idealistic young; she must work harder because death had stopped him from working. He must help her to go on; if only the mist through which she saw him might clear. She knew he was there and she dreaded the distance becoming greater, the memories more vague; he must stay. On 15 February 1915, she told Hans that she doubted now what she had previously thought – that egoism had to end, that the Fatherland had the right to ask for a life. Work she saw now as even more vital. The artist Max Liebermann wrote to her that she must go on working. Again, she recalled her grandfather Rupp's words, 'A gift is a duty.'

Käthe Kollwitz's journey from patriotic emotion to pacifist internationalism had begun yet she couldn't accept that Peter had died for criminal madness because this would make his loss pointless. She thought of Goethe's line, 'Seed corn is not for harvesting.' Had it been wrong of her to plead with Karl to let the boy go? She told Hans that his father and she would gladly have given their lives so that their sons could live. But she had liked the patriotism Peter had shown, its pure emotion. The Fatherland *did* stand at the back of everything, overshadowing each individual life.

On 2 January 1916, she wrote in her diary of the year without Peter, how, like him, she loved Germany. Had their positions on the war been close? In 1915 she noted in her diary the taking of Warsaw by the Germans, but she also drew two grieving parents round the mocking symbol of a joyful family festival – a Christmas tree. The death of her son made her work more sombre. A theme for the rest of her life was the betrayal of the young by the old who had exploited their idealism. It was as if grief became her closest companion, her most intense love, so personal that it was a barrier between her and Karl, even between her and Hans. Grief and guilt could, she thought, be soothed by art – by absorption in making a heartfelt work.

The self-portraits begin to show age and stoicism, a wish not to hide suffering but to give it dignity and beauty. Peter's friends began to call her Mother Käthe. Another sentence from grandfather Rupp came back: man is not born for happiness but so that he can fulfil his duty. On 11 October 1916, as winter came to the battlefields, she wrote of the madness of the youth of Europe killing each other: of how the love of country inflaming German, British, Russian and French boys had been betrayed. Was it disloyal to Peter to think like this? He had died believing the ideals for which he – and they – had gone to fight.

In June 1916, Käthe and Karl had their silver wedding. She had stayed with him yet could feel, as in the past, stifled by his love. The next year she started to dream of a simple life, away from Berlin, in a country cottage with a garden, a dream – not reflected in the urban, committed atmosphere of her work. Her fame should, she felt, have been more consolation – and she did like it: the celebrations of her fiftieth birthday in 1917 with exhibitions in Bremen, Berlin and, in July, Königsberg which she went to see. A review in the *Königsberg Hartungsche Zeitung* said what Gerhart Hauptmann also now thought – that the works were relentlessly serious, full of the heart's suffering, conveying exhaustion, despair, apathy, showing that humanity's way is 'hard, awkward, haggard', its forms 'emaciated, unlovely . . . The ugly and unpleasant is predominant; the gentle, soft and kind fail.'

She herself wondered if her art might be too hopeless and when Hans won the Iron Cross, her joy briefly eclipsed her horror at the war. To Hans, on New Year's Eve, she wrote of sitting alone (for the first time on this night for twenty-six years), with a glass of wine, not sad now to think of the two sons and Karl, the people she loved most, as the bells celebrated the arrival of 1918 and the end of another year of war. But on 20 March, the day before the launch of the last German offensive in the west, she thought again of how Peter and many millions like him had been betrayed.

It was the eastern victories that made this huge attack possible. In September 1917 the Germans took Riga, in their last battle with the Russians. The October revolution made any further advance unnecessary, for the new Bolshevik government was pledged to seek peace. In Riga the conquerors found what looked like a German city, dominated by the Baltic Germans who could trace their origin there to the Teutonic Knights. Russian Latvia seemed to have had a colonial world imposed upon it of Lutheran churches, classical manor houses, ordered forestry and farms and a legal system mostly administered by landowners and businessmen who often barely spoke the local language. The Bolsheviks had abolished all this but the Treaty of Brest-Litovsk, signed on 3 March 1918, revived it. Estonia, Latvia and Lithuania came under German control, as did Russian Poland and most of what is now Belarus; Finland and Ukraine were made independent, under German influence. The Baltic Germans found themselves once more in charge, under Ober-Ost.

7: 'Seed corn is not for harvesting'

In 1917 – and for the next three years – Alfred Knox saw the chaos that shaped his political views for the rest of his life. Communism would come to mean, for him, the end of civilization. His pre-Bolshevik Russian world – journeys to the front in the railway carriages of Grand Ducal army commanders, dinners in St Petersburg where whisky was served with real Schweppes soda, confidence in the decency and loyalty of the Russian soldier – was blown apart.

How hard it was, though, to foretell the terrifying violence of the collapse. Even in March 1917, Mikhail Rodzianko, the leader of the Duma, or parliament, told Knox not to worry about Russia making a separate peace with Germany because 'Russia is a big country, and can wage war and manage a revolution at the same time.' The ground shifted with extraordinary speed. The Tsar abdicated and Knox quickly became disenchanted with Alexander Kerensky, the most charismatic and visible member of the provisional government. From 3 June, Knox was at the southwest front, where another offensive failed; by the end of July he was writing of an economic and food crisis – with officials being murdered, peasants holding back grain because of plummeting prices, landowners being expelled, the railways paralysed.

Petrograd – as the German-sounding St Petersburg had been known since 1914 – descended further into chaos. When the Winter Palace fell to the mob, two Russians from the Women's Battalion who had been part of its defence reached the British embassy and pleaded for help: a hundred and thirty-seven other women had been captured, beaten and tortured and were at risk

of rape and death. Knox drove to the Bolshevik headquarters in
the Smolny Institute, once St Petersburg's most fashionable girls'
school, and, in an astonishing display of browbeating, demanded
the release of the women, threatening that he would set the opinion of the civilized world against the Bolsheviks. He fell into
anti-Semitism again in his description of one of the revolutionaries – 'a repulsive individual of Semitic type . . . of a race which
has been oppressed for centuries but now holding all the cards,
not arrogant but determined.' Later, the women were freed.

In November, Lenin and the Bolsheviks formed a government. Counter-revolutionary moves failed; the coup held and on
3 December, the new rulers met the Germans at Brest-Litovsk
to discuss an armistice. Terror strengthened the Bolsheviks' grip;
Knox heard that several of his old friends, senior officers in the
Russian army, had been murdered. Later he recalled the attacks
published by Trotsky on the Allies, especially on British imperialism in India, to which Knox had given much of his working life.
This proved, he thought, that Bolshevism was internationalist,
intent on bringing world revolution. On 7 January, Knox and
British diplomats and military and naval personnel left Petrograd
for the last time, two bottles of brandy having secured them a
comfortable carriage on the train. Only one Russian dared to be
there to see them off, a woman whose name, even in 1921, Knox
dared not reveal lest she face reprisals.

Alfred Knox believed that the Allies had to move quickly to
stifle Bolshevism, for the sake not only of Russia but of the rest of
the world. Leaving London again in the summer of 1918, he went
east, as head of the British Military Mission to Siberia. Counter-
revolution was thought to have a chance in Siberia partly because
there were already the foundations of an anti-Bolshevik or
'White' force in the form of Japanese troops and the Czech
Legions, released Czech prisoners of war who had been captured
by the Russians while fighting for the Austro-Hungarian Empire,
from which they now wanted to be free. In Tokyo, Knox met the
possible Russian leader of this force: Admiral Kolchak, whom he

knew slightly and respected as an honest man of reputedly strong character.

By September he was in Vladivostok and went on to Omsk. But gradually the White movement degenerated into corruption and brutality, with the Admiral – whose strength had proved to be an illusion – unable to control his grim subordinates. Knox, at odds with the French commander of the international force, General Janin, came to be seen as Kolchak's puppet-master, especially when the Russian wore a British great coat and 'God Save the King' was played on formal occasions after the Tsarist anthem.

It was an extraordinary war, seemingly at the furthest end of the earth. Omsk filled up with exiled princes, vagrant writers, scheming politicians, black-marketeers, White officers with mistresses in private railway carriages and an enormous consignment of Tsarist gold. Knox had the title of *chef d'arrière*, in charge of supplies and training schools set up in Vladivostok, Irkutsk and Tomsk – officially under Janin but independently powerful because of the prodigious distances. In the rough world of White Russian politics he tolerated Kolchak's suppression of dissent, fearing that the Admiral was in fact not tough enough. But a spring offensive, which Knox had opposed, failed. By August Kolchak seemed to be an obvious loser. The supply position was chaotic; consignments went astray or were captured or sold on the black market. In one of Kolchak's army corps, the only equipment issued to the officers during six months was a thousand pairs of braces.

In all this, Knox symbolized order. A Russian diplomat praised his truthfulness and energy and a British colleague wrote, 'This is a type of British officer one meets occasionally. They make one proud to belong to the same race and eager to spare no effort to work for the patriotic and unselfish ideals which evidently form the mainspring of their lives.' Greed and weak leadership, however, wrecked Kolchak's crusade. Both Whites and Reds were brutal – but the Reds were hard in pursuit of victory whereas the

Whites took what they could in what came to be seen as opportunism or a reminder of the old, unloved regime.

The end was bleak. Kolchak was captured and executed by the Bolsheviks in Irkutsk on 7 February 1920; his mistress, Anna Timireva, imprisoned nearby, heard the volley of the firing squad. The train load of gold fell into the hands of Lenin's revolutionary government and the next month Knox and the British Military Mission left Russia. The truth was that after the armistice in November 1918, Allied governments had gradually lost interest in the expensive and unpopular military intervention in Russia. Only a few politicians like Winston Churchill pressed for a war against the Bolsheviks, who were often wildly underestimated, as Hitler would be a decade later. To Knox, the collapse seemed particularly grim. He had failed in everything, he told an American officer. Such a humiliation – for a man full of the pride and self-esteem of an Edwardian imperialist – was devastating. He had, he wrote, begun retreating at Tannenberg and had not stopped for the next six years.

*

In the west, the huge German spring offensive, after startling initial success, was contained and the Allies counter-attacked, crucially aided by growing numbers of American troops. On 1 October 1918, Käthe Kollwitz wrote that Germany had clearly lost the war. Enough: this was the feeling that overwhelmed her. On 28 October she protested in a letter to the paper *Vorwärts* against more young people being sent out to fight and quoted again from Goethe, 'Seed corn is not for harvesting.' At least Peter had been killed at a gentler time, before the slaughter of the great offensives.

A memorial would be the best expiation. Into it went her guilt at having let Peter go, the loss and an offering of regret from an older generation to the young. She worked against doubt, difficulty, depression and pain – with intervals of inactivity, as if to regain her strength. Her duty was to finish this expression of what she and millions of others throughout Europe had felt: the enshrining of a moment in lasting art. Käthe Kollwitz held to a scene: the dead boy lying between the father and the mother who kneel below the body – whose eyes gaze at the sky, as on those romantic wanderings before the war. The lips part as if in laughter; on his breast is a representation of a flower that she had once given him.

She thought of possible inscriptions: 'The Death for the Fatherland' or 'No more beautiful death in the world'. The group is like a Christian image – the mourning for Christ or the farewell of Mary to her dead son – a secularization of her own childhood faith, also giving a sacredness to Peter's belief in the Fatherland. The mourners show humility as well as grief at what he had sacrificed. The group brought back the enthusiasm of August 1914, a selfless, innocent joy. Surely she had been right to speak up for this on that August evening, even if it had led to his death. In a more intimate study – a tablet for Peter's gravestone above his body in Flanders – the parents bow low so that their faces are hidden as the mother clasps the apparently overwhelmed father who seems still isolated, the prehensile hands and heavy limbs showing raw misery. It is a shared mourning but also the pain of solitude and incommunicable memory.

All this at first brought a sense of 'good and calm'. But the war began to seem too much like madness; by 1919, in revolutionary times, Käthe Kollwitz had ceased work on the large memorial. After reading accounts of the pre-war crisis that contradicted Germany's claims of self-defence, she felt the idealism of 1914 had become tainted. What Peter had died for – a threatened country – seemed to have been at least partly a lie. She still worked on images of loss, of mourning and of isolation; *The Parents* of 1919, for instance, shows the man's knee awkwardly touching the thigh of the woman with the rest of their bodies apart in the empty air. In February 1916 she had gone to a Secession exhibition in Berlin and seen the wooden sculpture by Ernst Barlach of *Grief* – of a man and a woman facing emptiness, staring ahead without hope. Barlach resembled her also in his depictions of the poor and a romantic fascination with Russia which Käthe Kollwitz thought in her case came from her origins in the east.

She knew that East Prussia was the country of Kant, not of Tolstoy – more rational, cooler – yet she had a spasmodic longing to fling this off, to seek a wilder place. Like Barlach, she welcomed the Bolshevik revolution of 1917; like Barlach too she thought that writing and music – Goethe and Beethoven – were stronger than her own art. Although he said it was coincidental, Barlach made one of his carved figures in Gustrow cathedral resemble Käthe Kollwitz. After the armistice in November 1918, with Germany in a state of revolution, Käthe instinctively feared society's breakdown and what revolution might bring. When the Emperor abdicated and Hindenburg was said to be working to prevent chaos, she wrote, 'Bravo Hindenburg.' At the war's end, the Germans, still occupying large parts of Belgium, were not far from where Peter had fallen.

8: East Prussia's Versailles

At Slobity I become lost while driving in a car rented in Olsztyn for the day, having turned off the highway down an old cobbled road, the tyres on the stones sounding like low thunder. The Dohnas had once owned thousands of acres here. They planted woods – partly for forestry, partly for sport – that still break up the rolling landscape; their trees are an older presence than the group of abandoned buildings, of corrugated iron and pre-fabricated blocks, low like long chicken sheds, that marks the remains of communist collectivization. It has started to rain, bringing desolation to the scene. In a nearby field, a man on a tractor is ploughing, up and down, reaching the end, where I am, before moving off again. To ask him to stop is inconsiderate yet I raise my hand. He will have to get out of the tractor's cab if he wants to help me and soon become as soaked as I am – for the rain is heavier: relentless. Now I see him clearly – a wide, brown-reddish face, his hand now raised as well, as he smiles and gets down.

I manage some questions, in phrase-book Polish: his land? Yes. Good? OK. What next, he must have thought, his smile fixed; and I ask for Slobity. 'Locomotive?' he replies, thinking of the train station close by and I said no, *Zamek* or castle. It is clearly the least likely place of the two – the castle and the station – for people to want to find. I say the name 'Dohna' and he again looks mystified; then I add 'German' and he knows and points me on my way. It's the same with some young people whom I ask for directions, in the village now called Slobity, only a few hundred yards from the Dohna house's wrecked lodge gates. At first they look at me as if I'm mad.

The land around the ruins is soft and muddy after the rain. Weeds and high brambles and bushes grow through the pane-less windows of the side pavilions that, unlike the mansion, still have the remains of roofs. The wide, three-storey-high façade faces me – the oblong holes of windows revealing vegetation and a blank, crumbling rear wall, like a stage set's contrived glimpse of decay. At the centre, above the façade, are the remains of a decorative trophy, a last sign of ownership and power, its carved stone work framing an empty circle where once, probably, the Dohna arms had been. On the house, the stone stucco had chipped or peeled back, revealing patches of red brick beneath, harsher than the pink that had once been thought soft and beautiful. Thin saplings sprout from the walls. Among the ruins are some young birches, the tree of the endless lands of Russia, whose frontier is just a few miles away.

Two wings break the monotony of the façade at each end of Schlobitten; green foliage spills out of the top of a high chimney, a good place for a stork's nest. The formal gardens are on the other side. At the front, facing me, is a damp ditch and some ploughed land perhaps used by the villagers. Above the ditch and a shallow pond is a cracked three-arched bridge, lined on top with stunted pillars, that leads to the centre of the house, the point of entry for guests or returning members of the Dohna family. The Emperor William II had arrived here, the last of a succession of Hohenzollerns who had royal apartments set aside for them at Schlobitten. These visits must have seemed to confirm the place's solidity through the presence of a high, even sacred, hereditary force that, like the Dohnas, had survived.

The desolation has a beauty, partly in the wild growth over an earlier formality that, as bullet or shrapnel scars on the walls reveal, had ended in terror. The rain stops and the house is struck briefly by sunlight, before stifling white and then grey cloud drifts in; again the place seems like theatre, an idea of what once had been. To the left, in front of one wing, some soil, perhaps dug from the pond or simply dumped on a now useless space, forms a mound that is already speckled with weeds.

The village is small: really just one curving street, the big house set apart, up what has become a track, yet near enough for small children to be able to play among the ruins. The next most prominent building is the church, again red brick, once under the patronage of the Dohnas, now, in its Polish identity, Roman Catholic. Outside the church – opposite the short spire at its eastern end – a smartly dressed middle-aged woman is getting out of a car with some flowers. She has a key that opens the church door and when I walk in behind her, she turns, surprised, not pleased. But she smiles when I ask some questions, and we speak together, in a mixture of English, German and my phrase-book Polish.

The Dohnas? She shrugs. I look at the church's interior, now adapted to its new Roman Catholic identity. There had been, I recall from Alexander Dohna's memoirs, an altercation with one of the Roman Catholic priests who had been out of sympathy with the idea that the Dohna monuments should be uncovered or partly restored. She took me outside again, and pointed to the wall of the church and a grey stone tablet on which is a carved tree, with roots below. On either side of the tree's trunk are branches with birds in them and a curving stone pennant or banner with the words 'In the world war 1914–1918, they died for the Fatherland' – then, under the roots, 'to our fallen heroes'. Several Dohnas have their names on the stone.

Alexander, the last Dohna to live at Schlobitten, went west in the snow in 1945 – leading a great trek of hundreds of refugees, some driving tractors, some in carts or on horses, others on foot. For the rest of his life he was proud not to have abandoned his people although this paternalism now has few admirers. In 2003, a critic wrote in Germany's conservative newspaper, the *Frankfurter Allgemeine Zeitung*, that no one likes the Junkers, the landlords who once had their way east of the Elbe. He may have been thinking of the caricature, based on Alexander Dohna's grandfather, in a 1912 issue of the satirical magazine *Simplicissimus*, of a booted and spurred fat man drawn from the rear – with a bulging neck, a small hat jaunty over close-cropped hair, some loud-checked jodhpurs and a horseman's bow legs; at his feet, a thin greyhound has its tail down, perhaps in reaction to abuse. We don't see the man's face – only those of some fawning workers in rags in front of him, two doffing their caps. Behind them is Schlobitten, East Prussia's Versailles, with its pavilions, its mansard roof, its tall symmetrical chimneys and broad immaculate lawns.

In East Prussia the castles of the Teutonic Knights had evolved into country houses, their fortifications softening into elegance and art. But farming – principally cattle, horses and corn – and forestry were the life blood of families like the Dohnas, the Dönhoffs and the Lehndorffs. In other parts of eastern Germany, notably in Silesia, coal, iron ore and other minerals made landowners vastly rich; in East Prussia there was none of this. Alexander Dohna's ancestor, for whom Schlobitten was enlarged at the end of the seventeenth century and start of the eighteenth,

Schlobitten: East Prussia's Versailles.

had asked for a plain exterior, as if to keep the place grounded on the earth that had yielded up the money with which to build it. The resulting façade was coolly classical: what Marion Dönhoff, in her book on her old homeland, claimed was the essence of Prussia.

Inside, however, Schlobitten erupted into a palace. There was elaborate plaster work, sculpted decoration and large murals; and over the centuries the house filled up with Chinese and German porcelain; English, Bohemian, German and Dutch glassware; faience and seventeenth-century Danzig and Elbing silver; furniture that included a seventeenth-century amber chest from Königsberg; armour, coins and medals and one of Frederick the Great's snuff boxes. Berlin tapestries of oriental scenes were commissioned for the royal apartments. There was a library of over fifty-five thousand volumes and an archive that included a book of songs by the English composer John Dowland, correspondence with the Vatican (where a Dohna had gone on a mission in the seventeenth century) and with the Reformer Philipp Melanchthon and the rulers of Brandenburg, Prussia and other German princely states. There were family and royal portraits – one of King William III of England and Orange, to show the family's Dutch links – and pictures by Jan Mytens, van Loo, Madame Vigée-Lebrun and a small silverpoint drawing of Kant.

The Dohnas had served the Hohenzollerns, as generals and courtiers and ministers. A reminder of the last years of this was a warlike image of the last Emperor leading a cavalry charge in 1895, leaning back in the saddle, apparently complacent rather than aggressive – which was appropriate for he never saw action. William II showered gifts on the family – ornately framed land and seascapes, a silver Jugenstil tankard, an enormous heraldically decorated window and a massive portrait of the Emperor himself in uniform thought to be too warlike for the German embassy in London. Even in a house as large as Schlobitten the imperial generosity tested the limits of the storage space for the Dohnas had kept almost everything, accumulating a mass of clothes and costumes (used in performances in the house's small theatre), kitchenware, the papers and books and keepsakes and gifts from over four centuries – an astonishingly complete record.

Some of this mass of possessions was destroyed in the looting and fires after 1945; some was sent west early enough and can be seen in the Berlin Schönhausen Museum or a former town house of the Dohnas in the Polish town of Morąg (formerly the German Mohrungen). In Berlin and Morąg, visitors tend to pass quickly through the Dohna rooms, for there are no obvious masterpieces. In Berlin, an attendant stared at me when I made notes, a sign perhaps of the rarity of such interest; at Morąg, in the restored town house, it is the section dedicated to the philosopher Herder – who was born in the town – that is popular, not the Dohna china or family portraits. Sometimes a piece from Schlobitten surfaces at an auction or in a dealer's catalogue; there may be questions of looting or dubious ownership but usually a new owner gets what he or she wants before silence, once again, engulfs an old idea.

The atmosphere of the youth of Alexander Dohna, Schlobitten's last hereditary owner, was military. Born in 1899, he lived with his parents at Potsdam, where his father was adjutant of the Garde du Corps, among the uniforms that represented Prussian, then German, power. The last Hohenzollern ruler, William II, cherished this as vociferously as any of his predecessors – and the Dohnas were with their emperor. In his memoirs, Dohna wonders what had made his nineteenth-century forebears abandon an earlier more liberal tradition and move to the right. Could it have been the shock of the revolutions of 1848 or the nationalistic euphoria that accompanied Bismarck's remarkable expansion of Prussian and German power?

During his lifetime, Alexander Dohna became a symbol of this power and of its loss. Near the start of his memoirs, there's an early photograph of the little Alexander on an ornate chair in front of Schlobitten, a peaked officer's cap on his head, his legs crossed and an unyielding gaze directed away from the camera.

Towards the book's end, there is a quite different scene: the shop-keeper Fürst behind a counter, courteously taking in a pile of dirty clothes.

The old world watched over the boy's christening. The Emperor was his godfather but could not come to the ceremony so was represented by General von Moltke, from the family of Prussian field marshals. Alexander's early childhood was spent not only at Potsdam – until his father left the army in 1906 – but also on the Dohna estates in East Prussia: at Behlenhof, Prökel-witz and Schlobitten, the largest of the family's houses. During the army manoeuvres near Schlobitten, the Emperor came to stay and there were other imperial visits, sometimes for hunting when as many as five hundred roebuck were killed; Dohna's grand-father, Richard Wilhelm Dohna, a conservative member of the Reichs-tag, is said to have introduced William II to the artistic, sentimental Philipp von Eulenburg – a friendship that later col-lapsed after the exposure of Eulenburg's homosexuality.

The Dohna atmosphere was sporting, not artistic; even the librarian had to learn to ride. It was also old-fashioned; Richard Dohna's marriage to a cousin had been arranged by his father. Structure was important, as the timetable at Prökelwitz for the Emperor's pleasure shows: breakfast at 3.30 or 4.00; the morning roe-deer shoot; back for a sleep before lunch at 4.00 p.m.; another outing to the woods; then a 'simple' evening meal and anecdotes before bed at 10.30. A withered arm – the result of a mishandled delivery at his birth – did not curb the Emperor's enthusiasm for sport. At meals he used a special large spoon to allow him to eat as fast, and as much, as anyone else.

In old age, Alexander Dohna declared that the years before 1914 had been the best of his long life for families like the Dohnas. A monarchy put the imprimatur of the state on heredi-tary power, as did the Prussian Herrenhaus, a hereditary upper chamber similar to the old British House of Lords. Royal visits and rituals seemed also to confer legitimacy on the great houses. During the military manoeuvres of 1910, over the flat empty country that would be the first victim of a Russian invasion, ten thousand soldiers took part and field-grey uniforms were worn for the first time. The eleven-year-old Alexander noticed the enthusiasm of the locals and the pride of the troops. Years later he recalled this, after German patriotism had been tainted by the enormities of the Nazis and the national identity had changed.

On the estates of East Prussia, the Emperor and his friends returned to a pre-industrial age. The walls of the grand houses were covered in thousands of deer heads, the bleached skulls sprouting the horns that were the trophies of the sport, bringing a wild land into interiors decorated with bosomy nymphs, painted ceilings and classical statuary. The woods near the ruins of Prökelwitz and Schlobitten are still spotted with tablets commemorating notable kills, some visible beneath undergrowth or in forest clearings, signs of an earlier possession, like the soldiers' graves. At Schlobitten, on September or October nights, you still hear the roaring of the stags.

Alexander Dohna remembered the pale-blue East Prussian sky; the breezes from the Baltic; the journeys in a horse-drawn trap in summer and a sleigh through the long winter snows; the ancient oaks near the great houses; trips to see his cousins the Dönhoffs on one of their estates at Quittainen, near Schlobitten; the tutors and governesses; his grandmother's brothers, both veterans of the Franco-Prussian War, who came to stay. He felt moved by Sedan Day each September when his father made a speech to celebrate the 1870 victory over the French and the crowd sang patriotic songs. William II was toasted not as the Emperor of Germany but as the King of Prussia.

In the summer of 1914, the Dohnas were on holiday on the Frische Nehrung, the western spit on the Baltic. During the talk of war, Alexander recalled feeling a surging wish to do his duty to the Fatherland and to the royal family. More than fifty years later he thought that from that day the foundations of his life – the world of his happily married parents and their five children – had begun to break up.

Fearing a Russian invasion, the Dohna parents sent their children west, to relations in Darmstadt. After Tannenberg, when the saviour Hindenburg had made East Prussia safe, the children returned for Christmas at Schlobitten. Alexander Dohna went back to Darmstadt, to live in a pension and to go to the Ludwig-Georg-Gymnasium where he made friends with a boy called Karl Wolff who later changed his life. In 1916, he moved to Switzerland, to a school in Davos. In 1918, he was at Potsdam, as a young officer in his father's old regiment, going into the field in September, to Kursk, near Kiev. There was no fighting; in March the Treaty of Brest-Litovsk had been signed with the new Bolshevik government. On 10 November, in Ukraine, he heard of the Emperor's abdication, feeling relief because it must signal the end of the war. On 18 November, his father died and Alexander became the Fürst. The next month, sick with diphtheria, he took the train west and, on arrival at Dresden, saw the new defeated Germany: a banner that declared 'Proletarians of the World Unite'. At Potsdam, he left the army and in January 1919 arrived at Schlobitten, now the centre of his world. In the hall was part of his dead father's collection of hats, symbol of the age's formality. At that date, it was inconceivable that anyone should be seen outside the Dohna house without a hat.

9: 'Names that are named no more'

Dr Tadeusz Iwiński, the member of parliament for the once-German north-eastern part of Poland (that includes Slobity, formerly Schlobitten), agrees to see me in a Warsaw hotel. He's been hard to reach because of an election campaign. When we meet, I recognize him because I've just come from Olsztyn, his constituency's largest town, where I'd seen a poster of his smiling face to which someone had added two long, curving vampire's teeth.

A professor at Olsztyn University, and a brilliant linguist who speaks Mandarin Chinese, Tadeusz Iwiński now leads one of the parties of the left. His family had roots in Olsztyn during the German times (when it was Allenstein) and after the region became Polish his father worked there as an engineer. Born in 1944, Tadeusz had a soaring academic career, obtaining a Ph.D. at Warsaw University in international relations and scholarships to Harvard and to Berkeley.

Tadeusz Iwiński is interested in land tenure in British colonial Nigeria and I try to stop him talking about this although his knowledge of it is phenomenal. Did I know, he says, that the Portuguese had been the first into Africa and the last out? Small and energetic, he gesticulates a lot, once knocking over his cup of coffee. That day he has already been three times on television and has another interview lined up for this evening. He thinks that as a politician today you can do nothing without the media. It means he's recognized all over the place, even recently by some Polish visitors to Cape Town, where he was attending a congress.

Why am I interested in north-east Poland, he wonders? He seems pleased. Have I been to Olsztyn already? Where did I stay?

The hotels were full but I'd found a room near the castle, in the Polish–German House of Friendship used mostly by youth groups. Here I'd felt conspicuous, old: aware of cool glances from staff and guests.

Olsztyn mixes Poland and Germany. There's the old centre – the red-brick castle of the Teutonic Knights and the churches, the gabled houses round a market square (where a Prussian marksman nearly shot Napoleon) and fortified walls and historic gates, a place for tourists: then the nineteenth-century and Communist-era town that blends into the ring road, the new university and the Michelin tyre factory that show the modern Poland of the European Union. On the outskirts, you see a signpost to Kaliningrad. The Russian border can take hours to cross because of visa inspections and searches to stop smuggling.

Tadeusz Iwiński talks about the region's history, about the exodus of Germans at the war's end and the influx of Poles from the territories further east that had been taken by Stalin. He speaks of his constituency, what it was like and what it has become – different to the Dohna story of a feudal order maintained even in devastation and retreat. After 1945, hundreds of thousands of Poles were moved into the former East Prussia. The new Poland had new frontiers; these were pushed west to the River Oder – bringing in a swathe of the old Germany, including Breslau (now Wrocław) and Danzig (now Gdańsk) – but they contracted in the east. Much of what had been eastern Poland between the wars – Lwów, for instance, and Wilno (now Vilnius) – became part of the Soviet Union.

Stalin wanted the Poles out of his new lands. Poland needed settlers for its own new territories where millions of Germans had been expelled or killed. So Poles, many either town-dwellers or from some of the poorest parts of eastern Europe, were shifted into the wrecked landscape of what had been eastern Germany. They entered Silesia with its mines and industry, Pomerania – a mostly agricultural province – and the most rural area of all: East Prussia. The former German East Prussian land had been well

cultivated, with field drainage begun in the eighteenth century
on the advice of the Dutch. The cataclysmic war had destroyed
much of this; and the new communist Poland imposed collectivization, run by people who didn't know the land. Inefficiency or
destruction ruined farms that before 1945 had been Germany's
breadbasket. It was the same in the new Russian district of Kaliningrad, formerly Königsberg.

Now, in the new Poland of privatization and the Common
Agricultural Policy, Tadeusz Iwiński says, you can see much more
cultivation, sometimes by big, highly mechanized farming companies, from the United States and western Europe. But, he adds,
the workers on the old state units have suffered. In parts of
Masuria, the unemployment rate is over 20 per cent, one of the
worst in Poland. The old, admittedly over-manned collective
farms, he says, at least looked after their workers. Since Poland
joined the European Union, the subsidies go to the new farmers,
not to the unemployed. Some of the land is good – like the black
soil of Ukraine. And the farming companies benefit from the EU
Common Agricultural Policy. Is it true that the Queen of England,
who owns so much land, is one of the greatest beneficiaries of
this? Tadeusz Iwiński's eyes glint like twin blades.

Communist Poland hadn't been like the Soviet Union, he says;
you could travel abroad, the Roman Catholic Church was strong,
there was some private ownership. Is it surprising, he asks, if
some older people feel nostalgic for the old days of full employ-
ment? Parts of his constituency are like the Kaliningrad region:
poor, left behind. To Poles, Kaliningrad is a strange land –
Russian but cut off from the rest of Russia, unknown yet so near.
An exhibition of photographs called 'The New Europe' in a
Warsaw square has a section on Kaliningrad. Pictures of proud,
bemedalled Red Army veterans are mounted alongside others
of bleak Soviet housing and military parades. The text describes
a place filled with missiles, nuclear weapons, cemeteries, war
memorials and a seething insecure people: a danger, it is implied,
to the world.

Three great reconciliations are needed for Poland now, Tadeusz Iwiński thinks – with Germany, with Ukraine and with Russia. Many remember the Fourth Partition of Poland – the Molotov–Ribbentrop pact of 1939 between Germany and the Soviet Union that divided the country between the two monsters of twentieth-century Europe. This was followed by the murders of the war and its aftermath – Poles killed by Ukrainian nationalists, by the Soviets and by the Germans.

Iwiński says that a huge change in Poland has been the fall in the size of its minorities. Before the war a third of the population were Jews, Ukrainians and Byelorussians. Now minorities make up only 1 to 2 per cent of Poland; in his constituency, most of the Germans (or German Poles) who had stayed after 1945 had gone to Germany, lured by the German government's grants for resettlement. The Holocaust had ended seven hundred and fifty years of one of the world's largest Jewish communities. The few post-war Jewish survivors mostly left because of continuing persecution by the communist regime. Of the hundred and twenty MPs in the first Israeli Knesset, sixty-two spoke Polish; among these were great personalities like Peres, Begin, Dayan and Golda Meir.

Tadeusz Iwiński is keen on the new Europe. He was part of the Polish delegation to the Dublin summit in 2004, when Poland joined the European Union. But this closeness brought problems, such as Germans claiming back land in the old East Prussia. The legal basis for these claims was said to be a failure to put the change of ownership into the Polish land registry during the communist times. A European aim was to have free movement of land ownership – with member states open to buyers from anywhere in the EU. But this wasn't a reality yet, at least not in northern Poland. You still have to buy through a Polish nominee.

The loss of their old property where their ancestors and fellow countrymen had been for centuries was a wound for many Germans, Iwiński says; he can understand this. Had I known the Countess Dönhoff, he asks? He'd been one of the Polish representatives at Marion Dönhoff's funeral in Hamburg in 2002. Yes, I'd met Marion Dönhoff a long time ago. There was a time when if you wanted to know about East Prussia you went to Hamburg, to call on one of the most famous, and most admired, women in Germany.

*

Born in 1909, into one of those three historic East Prussian families – Dohna, Dönhoff and Lehndorff – the Countess Dönhoff, often known (usually with affection) as 'die Gräfin', was one of the founders of the great post-war German liberal newspaper *Die Zeit*. Now, some seven years after her death, a large photograph of Marion Dönhoff hangs above the reception desk in its Hamburg offices: the first image, for a visitor, of what the paper should be. Her determined, tense lips hint at a smile, her round

Marion Dönhoff.

face is wrinkled beneath shortish grey hair that curls up slightly at its edges. It is an austere image perhaps – although I may be imagining this after hearing her described often as 'very Prussian'.

She was a writer. She couldn't, she told me, think of life without writing – it came naturally to her. Much of what she wrote shows pride in her old homeland, evoking a different past to Elard von Oldenburg-Januschau's contempt for democracy or the shameful Nazi time. Her theme is often the Germans in the east, how, since the Middle Ages, most, if not all, intellectual development had been brought to this part of Europe by them: Christian belief, Luther's Reformation, the Enlightenment, humanism. Until the Second World War, German had been the lingua franca in eastern Europe. She points to the great romantic Polish poet Adam Mickiewicz's fascination with Schiller, to Nicholas Copernicus's mixed German and Polish ancestry. Her best books are about her early years in Friedrichstein, the vast house on one of the Dönhoff estates some fifteen miles from Königsberg, before her flight west in January 1945: *Names that are Named No More* (published in 1964) and *Childhood in East Prussia* (1988). They are unsentimental but loving depictions of a beautiful place, of a world of integrity and duty.

From 1709 to 1714, Friedrichstein was built for Otto Magnus Graf von Dönhoff, a general in the Prussian army. Designed by the French architect Jean de Bodt, who had worked at Berlin and Potsdam, its neo-classical façade covered a baroque interior – as at Schlobitten, an outward plainness over an inner extravagance. Like the Dohnas, the Dönhoffs installed elaborate tapestries from Flanders; rococo commodes and Danzig cabinets; collections of porcelain and medals; an accumulation of stiff images of ancestors: and, in the taste of Marion Dönhoff's father, statues and pictures of naked nymphs, goddesses and, in an unconscious glimpse of future horror, the rape of the Sabine women. There were formal gardens in the French style and some landscaping like an English park. It was Schlobitten again – a palace, even further east, nearer to the Baltic.

Marion Dönhoff's books show that with all this came the family's idea of duty, brought to what sounds like a Kantian pitch of importance. The Dönhoff children's lives at Friedrichstein were not luxurious, she writes; sometimes they went hungry because there wasn't enough food to go round, and ostentation was despised. It was a good and austere world, of responsibility for the workers on the property, of pride in the Dönhoff history, of an absolute integrity. Was it any wonder, she implies, that many of those involved in the July 1944 bomb plot against Hitler came from such a background? They had seen it as their duty to act against evil, even if this meant risking their own lives.

I've wondered often why they didn't make a move earlier – and when I met Marion Dönhoff in Hamburg in 1992 I asked this, not at all in a challenging way. It made her quite – but not very – angry. How hard it is, she said, for someone who hasn't lived under a totalitarian regime to understand the difficulty of any kind of opposition. Hitler was very popular; she conceded that. During the war, when she managed the family's properties, one of her secretaries was an ardent Nazi and several of her relations were in the party. You were watched all the time, especially someone like her whose views were known to colleagues and acquaintances. She realized from early on that her flight west in 1945 was inevitable – it was just a question of how soon.

You can buy books of photographs of the routes she took on her journeys – not only on the flight of 1945 but also during a ride through Masuria with her cousin in the early autumn of 1941, when Hitler's Germany was at its most triumphant. I told her that I was going to see that country – still, in 1992, not easy to reach. I asked if she knew what had happened to the house of her Lehndorff cousins, Steinort, where the last owner, Heinrich von Lehndorff, was arrested by the Gestapo in 1944, in front of his wife and children. The property had been called the great wilderness – and Heinrich had fled across it, trying to escape his hunters and their dogs. She said she'd heard that the place is a ruin.

Dönhoff never fell for what lured many of her class to

National Socialism: its power to protect them from communism, its restoration of order and prosperity, the cunningly dangled hope that the monarchy might be restored, its revival of national pride. She was a clever, hard-working student, studying economics at Frankfurt and, after the Nazis came to power, going to Basel in Switzerland for her doctorate. In Basel she had wanted to write on some aspect of Marxism but the professor suggested that the history of an East Prussian estate, based on the archive at Friedrichstein, would be a more original subject; the research brought her even closer to her home. Her family's money also let her travel before the war – to Kenya, to the United States and to see her older brother Heinrich in the Berlin of the artistically exciting Weimar years.

Heinrich took over the management of the family estates and Marion helped him; this, in addition to her studies, was her work. Their efforts were made easier after 1933 by the National Socialist government's support for agriculture, even if, at the harvest celebrations, the workers toasted Hitler instead of Count von Dönhoff. National Socialism, however, could strike the Dönhoffs with vicious cruelty. Marion had a sister, Maria, who had been born with Down's syndrome. The family managed to protect Maria from the official murdering of the afflicted that began in 1939 and she survived in a home until the protests of the Churches led Hitler to curb the campaign.

Dönhoff's liberalism mixed with an older, more rigid world, even when she was young. In June 1938, her brother Heinrich married a Roman Catholic from the Rhineland, Dorothea Gräfin von Hatzfeld. 'Dodo' refused to give up her religion and the Dönhoff family decided that any Catholic child of the marriage should not inherit. Dieter, another brother, became the heir. Years later, Marion Dönhoff said that for a Catholic to be the squire of Friedrichstein had been unthinkable. Roman Catholics were thought of as foreign hypocrites; the head forester, for instance, would never have employed one.

Until June 1941, Friedrichstein and Quittainen (another Dön-

hoff property, south-west of Königsberg, where Marion Dönhoff
lived for much of the war) were far away from any fighting.
That summer, however, the bombers droned overhead in support
of the invasion of the Soviet Union. There was a service for the
newly confirmed young in Quittainen's onion-domed church,
with the congregation aware that these young boys would soon
be sent to the Russian front. Incoming soldiers, transferred from
the west, relaxed on the village green during a break in their
journey, at a time of farewells. In September, Marion went with
her cousin Sissi Lehndorff on a five-day autumn ride through
Masuria, the wild country east of Allenstein, near the battlefields
of Grunwald and Tannenberg and the Tannenberg Memorial. She
evoked this symbolic journey some twenty years later in one of
her books, mostly through her old letters to her brother Dieter,
Sissi's husband, who was then on the Russian front.

Already, the Dönhoffs had begun to evacuate part of the art
collection to the houses of friends. Some was lost en route or later
because it hadn't been sent far enough west. The family had imagined that the Red Army might reach the River Oder – but not the
Elbe. In September 1941, there would not have been much talk of
resisting Hitler, for Sissi's husband was a loyal soldier at a time of
German triumph. The land – the wide lakes, the changing leaves,
the silence, the softly lit horizon, the friendly people who must
often have recognized the riders' names – was what Marion Dönhoff loved, then and afterwards: a memory set apart from the
barbaric regime that had been celebrated by most of her fellow
Germans and almost all of her class. So among the tasks that she
gave herself after 1945 was to make two different countries – a
good present and a past that hadn't been nearly as bad as the
post-war view of Germany.

Dönhoff had stayed away from her homeland for some forty-
four years until, in 1989, the philosopher Immanuel Kant took
her back to Königsberg, now Kaliningrad. For her journey east,
she went in two guises: someone from an utterly foreign past
but also one of the most distinguished liberal figures in modern

Germany. Even someone of her impeccable reputation found it difficult to get permission to enter what was then the closed zone of Kaliningrad; only at the last minute did the Russians grant the visas. She travelled by car, in August, in a Citroën *deux chevaux* driven by a young nephew, Hermann Hatzfeld. Marion Dönhoff never had children or married, although she was several times in love.

It was Kant who allowed her to go back. A Dönhoff great-great-grandfather had heard the philosopher lecture in Königsberg, but her family's most recent link with him had been towards the end of the war, when a statue of Kant by Christian Rauch, his home town's memorial to him, was sent to Friedrich-stein for protection from the bombing. Her father had died, her brothers were in the army (one had already been killed), her other unmarried sister had Down's syndrome so Marion Dönhoff had taken over much of the management of the family properties. She placed the statue in a quiet grove in the park at Friedrichstein.

Then came her flight west, in January 1945, and the arrival of the Red Army. Friedrichstein fell into ruins and has almost completely vanished. With it has gone much of the family collection and an archive that had started when a Dönhoff settled in this remote land in the seventeenth century. It's important to remember that borders and allegiances often shifted. Marion Dönhoff's ancestors – and the Dohnas and the Lehndorffs – had, after coming east, served not only the dukes and kings of Prussia and the emperors of Germany but the kings of Poland as well.

Kant's statue disappeared after the war, with the old world. In the 1980s, Marion Dönhoff tried to find out what had happened, writing to her friend the communist poet Rudolf Jacquemien, one of the few Germans in Kaliningrad. No one knew anything about it but Jacquemien did his best to find out. A roistering, red-faced man, he'd come to Stalin's Soviet Union as an idealistic communist before the war, working as a seaman before service in the Red Army and imprisonment as a German. In the more relaxed late 1960s, he retired to Kaliningrad, drawn perhaps by what

remained of the German atmosphere, joining the writers' club
and writing his poetry about the sea and love and a joy in life
that had survived Stalin's labour camps. 'I didn't cry when I
was born,' he told a Russian friend, but laughed to meet the
world.

So Rudolf Jacquemien and some friends set out from Kaliningrad for what had been Friedrichstein – now the Russian
Kamenka – to try to find Kant. Marion Dönhoff had sent him
the plan of the grounds and directions to where the statue might
be, perhaps buried under the reclaiming earth. Quickly they
excavated remnants of her former life: cups bearing the Dönhoff
arms – for which they rapidly brewed up tea – small plates, a
jug, further remains of the Count's breakfast service, and some
silver coins (1935 Reichsmarks with Hindenburg's head on them,
the German eagle joined with Hitler's swastika). Suddenly one of
the Russians there, the writer Yuri Ivanov, felt overcome – in this
Soviet land – by the romantic idea of Marion Dönhoff's youth.

Yuri Ivanov had been near Friedrichstein before – in 1945
with the Red Army when he was attached to a unit searching for
East Prussian art treasures, for the Amber Room (a 1716 Prussian gift to the Tsar Peter the Great, plundered from Leningrad by
the Nazis) and the great libraries. He recalled what he'd seen then
on a German air field off the road out of Königsberg – the rows
of abandoned Junkers and Focke-Wulf planes (that would have
bombed his family's Leningrad house) with records of sorties
marked on their fuselages (Tallinn, Leningrad, Liepāja) and pin-
ups still stuck in the cockpits – then, further on, the former panzer
school named after Heinz Guderian, one of the pioneers of
Blitzkrieg. All this had been surrendered or broken into the detritus of defeat. It was further remnants of such destruction that he
found at Friedrichstein on the hunt for Kant some forty years
later, after turning into a long tree-lined alley that leads off the
main road into what had been the private Dönhoff domain.
Uncontrolled woodland, weed and wild flowers have taken over
the mown lawns and carefully placed statues or selected plants of

a planned landscape that had once been its owners' idea of a civilized world.

With excited cries, Yuri Ivanov and the search party pored over a new discovery, a large stone head of the god Neptune. But Ivanov was surrendering to another past – different to his own of being bombed and starved during the German army's siege of Leningrad, or even the chaotic victory of 1945. He felt instead, in that bright Baltic light, the romance of the old German version of Friedrichstein – the pale stone, the family's arms above the entrance, the sun over the garden and the ancient oaks in the park. Inside had been the chain of rooms, the red room or the green saloon and the Gobelins or Flanders tapestries and (scrupulously stored and catalogued) the archives where Marion's research and writing life had begun: all the 'beauty, calm' and space brought by generations, Yuri Ivanov thought, before the bombers had flown over it, east towards Russia at the start of the invasion that had ended in destruction. How strange that this could move him, a former enemy. Another shout came from the search party – it was not Kant they had found but another stone version of a god, perhaps Pregel, a river god worshipped by the old Prussians who had been at least partly exterminated by the Teutonic Knights, the first Germans here.

In the evening, after their work, the party sat drinking more tea out of the Dönhoff cups by a small fire they had made. Wild duck flew overhead, seeking the artificial lake, Friedrichstein's most obvious remains. Rudolf Jacquemien read them some verses about the Lithuanian sea princess Jurate's love for the young fisherman Kastytis that had annoyed the sea king Naglys, the brother of Pregel whose head they had just found. Ivanov's romance took off again. These two Germans, Marion Dönhoff and Rudolf Jacquemien, had been brought together by destruction, for Friedrichstein was as far as you could imagine from Jacquemien's childhood in the cold rooms of a Roman Catholic children's home in Kiel before he began work as a gravedigger, miner and seaman. In 1932, fervently anti-fascist, he came on a freighter to the north

Russian harbour of Archangel, meeting a Russian girl there and deciding, on a second visit, to stay in Soviet Russia; later came the Red Army and a Siberian labour camp. Another member of the search party shouts, very excited, thinking she has found more treasure – but it turns out to be the top of a used anti-tank shell.

The Russian search party never found the statue – so Marion Dönhoff decided to give a smaller copy to the Russians and to take it to Kaliningrad herself. In Berlin she tracked down a cast of another Kant statue by Rauch, practically identical, and paid for a bronze copy of this from an award recently given to her: the Heine Prize, named after the poet who, ironically, had written scornfully about Kant. The gift was a restoration of a tiny part of a city that is described sometimes as having been almost completely lost. In fact there are many survivors in Kaliningrad from the German times such as the cathedral, the red-brick fortifications, the city gates, the former Prussian government buildings and the tomb of Kant. Before she went back, Dönhoff couldn't have realized how much of Königsberg had lasted, outside the bombed centre. As with the contents of Friedrichstein, she may have wished to think of a total destruction.

She had a unique place in post-war Germany. I knew this when I went to see her in 1992. Biographies of her – there have been several – show a photograph of 'die Gräfin' with other journalists meeting the Indian Prime Minister Nehru in the early 1960s; it is Dönhoff who is talking, her hands together in her lap, her face slightly tentative but severe and thoughtful as she sits in the most significant position, opposite the Prime Minister, the only woman there, with the others on both sides of her. Nehru smiles at an ashtray, a little awkwardly, apparently stubbing out a cigarette. It could be two heads of government on equal terms. There were rumours that Marion Dönhoff was once offered the presidency of West Germany.

With me she is kind and practical. We meet in her modest room at *Die Zeit* where the only apparent evidence of the past is a small picture of Friedrichstein that's easy to miss. When am I

going to East Prussia? In the spring? It is, she says, important not
to go too early, ideally not before May. The frosts and the cold
and the rain can linger past April, muddying the roads, covering
the land with mist and fog. Where am I thinking of going? She
unfolds a beautiful pre-war map, backed on linen, with the old
German names; then begins to trace possible routes, her small
brown hands moving quickly over the region's former identity.

I find her smaller than I had expected, and more humorous:
agile and spare, quick in movement. She is severe only occasionally, once when I ask what she must have been asked hundreds of
times – if she had thought after 1945 that her old homeland might
be German again. No, she answers sharply, it has gone for ever,
as if the question had been entirely about the present. The telephone rings once, a call that she says she must take. I hear the
conversation, about a conference. Will Dr Kissinger be there, she
asks? The answer seems to be yes. In that case, she says, she may
go.

The worlds of politics and of writing were natural places for
her, I think, for the recent history of her family shows culture and
responsibility. Marion's father, August von Dönhoff, was sixty-
four when she, the youngest of seven children, was born in 1909.
He'd been a soldier in Bismarck's Austrian and French wars,
then – after German unification – a diplomat in Paris, St Petersburg, London, Washington and Vienna and later a conservative
member of the Prussian and German parliaments. She talks of
him also as an art collector, a friend of the Berlin museum director Wilhelm Bode, who liked the baroque, the rococo, and
Renaissance sculpture, bronzes and coins. Political perhaps from
duty, he became more nationalistic during the First World War, in
which one of his sons fought. His daughter doesn't mention this
– or that August von Dönhoff was at a meeting at Königsberg
castle in 1917 convened by the right-wing agitator August Kapp.

August von Dönhoff died in 1919. Marion didn't know her
father well; he was often away in Berlin although she remembers
him reading late in his study at Friedrichstein on long winter

evenings, the lamp a bright speck down a dark passage. Her father was worldly and cultured. Her mother, Ria, twenty years younger than August, was a lady-in-waiting to the last Empress, Augusta Victoria. Like her mistress, Ria was devout yet, unlike the philistine Empress, musical, organizing concerts at Friedrich-stein by artists of the calibre of Fritz Busch and Edwin Fischer. Marion's childhood world was, she believed, intensely Prussian, with an atmosphere that went back to her grandfather, also called August, who had been, briefly, the Prussian Foreign Minister before the unification of Germany. In her short book about Prussia, she quotes August's letters from post-unification Berlin to his sister that lament the loss of what he sees as the Prussian virtues of thrift, of frugality, of the elevation of duty above personal profit: how these had been replaced by ostentation and greed in the feverish years after the Franco-Prussian War. The book shows also Marion Dönhoff's distaste for the last Hohenzollern ruler, the Emperor William II. He had, she thought, the vulgarity and crassness of a parvenu.

It's as if she seeks to vault over the Nazi years, the Weimar Republic, the First World War, the brash Wilhelmine time, even Bismarck's victories. Beyond these lie what she admires – the reformers of the early nineteenth century like Stein and Harden-berg, whom she saw as having created a state that was not only powerful but responsive to its citizens. Hadn't Frederick the Great, the autocratic imposer of tolerance, welcomed immigrants and other religions (unlike Britain, where Roman Catholics did not have the same rights as other citizens until 1829) and pro-moted education? At the book's end, she claims that these traditions had moved the conspirators of July 1944, most of whom she had known. Weren't many of them descended from the great Prussians of the past? In a Shakespearian lament, she lists the names: Moltke, Schwerin, Schulenburg, Lehndorff, Yorck.

Not all of Marion's relations shared her liberalism. After the defeat of 1918, as Germany descended into revolution, her eldest brother Heinrich, who had fought in the war, joined the Freikorps, the private army financed by right-wing business interests, to fight Bolshevism in the Baltic. Such fear of a breakdown of order is understandable in a family that had much to lose and was linked to the Hohenzollerns and a world now tainted with failure. As with the Dohna *Schloss* at Schlobitten, the Emperor and his entourage had often stayed at Friedrichstein on eastern visits. In 1916, Hindenburg came for a week, two years after Tannenberg and the battles of the Masurian Lakes. So in 1919, with her husband too blind to write and near death, Ria wrote to the commander of the German troops still on the north-eastern frontier, about her fear of revolutionaries from Königsberg or invasion from the new Poland or Bolshevik Russia. She asked the General to take Friedrichstein under his personal protection and approached Hindenburg himself – whom she recalled had 'loved' the place. Troops were moved there soon afterwards.

Marion Dönhoff's memoirs tell of an apparently idyllic upper-class childhood of that time, with no sign of rebellion against its feudal roots. A large family of brothers, sisters and cousins – Lehndorffs and Dohnas among them – and tutors and governesses and school in Königsberg made a world whose defences were not easily breached until September 1924, when she was fifteen. The car that was taking a group of them home from the seaside village of Cranz crashed into the River Pregel. Marion swam free but two of her cousins, a boy and a girl, were drowned. The next morning the two coffins were laid out in the garden room at Friedrichstein.

Her mother thought that she needed to be sent away, to have her mind filled with new experience: to schools in Berlin and Potsdam. It was while at university in Frankfurt that she saw the brown-shirted young men celebrate the appointment by President von Hindenburg of Hitler as chancellor in January 1933. Marion Dönhoff realized, she wrote later, that this meant the eventual destruction of everything that she loved.

10: A Lost Victory

A carved stone lion stands in the main square of Olsztynek (once the German Hohenstein), its solemn face blurred by years of severe winters. This is the most obvious remnant of what was once a memorial to the victory at Tannenberg and to the German dead. The vast structure itself has become a shallow pit of rubble and grass, dotted with empty bottles, grey ashes and patches of burned ground – the detritus of moonlight parties. On a wet morning, I slither across all this, watched by a Polish taxi-driver.

He had said that the battlefield of Grunwald, the fifteenth-century Polish–Lithuanian victory over the Teutonic Knights, is nearby – easy to reach. Would I go there next? He could do me a nice tour: Grunwald, then Olsztynek, then the open-air museum outside the town – fascinating wooden buildings, barns, milking parlours, a church – then the Stalag 1B prison camp and finally to the station or the bus stop so that I could catch a train or bus back to Olsztyn. Or for a little bit more he could drive me all the way: better, really, in the rain. He looked at me, confident, the German words rolling along to show he had done this often for visitors from the country that had formed this landscape.

It's difficult still to get around in this part of Masuria, especially when you go north or east. Quite fast trains reach Olsztyn, the regional capital, from Warsaw and other big cities; then you can get slow local trains to some of the bigger resorts like Mikołajki, which Tadeusz Iwiński compares, not altogether accurately, to Venice. There are buses, less frequent than when I first came in 1992 for the timetable has been cut. So I take up the offer of the round-trip to Grunwald, the open-air museum and the prison camp.

Masuria is a land of battles. German wooden or metal crosses rise above uncut grass in fields, often on the edge of a wood, out of the way of crop-harvesting, or neatly lined up in cemeteries, some of which have been restored to mark reconciliation in a new Europe. The Russian memorials are more obvious, although unloved by the Poles – like the huge Soviet war cemetery further north, on the Baltic, near the Russian border, at Braniewo where the names and pictures cut or stuck on each stone have either gone or faded into a few vague lines. Braniewo still has a tall white triumphal column and sculpted figures of Red Army soldiers. It was rumoured that Putin would come there in 2009, when he was in Gdańsk for the anniversary of the outbreak of the Second World War, but he went back to Russia instead. At Braniewo, you're usually alone among the dead.

'You like our weather?' the taxi driver asks, on the way to Grunwald. The rain has stopped, and the sun lifts the flat land, catching a machine harvesting maize from a field. 'You know we have the most beautiful autumns in Europe – they just go on and on.'

I ask how many people come to what's left of the Tannenberg Memorial and he says hardly any – just a few Germans. 'It's gone,' he says. 'Over.' Grunwald is popular, however – not very popular, but school groups come because it's an important part of Polish history. Had I been to Kraków? There's so much history in Kraków. Warsaw is fine but it's been rebuilt so you haven't got the feeling in the bricks and stones, in the walls and doorways. He knows that some of the stone used to rebuild Warsaw came from here – German stone.

The Grunwald site brings back two periods of history – the fifteenth century and the communist post-war years when, in 1960, the memorial was built. First you have to go through the avenues of stalls selling plastic swords, armour, tabards, helmets, mugs, and miniature knights on horses and fast food. There's no other tourist around so each stall-keeper stares at me as we pass – or at the two of us, for the taxi driver comes too which I don't mind at all because he's very easy: a fat, short, funny middle-aged man.

'Not for you, eh?' he says, pointing at the plastic swords that hang on a line or lie flat on a stall's counter in front of coloured tunics stamped with lions or eagles or the black cross on a white background of the beaten Teutonic Knights. Not really, I say. 'Any children?' he asks. Yes. 'Well, why not buy them something?' They're a bit old for this, I answer. 'Oh, and I'd thought you were a young man!' We walk on. 'What about these?' he asks. There's a display of real axes and heavy swords and shields and one vicious-looking weapon of an iron ball with spikes protruding from it like tiny dark daggers. 'Grown-up games!' he says. In summer the region stages mock battles or tournaments for the tourists. Occasionally a sword strikes too hard and someone is really hurt.

On 17 July 1960, the victory's anniversary, the Polish Communist Party newspaper described Grunwald as a catastrophic defeat for German military feudalism – and it was easy to recall that the terrifying German invaders of 1940 had had the black cross of the Orders on their tanks. The high steel lances that dominate the Grunwald monument loom as if in perpetual warning. To reach them, you walk up a hill, past scattered stones – some inscribed with the dates of commemorative gatherings – to a flight of stone steps. At the top, across from the lances, is a thick column carved with impassive warrior faces looking out from stone sculpted to resemble a helmet's open visor. The grey-fronted museum – a low curving stone and concrete building, with serrated boulders on its outer wall – forms one side of the complex; facing it is a menacingly empty stone semi-circle, like a classical amphitheatre. On another side, in a further classical allusion, there's a carved stone frieze of battling horsemen.

Inside the museum – opposite a fading abstract mosaic – cannons, pikes, more lances and models of knights in real armour divide display cases crowded with weapons, tunics and crosses or interpretive maps of the Polish victory. A recurring motif is that of the two eagles, their wings spread for ascent: white for Poland and black for the Teutonic Knights. A white crowned bust – presumably of the triumphant Polish–Lithuanian King – seems suddenly startling against the grey walls and the outside cloud. Flanking the bland-faced monarch, under the carved date of 1410, are two wreaths of plastic flowers.

The land stretching away below the hill has single trees or occasionally a clump on it – pleasant invaders in the rolling pasture. The only human activity is a tractor and a cutter harvesting maize. 'Grunwald was a feudal battle,' a German historian told me. 'You can't think of a national victory or defeat. There were knights on both sides from all over Europe – Germans fighting for the Polish–Lithuanian King, Poles with the Teutonic Knights.' Fritz Gause, in 1960, asserted that Germans had the right to remember both 1410 and 1914 through memorials in both places. Both battles were in defence of Germany; both memorials stood on German soil. In 1960, there was still no treaty to confirm the post-1945 eastern frontiers.

The myth of Grunwald was appropriated by grandiloquent twentieth-century nationalism. In 1901, a memorial was put up there, still on the site today but not cherished, to Ulrich von Jungingen, the Teutonic Knights' Grand Master, who had been killed in the battle. After 1945, the German voices faded. In 1981, the patriotic communist Polish Grunwald Association was founded, under the patronage of the anti-Semitic thuggish General Mieczysław Moczar; soon it had over a hundred thousand members. In 1990, as communism was ending, the Polish President General Jaruzelski came to the monument, with representatives from Russia, Lithuania and Czechoslovakia – Slav lands that had suffered under the Germans – and the local Roman Catholic Bishop – because the battle had been a defeat for the Reformation. Annual celebrations are still held there. But Marshal Józef Piłsudski's miraculous defeat of the Soviet army outside Warsaw in

August 1920 – stopping the Bolshevik push into western Europe –
is now thought to be a more powerful symbol of Polish freedom.

*

In October 1918, Elard von Oldenburg-Januschau called for
a dictatorship, an immediate dissolution of the Reichstag and a
compulsory mass call-up. But, a month later, he was living in a
defeated Germany. Soon a revolution threatened even his own
estates. Returning to Januschau at the end of the year, he gathered
up ex-soldiers to defend the place and threatened troublemakers
with the whip, seizing one by the ear and asking, 'Who rules in
Januschau?' The man bowed down to the old authority.

The treaty negotiations pointed to a humiliation, like that
imposed by the Germans on Bolshevik Russia earlier that year.
Attempting to act as a unifying figure, Field Marshal Paul von
Hindenburg issued an appeal to the German people in February 1919. He evoked what, four years before, had been an
unquestionable victory: the defence of the eastern frontier
at Tannenberg. As Chief of Army Command he had, he said,
decided to make his headquarters in the east, a land that had
many memories for him. Germany had asked for peace because of
the numerical superiority of the enemy and the hunger blockade;
now the people must rally like the 'faithful ones' of 1914. 'Old
comrades and fellow fighters of Tannenberg and the Masurians,
hasten to my aid!'

The Treaty of Versailles, signed on 28 June 1919, took from
Germany some 13 per cent of its pre-war territory. In the east,
Danzig and Memel became 'free' international cities; a 'corridor'
of land between East Prussia and the rest of Germany was given
to the new Poland, as were parts of Silesia and Pomerania, some
of which had been Polish before the eighteenth-century partitions.
The victorious powers organized plebiscites in parts of East Prussia that adjoined Poland to ask if the locals wanted to be German
or Poles. The results were victories for the Germans, even in the
Roman Catholic districts of Masuria, mostly by huge majorities.

The new Poland, threatened by Bolshevik Russia, seemed to many too fragile an enterprise to risk joining. A delighted Januschau made a fulsome speech to German troops who were now allowed back into Deutsch Eylau, his local town. When August Kapp, from Königsberg, called on him to ask for support for his nationalist putsch, Januschau advised that it would be better to start this in East Prussia, not in Berlin.

Distrust between the two nationalities grew worse. Some Poles left the new East Prussia for the new Poland – which became a more secure place after the Polish Marshal Piłsudski's victory over the invading Russians in August 1920, a month after the plebiscites. Those who stayed found themselves seen as potential traitors within an increasingly uneasy land. The 11th of July, the day of the German plebiscite victories, became, like the anniversary of the battle of Tannenberg, an annual celebration. East Prussian towns and villages that sounded Polish – or not German – began to have their names changed.

Socialist and pacifist groups protested against Hindenburg's 1922 triumphal tour of East Prussia, which resembled an imperial progress, celebrated particularly by nationalist groups. Elard von Oldenburg-Januschau suggested that no Social Democrat or even any representative of the centre parties should be allowed to shake hands with the hero because they had betrayed the armed forces by making peace in 1918. Hindenburg demurred at this but, in general, he avoided contact with the left. Planning began for a new monument – one of the most obviously symbolic constructions in modern European history – to be built on the Tannenberg battlefield, provocatively near the post-Versailles Polish frontier.

On 31 August 1924, the tenth anniversary of the battle, Hindenburg laid the foundation stone, and the vast assembly showed the wish, or need, to recall victory. Crowds had begun to gather in the middle of the night; by midday, the hour for the ceremonies, the correspondent of the London *Times* thought there might be as many as a hundred thousand, with thirty thousand veterans and members of patriotic organizations. It was an occasion of imperial ceremony. Hindenburg had declared that he was a monarchist, in spite of his role in getting rid of the last Emperor in November 1918. Banners were brought forward; two services – Roman Catholic and Protestant – were held on the battlefield, and the Governor of East Prussia, Ernst Siehr, expressed the hope that this commemoration would help to awaken a national spirit in the Fatherland. The memorial symbolized the fear of the Poles and of Bolshevik Russia, of East Prussia's new isolation from the rest of Germany and thankfulness for an earlier deliverance. The Social Democrat government of Prussia reluctantly became involved in the financing. After Hindenburg's election as president of Germany in 1925, the national government gave direct support.

The competition to design the new monument was won by two architects from Berlin, the brothers Walter and Johannes Krüger. The Krügers had already built a war memorial at Leer in East Friesland – a defensive circle of brick and stone enclosing a tall cross. The commemoration of Tannenberg was to be a much bigger affair, on a site of some forty acres; for it, the Krügers again used the concept of defence, designing a vast octagonal circle of red brick – the material of the castles and churches of the Teutonic Knights – whose enclosure could be a theatre or a stadium with room for thousands. Eight four-sided towers sixty feet high stood at intervals in the wall, again like fortresses, with small, slit-like windows. The design resembled another imperial German monument, at Castel del Monte in Apulia, also with eight towers, erected in 1240 to mark Frederick II of Hohenstaufen's southward expansion. The Krügers mentioned their debt to Stonehenge and the massive block-like look must have seemed elemental and prehistoric; other historical links were to the ziggurats of ancient Persia and the Aztecs. Beneath the brick, much of the interior was concrete, shaped within the towers like giant artillery shells. Other contemporary touches were some fluorescent tube lighting and mosaics of soldiers that resemble the work of the Italian futurists. Later, under National Socialism, came the introduction of totalitarian symbols, typically communist or fascist, like the stone soldiers outside the entrance to Hindenburg's tomb where a slab of granite carved with the Field Marshal's name was put above the portal.

The building had a powerful sense of weight, of solid rootedness in the land, and was raised slightly so that visitors walked up to it, as if to a sacred site. The bricks must have resembled dark flames in the sun and yet have been almost black when the sky was overcast, as if they were alternately on fire or in a storm. Inside the towers, recesses held either regimental memorials or shrines to the unknown dead. Short passages led through rounded pre-gothic arches to soaring chambers. One chamber contained a semi-circle of busts of the Tannenberg commanders; others had staircases abutting from the walls with regimental standards hung along the edge; another was decorated with scenes from an imaginary soldier's life – from leaving home to death in battle. The Tannenberg Memorial was a mixture of imagery – of war and religion, of the Teutonic Knights, of an undoubted victory, evoking not tranquillity but a sense of brooding threat. The stone eagles inside looked angry and alert; long slits or patterned small windows rationed the light; models of swords decorated a part of one outside wall. Much more than the commemoration of individual deaths, it was the German equivalent of the Lutyens monument at Thiepval to the missing of the Somme but at the same time political and bombastic: an unquiet place rather than one of peace and regret.

People were invited into the memorial, as if to intensify its power; two of the towers were at first used as youth hostels and another was filled with evocations of the distinctive East Prussian landscape and history. Originally the plan was for the centre of the courtyard to stay uncluttered to allow sizeable gatherings. Eventually, however, a tall cross was put in its centre, a larger version of the simple cross the Krügers had built at Leer, and paid for by the local builder Gustav Leipski whose firm built much of

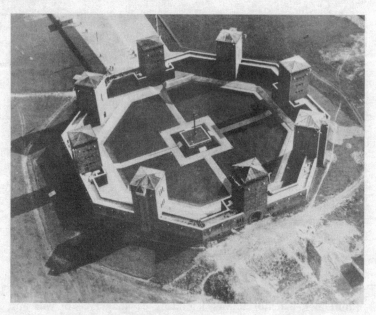

Red-brick defiance: the Tannenberg Memorial.

the memorial. The Krügers had thought of imitating a design by
Reginald Blomfield for the British cemeteries, of a stone cross
embedded with a bronze sword. But the swords on the towers
stood alone, unmixed with crosses. The architectural drawings
included a rising sun, as if to indicate a new national consciousness. The monument had a clear message – of defensive purpose
and past victory, reflecting Hindenburg's claim that Germany had
fought against aggression and his challenge to the war-guilt clause
of the Treaty of Versailles, even to the acceptance of defeat.

By September 1927, the building was ready to be dedicated,
although not quite complete, and Hindenburg, by now President
of Germany, came on a symbolic journey. Avoiding the Polish
territory of the Corridor – which he would have had to cross
if he had come overland all the way – he travelled on a warship
from Swinemünde to Königsberg and then by car through the

East Prussian landscape to Hohenstein, to the battlefield that had made his name: Tannenberg.

*

In Ypres, Reginald Blomfield's New Menin Gate also stands for victory. It shades into individual tragedy in the lists of the dead, grouped into their regiments, but seems to wait for a victorious army to march through its high arch. To escape this, you walk up on to Vauban's seventeenth-century ramparts – built when the French were campaigning in this part of Flanders – past a metal tablet engraved with some verses by Edmund Blunden, his poem 'Can You Remember?' written some sixteen years after the end of the Great War when comrades and the landscape could still loom shockingly through the fog of time:

> 'Those mists are spiritual
> And luminous-obscure,
> Evolved of countless circumstance
> Of which I am sure;
>
> Of which, at the instance
> Of sound, smell, change and stir,
> New-old shapes for ever
> Intensely recur.
>
> And some are sparkling, laughing, singing,
> Young, heroic, mild;
> And some incurable, twisted,
> Shrieking, dumb, defiled.'

Blunden wants to hold on to memory's sharpest definition. War had been, he felt, in some ways ennobling ('when will such kindness come again?'), yet so horrific and wasteful that he had been prepared to trust Hitler, a fellow veteran, who (Blunden thought) must be determined that it shouldn't happen again.

The path leads up to the top of the city wall where some leaf-less trees are no shelter from increasing rain and a track-suited jogger splashes past. Now the town centre is on your right, with its precise reconstruction of towers, spires and gables; to the left the ground drops away towards the moat, a busy main road and newish buildings – Ypres' modern life. Vauban's fortifications now protect the old – and here, clear through fading drizzle, is a British cemetery: quite small with a tall cross above rows of smaller crosses on short grass as smooth as a cricket pitch. It's overwhelming: an outpouring of collective memory, outside reason: first the pompous gate, then Blunden – the Kentish boy who hadn't wanted to go – who brings back individual experience before you reach the buried dead.

At Ypres, it's still the victors' story. You have to search for the field at Esen, where the Roggeveld cemetery was, where Karl and Käthe Kollwitz came in 1927 and 1932. The place is now enclosed by a wire fence beside a road near a shed and some silage covered in black sheeting, kept down with tyres. A pylon looms beyond gates that are tied up with blue binder twine – a rare flash of colour. The field looks derelict, as if the graves have only just been removed; scattered stones might be broken bits of head-stone, the small rise in the centre perhaps a burial mound of some neolithic chief. Some fruit trees nearby, possible pre-1914 plant-ing, suggest an orchard – against the flat Flemish landscape of grass, plough and coppices where troops could have hidden. A hill, a mountain for this part of Europe, rises in the distance.

This place was emptied of bodies after 1945 and the dead moved to Vladslo, a few miles away from Esen, where they lie under rows of stones, groups of crosses, darkening oaks and, on the edge, even darker rhododendrons. Vladslo is also quiet, and in flat country. The statues, *The Grieving Parents*, are near Peter's grave – where he shares his stone with nineteen others, their dates of death ranging from September 1914 to September 1915. For him, the inscription reads, 'Peter Kollwitz Musketier. 23:10:1914.'

11: Fallen Oak Leaves

Käthe Kollwitz is now a part of her country's good past. The place where she lived for years with Karl, where Hans and Peter grew up, has been named after her – Kollwitzplatz, a pleasant nineteenth-century square in Berlin's Prenzlauerberg. It has survived the bombs, the hideous post-war development and its years in the communist east to become a place of bohemian prosperity. The Italian coffee shops and Asian and European restaurants are full; the brewery that Peter's room looked out on is now an arts centre; sensibly dishevelled mothers wheel babies around in buggies and a weekly market is impeccably organic and 'fair-trade'. If someone is described as being 'sehr Kollwitzplatz' it means liberal, worried about the planet, pleasantly earnest, decent and (because of rising property prices) quite rich.

In the garden in the square's centre, near a children's play area and a grove of trees, is a black statue of the artist, the cast of a self-portrait. Käthe Kollwitz sits in a typically prehensile pose, bulky and hunched, resembling a nun in a shapeless habit, one hand holding what looks like a sculptor's tool. Someone, in a gesture of freedom, has written on the statue, leaving a blue scrawl across her breast that says 'Kranke Kollwitz', sick Kollwitz.

It's true that Peter's death left her wounded for ever. There *were* distractions from mourning as Berlin became a centre of post-war turmoil and, rooted in Prenzlauerberg, with her husband's medical practice and their surviving son Hans, she became caught up in the febrile atmosphere. Her poster designs of the 1920s for campaigns against war and hunger show an intensifying of emotion: hypnotized youth streaming to the front led by the figure of Death in *The Volunteers*; the *Sacrifice* of a woman offering up her infant son; another woodcut of *The Parents*, this time clasped together in shared sorrow. For the religious imagery she went often, as before, to old masters like Holbein – his body of Christ in the grave – or to Michelangelo's *Pietà*. Her work still reflected a puritan sense that art should never be obscure. She used woodcut and (more and more) lithography, which made her work cheap to buy.

She was growing old. In her youth, she thought, she might have been a revolutionary but now she wanted change by evolution, without hatred. Her series *War* of 1922–3 reflects the suffering of mothers and children rather than battle, reminiscent of Goya's scenes depicting what Spain had endured against Napoleon. The memorial woodcut of the corpse of the revolutionary Karl Liebknecht (murdered by the right-wing militia, the Freikorps) and the mourners reflects Holbein's *Christ in the Sepulchre*. It was Liebknecht and his family and the mourners that she sympathized with rather than the revolution. For Käthe Kollwitz, the suffering individual was more important than abstract ideals – and she herself was in anguish. In April 1921 she wrote of depression, of a sense of uselessness as an artist and of difficulty in loving Karl and her family although that same year she found a new reason to love – Hans's newborn boy, her grandson, also called Peter.

Not until January 1924 did Käthe Kollwitz return to what had once obsessed and comforted her – a memorial to her dead child. This was prompted – at least partly – by the fact that Peter, after the allocation of land for the dead, had reached his resting place, at Roggeveld cemetery. Her ideas had changed; she thought now of two reliefs on either side of the door to the cemetery with the inscription 'Here lies the most beautiful German youth' or 'Here lies flowering youth' – or two gigantic free-standing figures, like monoliths from the Egyptian temple at Abu Simbel. By October she was thinking of the free-standing mother and father, both kneeling, the mother looking out across the graves, her arms open as if to embrace all her 'sons', the father with his hands clasped in his lap. A year later this had changed again, the mother kneeling but with hands crossed in a 'loving position' under her face, still looking at the graves, apparently happy in her love.

The work was interrupted in the summer of 1925 when her mother died. Käthe Kollwitz went with the ashes from Berlin to Königsberg, where they were buried in her father's grave. About thirty people gathered in the churchyard – mostly relations and representatives of the Free Church. A hymn was sung – 'Our Dead Live On' – and Konrad, Käthe's brother, spoke of what they had loved and learned not only from their mother but from her family, the Rupps, and from the Free Church. Käthe followed, saying that she had asked her mother if she believed another life was waiting after death and the old lady had answered, 'It is enough.' This was true, the daughter felt, when a life had been lived to the end, like that of her mother. They gave her, Käthe said, with feelings of honour, back to the earth. The words express pleasure in remembering the fulfilment that Peter had never known.

The memorial would embody grief and guilt and anger. By March 1926, the composition was still of two kneeling mourners. She felt uncertain about the position of the heads and hands, although she was sure that the piece should represent not only the sadness of their own son's death but the loss of those buried alongside him. In June the Kollwitzes visited Peter's remains in Flanders for the first time. She described the scene to her son Hans – the rows of graves, the low wooden crosses with the names of the dead on metal plaques, the cemetery among farm land, the silence broken by the larks. The only ornaments were a short pillar on a plinth without an inscription and a regimental memorial, also shaped like a pillar. His parents cut three small roses from a wild plant and put them beside Peter's cross.

The land's shape and an awkward entrance made it impossible to put the figures by the cemetery's gate; a better place might be near the boundary hedge. Back in Berlin she thought about this, still not certain, and had the idea of a stone on the ground in front of them, inscribed with 'Here lies the most beautiful German youth', perhaps beside the names of Peter and his dead comrades on another plinth. She changed the mother figure again, making the head bow lower, folding the arms over the breast in the shape of the cross bar of a Christian cross. Many attempts at women's clothes disgusted her before she settled on an all-encompassing cloak, shapelessly self-denying. It reminded her of a letter she had written soon after Peter's death to a friend to thank for the present of a shawl, saying that her son would no longer need it because he had been killed. The image seemed right; in March 1928, she wrote of the cloak of pain, of love and yearning that seemed to cover her when she worked, of the sense of a living Peter that made her cry. She had chosen Belgian granite for the statues. The German government would give her enough money to finish them.

In 1927 there was another interruption. Käthe Kollwitz's fame as an artist of protest interested those in the Soviet Union who wished to have contacts in the west – and the Russians invited her to Moscow for an exhibition of her work. Photographs capture the apparently impassive artist, flanked by admirers, some dressed in the dark suits of Soviet officialdom. She grew tired, thought of Peter, felt admiration for what seemed to be the achievements of the revolution but also a detachment from all this because of the work waiting for her back in Berlin. By April 1928, the face of the mother-figure had become her own face: a stark portrait of an old, lined woman and just impersonal enough to represent universal mourning. The father, less obviously Karl, clean shaven instead of bearded, gave her trouble. Early attempts seemed 'soulless', although technically adept; by October 1929, still dissatisfied, she had begun again. In the finished group, the father is not looking down, like the mother, but has his head pointing ahead, eyes open, his look glazed, painful but disconnected. His arms are crossed, his hands clutching them, as if to shrink the upper body or hold on to it, fearful of loss. To lose memory,

Käthe Kollwitz felt, would be another betrayal, like that of letting Peter go to his death in August 1914.

There was great interest when the statues went on show at the Berlin National Gallery in June 1932 and casts were simultaneously displayed in the old Crown Prince's palace. During the Weimar years Käthe Kollwitz's fame had grown. She became a professor at the Prussian Academy of Art and, although cautious about active political involvement, signed a public appeal in 1932, asking that the communists and Social Democrats should unite against fascist extremism in the forthcoming elections. Other signatories included Albert Einstein and the novelists Heinrich Mann and Arnold Zweig.

Later that summer, the pieces made the journey to Belgium, travelling by train through Cologne and Ostend, and were placed at Roggeveld. The work was overseen by the Kollwitzes and there's a photograph of them in the cemetery, with the workmen and an architect from the German War Graves Commission on what must have been a cool day. Karl and Käthe wear raincoats, and she is in a hat, leaning against the plinth of the statue of the father. Karl has a solemn, puzzled look, stiff but calm; Käthe seems resigned, one hand drooping from the plinth where her arm rests, the other arm at her side. Karl's hands are clasped in front of him, not so tightly as in the statue.

She found the cemetery changed since 1927. The ground had been levelled and planted up, covered with large wooden crosses, shielded by a higher wall. Perhaps it seemed a more orderly and official place, as if time was gradually smoothing away pain; it was to stop this that she had made the statues. Roses were in flower, some on Peter's grave, and she had to admit that the mown lawns were beautiful. The Belgian workmen and the locals – former enemies of the Germans (Peter was killed by a Belgian) – were friendly, as in 1927. When the statues went up, she thought the father's gaze from the strong, angular, almost square head was not wide enough; it should perhaps have taken in all the graves. The memorial still seems angry, not consoling – different to any idea of worthwhile sacrifice, endless rest or the Glorious Dead: more a personal expression of pain and of the difficulty in sharing it. The separation of the mother and father, the distance between them, is a reminder, subconscious perhaps, of how Karl Kollwitz had tried to dissuade Peter from enlisting while Käthe had persuaded him to let their son go.

The most beautiful time was the last afternoon, when they were alone with the statues – when she stood in front of the woman, saw her own face, stroked the stone and cried. All seemed to be living, what she had wanted for so long. Karl, standing behind her, acknowledging that the piece was her suffering, perhaps also that she had been right to show them apart in their mourning, whispered, 'Yes, yes' – and they both, as Peter's parents, felt now, in spite of the separated images, what only they could feel.

On their last day at Roggeveld, the Kollwitzes saw the first visitor – a young man on a bicycle who slowed down on seeing the statues from the road and came into the cemetery to look. She hoped it might become easier for people to get to the place. Buses took tours to the British, American and Belgian cemeteries but not yet to the German. The country around was full of the dead; although moved, her heart seemed to grow heavier at the sight of all the crosses on the graves and the symbols of remembrance. By the Yser Canal was the Flemish tower that had on four sides the inscription in four languages – an echo of one of her post-war lithographs – in English, French, German and Flemish – 'Never Again War'. Käthe Kollwitz preferred the dark, unrelenting, gothic atmosphere of the German cemeteries to the open, bright feel and planted blooms of the British ones. 'The war was not a pleasant affair,' she thought. 'It isn't seemly to prettify with flowers the mass deaths of all these young men. A war cemetery ought to be sombre.'

Back in Berlin, in August 1932, she thought of the Christian imagery of her childhood, of those Königsberg days inspired by Grandfather Rupp, of Bach's music to the text 'O great love – love without measure, that leads to you from this martyr's way'. The statues were without texts from the Bible or scenes from Christ's martyrdom, yet the crosses in Flanders – British, French, German, Belgian – seemed appropriate as a symbol of suffering, made more human by the absence of a representation of Christ. She was glad that someone had noticed the faintly humorous look on the mother's face.

Unlike the French, the Belgians had offered the Germans land for their dead after 1918, as if to echo the often-quoted words of Albert Schweitzer that the soldiers' graves are the greatest preachers of peace. The brutalities of the Second World War and the Nazis tainted this reconciliation and when, in 1948, the leases at Roggeveld and elsewhere came to an end, the Belgian land-owners wanted to reclaim some of the hundred and twenty sites. The Belgian and German governments agreed that the bodies were to be moved into four larger cemeteries and Roggeveld was among those that were given up. Peter Kollwitz went not too far, to his present resting place at Vladslo where, in 1954, the statues were moved and the new cemetery landscaped. Käthe Kollwitz had wished for a sombre place, without prettiness or serenity. In autumn or winter, when the fallen oak leaves – the tree of Thor, god of war – drift over the gravestones like shifting memory, Vladslo feels desolate, with the two statues large enough above the grave of the artist's son to spread their grief over all of this place's dead.

12: The Need for Order

When Alfred Knox returned to Britain, he felt he must warn about what he had seen. In 1921, he published two volumes that combined a narrative of events with extracts from his diary. Called *With the Russian Army*, the book was advertised as being by Major General Sir Alfred Knox KCB CMG (he had been promoted and then knighted) and moves along briskly, leaving a picture that for years dominated the view of the First World War's eastern front – that of a Russian disintegration both on and off the battlefield.

With the Russian Army is occasionally unpleasant, particularly when Knox indulges in a contemptuous anti-Semitism that was completely unremarked upon by the distinguished military historian Sir James Edmunds in the course of a very favourable review in *The Times*. The book leaves an impression, through the explosions of impatience and disappointment, of a man of a superior type trying to control 'children' who can be charming, even bright, but need perpetually to be told to pull their socks up. 'The Russians were just too simple and too good natured to wage modern war,' Knox wrote. He could not, however, avoid one shameful truth: that they, like the French, had believed that Great Britain was leaving its Allies to do most of the fighting.

At least this General could continue the battle. The next move, Knox decided, was to get into parliament – and his reason for this, as he made clear, was to educate the British about the Bolshevik threat. In March 1924, he was adopted as the Conservative candidate for Wycombe in Buckinghamshire, a mostly rural constituency that also included the town of High Wycombe, famous for the manufacture of furniture.

At the adoption meeting, the local Conservative chairman, Lord Desborough, read out details of Sir Alfred Knox's military service and his awards and medals – the British KCB and the CMG, the pre-revolutionary Russian orders and others from France, Italy, Czechoslovakia and Japan. Lady Knox, Lord Desborough said, was a worthy wife for this warrior – the daughter of a Scottish colonel and granddaughter of an officer who had been wounded at Waterloo. Then came extracts from Winston Churchill's recently published history of the war – *The World Crisis* – that called Knox 'an agent of singular discernment' whose 'luminous and pitiless despatches' had caused 'grave forebodings' in Whitehall in1914, after Tannenberg.

Knox addressed the meeting. He wished, he said, to do his best for his country, to convince it of the horrors of Bolshevism. He had seen the ruthless *coup d'état* in November 1917 and, some months later, the dark cellar in Ekaterinburg where the Tsar and his family had been murdered – and he was determined 'through all his life' to fight this evil. He stood for the maintenance of strong armed forces, for a strong British Empire, for opposition to the rule of the mob in industrial disputes, for 'orderly and constitutional' social reform.

Russia came up often in the campaign. Knox alluded to his experiences there, declaring that he 'loathed' the Bolshevik regime and opposed trading with it, and explaining that the Russian army could have fought on in 1917 but 'Jewish emissaries' came from Germany 'to demoralise it'. To talk about Russia, he said at one meeting, 'made him very angry and very hot'. His opponent, and the sitting member, was the Liberal Lady Terrington, one of the first women MPs but not at all formidable, 'completely uneducated' (according to a feminist observer), although extraordinarily well dressed. It was her dress sense that the *Daily Express* commented on and Lady Terrington thought this made her sound snobbish so she sued the newspaper, which prompted unhelpful publicity. Knox won the seat with a majority of over eight thousand, aided, a local paper suggested, by fear of socialism. The campaign showed that farce was a luxury which British politics could still afford.

*

Further east, in the borderlands of East Prussia, the mood was darker. The 1920 plebiscites delighted Alexander Dohna, with their huge majorities for staying within Germany – 92 per cent in Marienwerder and even only 13.47 per cent voting for joining the new Poland in Allenstein with its large number of Roman Catholics. He and his friends were German nationalists, against republican Weimar, for the restoration of the monarchy and angered by the French and the Belgians laying claim to the Ruhr district in 1923.

It was a time of revolution. The young Alexander found himself standing with a group on the road near Schlobitten, armed with hunting rifles and two machine guns kept back after the war, prepared to protect his property from a demonstration of angry workers which collapsed in bad weather. He stored weapons and munitions behind the organ at Schlobitten church and gave money to the Heimatbund, a nationalist organization pledged to defend the region from its enemies: the new Poland, Bolshevik Russia and communism. A local communist group was equipping itself with firearms and hand grenades. The Dohnas seemed to be about to suffer the fate of the landlords in Russia and searched for a force strong enough to help them. Alexander Dohna and a Heimatbund delegation visited Hitler in Munich, to find a man whom they considered a commonplace little megalomaniac. The failed Nazi coup in November 1923 seemed to confirm the ridiculous Austrian's irrelevance.

Alexander Dohna got married in 1926, to Antoinette Gräfin von Arnim (known as 'Titi'), who came from another Prussian land-owning family. After their honeymoon, the couple entered their new lives, arriving at Schlobitten in a coach pulled by six horses, to be greeted by the entire estate staff and representatives of the Bismarck-Jugend, the youth organization of the German Conservative Party. Ostensibly they were vastly rich, with their houses and art and land. But East Prussia depended on subsidized agriculture and these were inflationary times with low prices for wheat and timber. In addition the Dohnas had, like many patriotic Germans, invested in War Loan, a government bond that became worthless after the defeat. The Dohnas' lives were ruled by their unwieldy inheritance. Great blocks of land had to be sold and each year Alexander went to Berlin, to visit the banks that supported him.

Mostly their life was the daily routine at Schlobitten, among the more than seventy rooms: rising in summer at 5.30, waited upon by the staff, dealing with administration and visiting parts of the property, examining the figures: then hunting deer in the long, light evenings. There was also the care of the art collection and the immense, ageing house; advised by visiting experts, Dohna employed craftsmen from Berlin and stone masons from Königsberg or Elbing. He remained haunted for the rest of his life by the sounds of his family's possessions – the ticking of the ornate timepieces, their insistent chimes, the click of footsteps on the parquet floors: then outside, the deeper, louder bell of the clock on the stable tower. Hunting was more than a sport and had rituals of an almost sacred intensity. Stuffed or mounted heads of shot animals lined the walls at Schlobitten, even in the library – deer, buffalo and antelope killed on safaris in Africa; two large chamois given to the family by King Victor Emmanuel II of Italy; a spectacular series of stags bought from Rominten, the old royal estate: then, in his study, those shot by Alexander Dohna himself.

Tradition was this world's scaffolding, Dohna thought, and he felt that occasionally, at family weddings or christenings, he should reveal in its fullness the vision of those who had shaped Schlobitten. The best porcelain – one Berlin set a gift from King Frederick William II – and silver were brought out, all the grand rooms were opened up and water from the indoor fountain set into a wall in the painted hall cascaded gently down. The whole community took part in celebrations such as the harvest festival, with dancing and the crowning of a young village girl as harvest queen, and the Christmas party when a hundred children of estate workers were given toys and a Bible for those who had just been confirmed.

Dohna and his friends had been wrong about Hitler. With the rise of National Socialism, German conservatism was faced with a crisis and some of the Dohna family joined the new movement. Elard von Oldenburg-Januschau, while not following them, approved of this, thinking they might act as a brake on its more outlandish policies. Others persisted with their wish for the monarchy's restoration; Alexander Dohna thought this was unrealistic because of the poor quality of the last Emperor's heirs. The best hope seemed to be the semi-monarchical figure of Hindenburg. At the end of the 1920s, the Dohnas were asked to the presidential palace in Berlin, where the aged victor of Tannenberg shook the guests' hands with ponderous dignity, spoke slowly in a sonorous voice and retired early to bed. In the presidential election of 1932, Alexander Dohna voted for Hindenburg, although the old man was now eighty-four. In the parliamentary elections in July 1932, he and his wife voted for the German Conservative Party. In those of November 1932, they voted for the Nazis.

13: Kantgrad

Vladimir Gilmanov teaches German at Kaliningrad University and agrees to meet me in a coffee bar up a street from the theatre, near the statue of Schiller. Professor Gilmanov is a slight, intense, thin man in his mid-forties, with fuzzy, dark, longish hair. In his jeans and light-weight jacket and with his unruly hair, he has an academic look, with sharp quick eyes behind glasses. It's said that he can be so eloquent with German groups that they burst into tears. He grew up in Kaliningrad and remembers the angst of Soviet days: the restraint in the head if you wanted to tell the truth. That's gone – replaced by a coldness, by something hard. Society is colder. Post-modern civilization is cold.

The Professor sips his coffee. I ask about Rudolf Jacquemien, the German communist poet who came to the Soviet Union looking for a better place. Vladimir Gilmanov knew about him – it was sad but drink had finished Jacquemien. Those poems – did I know them? Not well, I say, but I did go some years to call on his widow because Marion Dönhoff had given me the Kaliningrad address.

Mrs Jacquemien was small, dark-haired, quite shy, and pulled her husband's books out from a glass-fronted case in the tidy living-room. She didn't want to talk much about him beyond telling how he had first come to Russia as a sailor, to Archangel, as a German communist. He'd been in the camps for eight years, sent there during the war for being German, and she'd only been able to visit him twice. Now, with communism over, they'd rehabilitated him. That was enough. He died in 1992, she said. Then we had sat in silence. Jacquemien had written in German and

Russian. The cheap paper of those books was already crumbling: the German editions had been published in the communist east. It wasn't the poems that moved me so much as the poet's life, the reality of what had been his dream as the ship approached Archangel – how this had crumbled into war and years in a Stalinist jail.

Vladimir Gilmanov agrees that it was sad about Jacquemien. But the poet had been right to retire to Kaliningrad. Jacquemien was a western European, and western Europe and Russia could mix more in Kaliningrad than in other places because of the past. I think again of Brodsky's image of the trees whispering in German, an insistent murmur against the attempts to make a Soviet city. The Professor says you can see problems in microcosm here – the problems of the European and the Russian pasts and of what is to come – in this Russian enclave bordered by Lithuania and Poland, both of which are now in NATO and the European Union. It could be a place for reconciliation or for missiles – a contact point or a fortress.

Professor Gilmanov respects the city's German past. He thinks that it's right to celebrate this, for instance in the plaque that had been put up on Agnes Miegel's old house. Did it matter, I ask, that she'd written a poem in praise of Hitler? The Professor says that some good poets had praised Stalin. He likes to see the groups of Germans at the place where the poet of East Prussia had lived – and he knows that her work has consoled them in their exile. Perhaps, I think, it is her articles, still in print, about Königsberg before the war – those puffs of sweetness and cosy sentimentality – that they read before coming back so that the new city is such a shock that they burst into tears.

In Kaliningrad, it was the city and its port that mattered, Vladimir Gilmanov says; these were what Stalin had wanted. Things are still not so good outside it, with as much as 80 per cent unemployment in some of the country districts. But, the Professor says, idealistic people stay in the villages; he knows a teacher who taught for a year without pay in Krasnolesye, the old Rominten.

Immanuel Kant.

Life is cold now but there are good tendencies. Vladimir Gilmanov knows western Europe. He goes often to Germany but he likes to live here.

Kant, he thinks, was a forerunner of globalization because his fame spread through Europe even though he never taught or lectured outside Königsberg. Kaliningrad might become Kantgrad: named not after a king (the thirteenth-century Ottakar of Bohemia) as in Königsberg or after an apparatchik (Mikhail Kalinin) but after a philosopher who bridged the Enlightenment and romanticism – or reason and spirit. With his dislike of nostalgia, Kant might not have approved of this commemoration. To him even wars led to progress; there never was a golden age. Until his death in 1804, he defended the French revolution with its blood-letting and terror.

Kant's own experience of war was quite calm. When the Russians occupied Königsberg from 1758 until 1762, the philosopher became a subject of the Empress Elizabeth, and young Russian officers attended his lectures. Prussian bureaucrats continued to run Königsberg; and, after Catherine the Great withdrew in 1762, they worked again for King Frederick the Great. So Kant had, briefly, been a Russian. But in the nationalism of nineteenth and twentieth centuries, he became a symbol of German greatness. He is one of the figures carved on the base of the statue of Frederick the Great in Berlin's Unter den Linden, although he had almost no contact with the King. In fact Kant's interests were international; he may never have left Königsberg, but he read French and English, was inspired by foreign philosophers like David Hume and probably saw himself as a citizen of the world rather than of Prussia. His closest friend – to whom he is said to have read most of the *Critique of Pure Reason* before its publication – was the English merchant Joseph Green.

Battered by the storms of Fichte and Hegel, Kant's ideas were accused of being lifeless. The poet Heine deplored the philosopher's dreary life, his low regard for music and painting, how he seemed to have been a thinking machine rather than a person. To Heine this was made more repellent by the life's concealment of a destructive intellect, as bad as, or worse, than Robespierre in its defence of terrorism. Kant came to be known as a man of fussily pedantic regularity by whose rigid routine people set their watches: obsessed by problems with his bowels, teeth and diet, betrayed and mocked by his servant, rigidly unadventurous in clinging to this remote land, increasingly eccentric in his thoughts of cats dying in Basel because of their propensity to attract electricity or of beer's power as a slow poison.

Kant believed in the elevation of duty, in the centrality of individual freedom and truth and personal independence. Perhaps he is most famous now for the categorical imperative – that you should judge each action in terms of a universal moral law – and for the separation of concepts that are beyond human understanding (such as freedom and the existence of God) from those that can be proved. Kant's belief in God, however, did not include the need for churches or Christ or prayer. Why, he asked, is it necessary to intercede with an all-knowing creator? The purity of duty should be the moral yardstick of an action, not the action itself or its result, no matter how admirable or beneficial these seem. A defender of the Enlightenment and – although a republican – an admirer of its despotic monarch, Frederick the Great, Kant saw reason as capable of rationalizing its own limitations. In his concept of the unknowable, he pointed to the romantic thinkers who followed him.

When Kant died in 1804, the church bells rang even though he had scarcely ever attended services and the funeral was held in a candlelit Königsberg cathedral before the corpse was lowered into the burial place reserved for notables of the city's university. What was the clue to Kant's genius? Over the years, his remains were disinterred, examined and reburied, his skull fondled and measured for clues – and he survived not only as a great philosopher but as a relic of a good Germany.

The greatness of Kant's reputation means that, since his death, he has been quoted often in support of views with which he almost certainly would not have agreed. After the defeat of 1918, for instance, he was exploited by the new, resentful nationalism. A symbolic tomb was built for him outside Königsberg cathedral, its pillared canopy designed by the neo-classical architect Frederick Lahrs, with the philosopher's sentence about the powers of nature and the need for a moral imperative set into it: 'Two things fill the mind with ever new and increasing wonder and awe, the more often and the more seriously reflection concentrates upon them: the starry heavens above me and the moral law within me.' At its unveiling in April 1924, the rector of Kant's old university declared 'the world must make up its mind to allow German thought and thoroughness their proper place in common labours for the advancement of civilization, or else decide that it could dispense with the works of Kant.'

Kant's body had already been searched for clues to his genius. The philosopher had disapproved of phrenology – but in 1864 an influential book, *Neuer Atlas der Cranioscopie* by Dr Carl Gustav Carus, analysed the plaster cast of the philosopher's face after death. Carus commented on the extraordinarily prominent forehead and the large head. He noted the shapes of the heads of (among others) Schiller, the art historian Baron von Rumohr, the poet C. A. Tiedge, Napoleon, Talleyrand, Goethe, a selection of retarded people, murderers and suicides, various 'Africans' and 'Orientals' and an Egyptian mummy. There's a sense of competition, particularly of the Germans against the French, with Kant representing the German genius for philosophy. Kant's skull, with its wide, high forehead and bulge at the back of the head, *does* have an almost deformed look. In 1880, his corpse was dug up, for reburial in a neo-gothic chapel. Representatives of the city government and the university's philosophy department watched the librarian and a professor in their shirt sleeves uncover the coffin on a hot June day to reveal a small skeleton approximately five feet in height. A photograph was taken of the skull, with the huge arching bulge at the back, the broad forehead, a lower tooth dark at its decaying root, and the open mouth curving upwards in what looks like a mocking smile.

Kant's small form was used to show that what came to be seen as Prussia's (and, after 1871, Germany's) most glorious times had been brought about not only by its army. In 1857, Rauch's statue of Kant went up in Königsberg and in 1901 the Emperor William II had his head placed on the memorial to Frederick William II, Frederick the Great's successor, although this monarch had tried to stifle the philosopher's criticism of organized religion. Kant, like Shakespeare in Britain, became a symbol of national greatness. Under the Nazis, who were obsessed by the idea of Aryan genetic superiority, Kant's skull was compared with that of the Slav Lenin which, the so-called experts thought, indicated organizational brilliance and mental derangement. A photograph exists of the director of the Königsberg Museum during Hitler's time proudly showing a cast of the skull to an awe-struck Japanese.

At the Kant exhibition in the Königsberg Museum in Duisburg

in 2004, marking the bicentennial of the philosopher's death, Klaus Weigelt, chairman of an organization that tries to keep East Prussian history alive, spoke of another anniversary: that of the RAF's obliteration of the city centre in August 1944. Kant's tomb at the north-east corner of the cathedral survived the British bombs, the 1945 siege and the Soviet dynamiting not only of the castle but of much of the Prussian past. It was the greatness and fame of Kant that had rescued Königsberg cathedral, Weigelt claimed. Since 1991, with money from the Russian government and from German companies, trusts and individuals, the cathedral had risen, Klaus Weigelt said, to a new beauty. The philosopher had reconciled Königsberg with Kaliningrad.

Another Duisburg lecture in 2004 was about what came out of Königsberg in the late eighteenth century, when East Prussia made intellectual history. This had been the age not only of Kant but of Hamann and of Herder. Herder was Kant's pupil but, partly influenced by Hamann, broke with his old master, to point towards Goethe's romantic *Sturm und Drang*. Herder disliked universalism, an Enlightenment concept. He thought people needed to belong to a group, to a local culture and language, and that these groups and cultures could peacefully co-exist. Herder held that imperial conquests, like those of the Teutonic Knights or Frederick the Great in Poland or the British in Ireland, were wrong because they let one culture rule, even kill, another. He admired the Slavs, the Balts, the Jews, the Indians and the Chinese and abominated western, particularly French, assumptions of superiority. He would have loathed Ober-Ost. A country, he recognized, is a mixture, with people leaving and arriving, as with the Salzburg Protestants coming to Prussia in the 1730s. 'To brag of one's country is the stupidest form of boastfulness,' he said. 'What is a nation? A great wild garden full of bad plants and good.' Herder was repelled by parts of Kant's thinking, such as the idea that individual suffering – the suffering of the less able – is needed for progress; Kant found Herder too much given to generalities.

Like Kant, Herder dismissed the idea of a golden age, of escape into myth. One should be oneself, in the culture of home, in the present. It was, he believed, impossible to absorb another culture, even through the learning of its language – and nostalgia and a yearning for home seemed to him to be natural and good, the mainspring of most popular movements. This exaltation of rootedness was later taken up by Fichte, by Treitschke and by cruder successors who grossly distorted it. Herder died in 1803, too early for the humiliation of Napoleon's victories over the Prussians and the rise of national feeling that followed the coalition's defeat of the French. He had rejected the idea of the Germans as military masters of Europe, seeing them much more as philosophers and poets.

Hamann's problem was that he was often incomprehensible. He had a crippling stammer and a dense, difficult prose that often obscures his subtle irony and sophisticated arguments; Herder and Kant begged him to be clearer. His thought encompassed a suspicion of science and a contradiction of the rational precision of the French Enlightenment. He believed in passion, saw rules as necessary evils, distrusted autocrats and the Jews – and believed it possible to throw off intellectualism and to have a direct understanding of the masses. Like Kant, Hamann stayed loyal to his king, Frederick the Great. But he denied that government measures could improve the condition of the poor because this went against the uniqueness of individuals. He did, however, foresee the failure of utopian systems such as communism.

The resonance of what began in the east echoed for centuries. Kant's elevation of the unique will was taken up by Herder, mutating into the concept of a powerful irrational self, exploding into the romantic cry, 'I am not here to think, but to be, to feel, live!' After this came Fichte and the cult of the hero; then Hegel, followed by a corruption of genius into nationalist hysteria and a terrifying end.

14: 'May every discord break against this monument'

Many thousands of people had come to Masuria, to Tannenberg, in September 1927, fourteen years before Marion Dönhoff's now famous 1941 ride through the early autumn landscape. The huge gathering of 1927 was by no means inclusive; Republican and Jewish ex-service associations were not asked and the Social Democratic Prussian government refused to attend what seemed to be a throw-back to the old monarchist days. The old First World War commanders were there but not the man who had been perhaps the true architect of the victory; Colonel Hoffmann, the brilliant staff officer, had died the previous July. Ludendorff, by now rabidly nationalist, was estranged from Hindenburg; they bowed stiffly to each other, brought together for this dedication of the memorial to their victory.

The legend that the German army had not been defeated in the field but stabbed in the back by treacherous politicians was already strong. Now Hindenburg, the President of the new German republic, spoke. Dressed as the Colonel-in-Chief of a Masurian regiment to which he'd been appointed by the Emperor, and using words that must have delighted the old guard like Januschau, and (to judge from the press response) much of his country, he repudiated Germany's admission in the Treaty of Versailles that it had started the war. 'The accusation that Germany was responsible for this greatest of all wars we hereby repudiate,' he declared. 'It was in no spirit of envy, hatred or lust of conquest that we unsheathed the sword' but 'with clean hearts we marched out to defend our fatherland'. This should be settled; 'Germany is ready at any moment to prove this fact before an impartial tribunal.' This place symbolized national unity. 'May every discord therefore break against this monument.'

Alarm spread through Europe. An editorial in the London *Times*, on 20 September, regretted that Hindenburg should have allowed himself to be manipulated by the German nationalists 'who have their stronghold in eastern Prussia'. The building and the ceremony seemed, to the writer, a frightening resurrection of another age: 'there is a medieval flavour in the very name of Tannenberg and it is hardly surprising that something resembling a medieval fortress . . . should have been erected even now in that centre of an ancient battle zone in East Prussia.' The enforced absence of a rabbi or of republicans was noted, as was the presence of the German Chancellor Wilhelm Marx; in fact ministers had helped to draft the speech. 'In that East Prussian atmosphere, which is still so strangely insensitive to modern facts', it seemed as if something entirely different was being said to the more conciliatory approach of the German Foreign Minister Gustav Stresemann. In the Nazi time, an extract from Hindenburg's speech denying war guilt was carved on to a bronze tablet and put into one of the towers.

The Krügers, architects of the monument, also designed an inn nearby. At first this was quite a modest building with broad dark beams, a heavy tiled roof and small windows – traditional in style, as if to show what had been saved in August 1914. It was later greatly enlarged when tourism grew under the Third Reich. First, though, the numbers of visitors dipped, because of the economic crisis; there began to be concern about the vast building's cost. Hitler came for the first time in April 1932, on a return journey from Königsberg during his presidential election campaign against Hindenburg. He lost the election but East Prussians greeted him hysterically. Hitler returned to Tannenberg after Hindenburg had appointed him chancellor, in August 1933, accompanied by the old President. The Nazis had enormous majorities in East Prussia in the elections of July 1932 and March 1933 as they exploited the fears in this frontier land. Their support was particularly strong in the poor rural districts, even among the Polish minority whom Hitler promised full inclusion in his new Germany.

Nineteen-twenty-seven, the year of the Tannenberg monument's dedication, also saw the President's eightieth birthday. Neudeck had been put up for sale by Hindenburg's relations and Elard von Oldenburg-Januschau and other East Prussian well-wishers set about buying the house as a birthday gift for the old man. With the President's son Oskar, they organized a collection, hoping to raise the money in East Prussia, but after an inadequate response from the beleaguered rural province, they had to go for help to rich industrialists in the west. The property was put in Oskar's name, thus avoiding future death duties – a scheme of tax-dodging out of keeping with traditional Prussian austerity.

Neudeck gave Hindenburg a stake in the land. During his visits there, he behaved like a caricature of a Junker, fond of hunting, a good trencherman, sparing with words, his hair clipped to resemble a stand of grey needles. On the terrace or in the sparsely decorated rooms, the *camarilla* – as the President's cronies were called – met to discuss whom they liked and trusted. Within this circle was the conservative Franz von Papen, a minor aristocrat and former cavalry officer whom Hindenburg particularly liked; Hitler himself seemed desperately uncouth. Januschau thought that the Nazis could be managed; they were, after all, 'quite attractive' young people and Göring was a much-decorated officer of the First World War. There were hints that Hitler would support farming and the estates in the east and restore the monarchy as well.

The Junker class was beginning to be an embarrassment, especially over the subsidies given to big landowners. In January 1933, on the eve of Hitler's confirmation as chancellor, the British Ambassador reported that the budget committee of the Reichstag had demanded to know more about 'the affairs of the notorious

East Prussian landowner and friend of the President of the Reich, Herr von Januschau', who 'showed no desire to provide parliament with any information as to the public funds which had been doled out to him.'

Much has been made of Januschau and other landowners influencing the President at Neudeck in May 1932. They were said to have encouraged his intransigence that brought about Chancellor Heinrich Brüning's resignation and the appointment of Papen, a process that led to Hitler's taking office some eight months later. In fact Januschau was on another of his estates at the time but the landlords – who loathed Brüning's scheme of encouraging more settlement in the east by moderate land reform – were delighted to see the Chancellor go. Not until after 1933 did Januschau see the true nature of National Socialist rule; by then, the fat, jovial figure who rode round his estate on a small pony, wearing a Lenin cap and letting a communist live in a cottage on his property because he thought the remote spot would keep the man out of mischief, seemed to come from another age.

In August 1933, some seven months after they had come to power, the Nazis laid on a massive demonstration at the Tannenberg Memorial, to commemorate the anniversary of the battle. Even the Polish authorities co-operated, allowing some fifteen hundred cars on a 'loyalty run' through the corridor to Hohenstein. Among the guests were Hitler, Göring (now Prime Minister of Prussia), Papen (the Vice-Chancellor), the army and navy commanders and several Lutheran bishops. Erich Koch, East Prussia's Nazi Governor, told Hindenburg that the state wished to present him with some six thousand acres of land that adjoined Neudeck and had a long connection with his family. Göring handed over the deeds and Hitler declared that this property would be free of taxation as long as it was owned by Hindenburg or one of his male descendants.

Hitler's speech at the memorial was a repeat of familiar grudges and resentment, including Hindenburg's 1927 repudiation of German war guilt. Tannenberg, he said, had 'accomplished' Germany's salvation: also that 'posterity will not understand that a nation, after the loss of a war which it never wanted, should have been unworthily oppressed and shamefully mishandled simply because it did not defencelessly surrender its freedom, but tried to defend its right to live and the independence of its territory while making untold sacrifices.' Hindenburg's reply evoked dead comrades and his loyalty to the monarch whom he had forced to abdicate: 'When I pursue my memories of the time in question, I think first in reverence and loyalty, and gratitude of my Kaiser, king and master, whose confidence and command first called me here.'

A year later, the monument became again a symbol of memory and renewal, after the death of the victor of Tannenberg. When on 2 August 1934 the black and white Prussian standard above Neudeck was lowered to half-mast, the planning of the funeral began. The old man had wanted a simple burial next to his wife (who had died in 1921) in Hanover; for his son Oskar and for Hitler's government, however, this was a magnificent chance for the Nazi propaganda team. Hitler told the architect Albert Speer to make sure that the day was spectacular. Any objections by the Krügers that the plans compromised their original vision were swept aside; they may have felt that they did well enough under the Nazis to forgive this.

Late on the night of 6 August the coffin left Neudeck on a gun carriage, travelling across the East Prussian landscape – one observer noting the storks overhead – escorted by infantry and cavalry on a route lined by torches. Early on the cloudless morning of the funeral – 7 August – special trains began to cross the Polish Corridor to bring mourners to Hohenstein. The guests poured in through the northern gate of the Tannenberg Memorial where an immense iron cross and a black banner hung by the southern tower; in the centre of the arena was another huge cross, with chairs lined up on three sides for the crowd. On the ramparts, between the eight towers, stood blue-jacketed sailors and steel-helmeted troops, outlined against the sky. Fires burned on the top of each tower, the black smoke curling southwards in the slight breeze.

Uniforms predominated: the old uniforms – the spiked helmets, the black cavalry busbies or the blue and scarlet of the foot-guards worn by Field Marshal Mackensen or Elard von Oldenburg-Januschau in his old Reichswehr ceremonial kit: then the new black of the SS bodyguard or brown of the Nazi storm troopers or the grey of the Stahlhelm, the other main nationalist paramilitary group. Never since the war, the London *Times* correspondent thought, had there been such a gathering of imperial uniforms. Wreaths, some so large that six men had to carry them, were banked up around the cross; colour parties held aloft the fifty-two standards of the regiments that had fought at Tannenberg. The Roman Catholic Bishop of East Prussia gave the Hitler salute and sat beside the Reich Primate, Ludwig Müller, who wore the sober black of the evangelical church.

The coffin was placed on a central slab by the cross, with the Field Marshal's baton and decorations. It was covered by the black, white and red army flag – onto which had been stitched an Iron Cross – and Hindenburg's *Pickelhaube* spiked helmet (that caricature of Prussiandom) and sword. After the Lutheran hymn 'A safe stronghold our God is still', Hitler went to the dais. An aide handed him a leather wallet. The Chancellor seemed to fumble while retrieving his text, thereby heightening the tension, before making almost exactly the same speech as he had given the day before in the Reichstag. Already he had declared that the offices of chancellor and president and commander of the armed forces would henceforth be combined in one person: himself. Now grandiloquent sentences once more retraced the dead President's life from his wounds in the Austro-Prussian War to the supreme wartime command and election to the presidency – 'the last triumph of the old army'. It was, the Führer said, 'a wonderful dispensation of Providence that during his Presidency the preparation for the national resurrection could be begun.' Now, he said, 'Go hence to Valhalla.'

Hindenburg's funeral.

Visitors started to come again to Tannenberg, making it into a national shrine. The theatre did not end with the old man's death. Two giant stone soldiers carved by Paul Bronisch were put as if on guard outside Hindenburg's tomb – and above the entrance glowered a massive granite stone, symbolically from Königsberg, with the Field Marshal's name carved on it. So heavy was this piece that railway bridges had to be strengthened to get it to the memorial by train. Again the Krügers claimed the influence of Stonehenge. A porphyry statue of the victor dominated the hall of honour above the tomb, by the East Prussian Friedrich Bagdons – a representation not of the dead, grey Reichspresident but of the defiant victor of Tannenberg. In the concourse, stone replaced grass; the landscape around was dotted with reconstructions or interpretive displays claiming that Aryan Germans had been in East Prussia at least since the Bronze Age.

On 2 October 1935 – the eighty-eighth anniversary of the Field Marshal's birth – another ceremony took place at the memorial when the body was moved to a final resting place in another tower. The Nazis may have seen this as a chance to demonstrate the consolidation of their power; the Night of the Long Knives – when Hitler had his old colleague Ernst Röhm and others murdered – had silenced internal opposition, a growing closeness to Mussolini's Italy had broken Germany's international isolation and German parliamentary democracy was dead. Hitler – accompanied by Göring, the War Minister General von Blomberg, the commanders of the navy, army and air force and the Deputy Führer Rudolf Hess – descended into the vault to lay a wreath. The family was led by Oskar, the hero's son, now a major-general, who had prospered under the new regime. Also represented were the 'organizations of the new Germany' – the SA, the SS and the National Socialist Party. The symbolism had changed, reducing Hindenburg's Weimar role to concentrate on the victor of Tannenberg, and the sarcophagus was covered with the wartime flag. In his speech, Hitler talked only of the victory, not of the Field Marshal's subsequent political activities. He declared the place a national memorial, to be paid for henceforth by the German government.

All this accompanied a resurgence in Masuria, the East Prussian region that included the Tannenberg Memorial. Increases in agricultural prices coincided with rearmament, a fall in unemployment and an unashamed nationalism; one newspaper evoked a glorious return of the Teutonic Order; Hitler declared that no district of the Reich was more loyal to his ideals. Nazi officials broke the grip of the landowners and the old Prussian bureaucracy. It seemed now as if a route to the top was open, as long as you joined the party. In 1939, Polish was banned as an official language in East Prussia and children were soon denouncing their parents and grandparents for speaking Polish or Lithuanian. The year before, the Nazi Gauleiter Erich Koch had set up a commission to rename places, even flowers, in German.

The Nazis proclaimed the symbolic worth of the borderland. In 1935 a series of stamps was produced to show East Prussia's principal monuments, journeys to East Prussia from the west were subsidized and from 1936 until 1939 an exhibition about the province, with particular focus on the Tannenberg Memorial and victory, toured Germany. The Baedeker guide of 1936 gave East Prussia much more space than had the edition of 1913, describing the Tannenberg monument – 'where President Hindenburg rests beside his fallen comrades' – as 'a place of national pilgrimage.'

To an English tourist, visiting the monument in September 1938, the eight brick towers linked by arcades with commemorations of the fallen, many of them (he thought) local men, seemed to be 'one of the noblest war memorials in Europe'. Bernard Newman, the travel-writer who was touring the Baltic on his bicycle, found many visitors wandering round the complex; among them a group of schoolmasters from central Germany, all (they told Newman) National Socialists. They believed that the German-speaking Sudetenland should be taken from Czechoslovakia and were certain that the Führer would make no further territorial demands. Surely, they asked, England would not go to war to prevent this act of national self-determination; no one in Germany wanted war with England for the true enemy had always been France. Why hadn't Newman responded with 'Heil Hitler' when they had saluted him at the memorial? He protested that when they came to England they weren't expected to say 'Heil Chamberlain'. But, after leaving Tannenberg, Newman felt reassured. He'd heard that East Prussia was a bastion of German militarism, the home of the dreaded Junker class. Instead he had found a fear of war, as had no doubt (he thought) existed for centuries in this anxious place.

A year later, in 1939, celebrations had been planned for Tannenberg's twenty-fifth anniversary but at the last minute – after the Anglo-Polish pact of mutual assistance had been announced – these were cancelled. Soon, after the Polish campaign of September, there was yet another German victory to commemorate. In April 1941 the Krügers made plans for the decoration of one of the memorial's towers with busts of the commanders and politicians who had brought about the defeat of Poland – Göring and Field Marshal Wilhelm Keitel and others – and tablets inscribed with extracts from Hitler's speeches dominated by a full-length statue of the Führer, like that of Hindenburg; but this never came about. The last state ceremonies at the Tannenberg Memorial were the funerals of two generals killed by Colonel von Stauffenberg's bomb in July 1944.

The end had a symbolic irony. When the Red Army advanced on the memorial, Oskar von Hindenburg was stationed in Königsberg, in command of the East Prussian prison camps, including the cruel regime at Stalag 1 B at Hohenstein where many had died. He was therefore on hand for the drama which began with the order from Hitler on 21 January 1945 that the Tannenberg Memorial should be destroyed before the invading Slavs reached it. Only a few days before the Soviets captured Hohenstein, the massively heavy lead coffins of the Field Marshal and his wife were taken with some of the regimental standards, like sacred relics, to Königsberg. They then went by sea from Pillau to Stettin, accompanied by Oskar, and by lorry to Potsdam.

Bombs were falling on the Potsdam barracks, parks and palaces of the Hohenzollerns whom Hindenburg had hoped to restore. The safest place was thought to be in a bunker beside the coffins of Frederick the Great and Frederick William I that had already been removed from the Garrison Church. When Potsdam came within range of the Soviets, these relics of Prussian glory went to a salt mine near Bernterode in Thuringia – from where American troops took the Hindenburgs to Marburg, to a castle owned by the Hesse family. In Marburg, they were buried quietly, with Allied permission, on 25 August 1946 – the thirty-second anniversary of Tannenberg – in the Elizabeth Church. Here they remain, marked by a commemorative stone, in a dim, dark aisle.

Hitler's order had been only partly carried out. Hindenburg's tomb and two of the towers were destroyed but a large part of the monumental structure had survived. The Soviets burned most of Hohenstein but, for some reason, left much of the memorial;

there was even a report that they had set up their own small monument within it. After the war ended, however, the destruction began again. The metal – the bronze or iron from the reliefs and tablets – was looted, the stone and bricks were used in the rebuilding of what had been Hohenstein and was now Olsztynek and the granite went for the Soviet war memorial in Olsztyn or to Warsaw for the new Communist Party headquarters. By the 1980s, almost all traces of the Tannenberg Memorial – once not only a building but a gesture of defiance – had gone.

Under the post-war German Federal Republic, Tannenberg became a symbol of a bad Prussia. In the 1980s teachers at the Berlin Tannenberg School (in the Ostpreussendam) wanted the name changed. But there's still a miniature copy of the Krügers' monolith, symbolically discreet for the new age – a memorial dedicated in 1995 at Oberschleissheim near Munich to the East and West Prussian dead of the two world wars. The architect Dietrich Zlomke was born in Königsberg; his design is a much smaller, lower version of the eight towers linked by walls, not in brick but in concrete, dominated by an oak cross twenty feet high with a much more modest, smaller iron cross on the low pale wall behind it. Initiated by East and West Prussian groups of *Vertriebene* (expelled people) it was built under the patronage of the conservative Bavarian state government to show a lingering of memory in a quiet place, appropriate for private mourning and regret.

15: *The Great Wilderness*

East and north from Olsztyn, you enter the lakeland, reaching the resort of Mikołajki with its masted boats on the water front, summer tourists and winter emptiness. German papers and books about the old times are on sale all year round in the shops, including a guide to the route of Marion Dönhoff's 1941 ride. Away from the lake, off the road from Olsztyn and Mragowo, is the austere evangelical church, said to have been designed by the Prussian neo-classical architect Karl Friedrich Schinkel.

The German Frank Dombrowski has taught in Mikołajki since 1991, in a private school named after Marion Dönhoff which she visited most years. We met some years ago, not long after he'd moved east. Frank Dombrowski said he loved the region and this was why he'd come, avoiding any suggestions of German guilt or duty or wish to escape. It was the history that moved him – did I know that Mikołajki was on an old Hanseatic route that led to Vladivostok? East Prussia had been fought over for centuries. You could learn about European history just by being here.

Dombrowski had been born in Königsberg, too late to remember the German city well. But he felt he had to tell me that the region had gone back since 1945 – mostly because the communists had wrecked it. Tourism seemed to be the best hope. People were open and kind – the children easier and more disciplined than in Germany and France where he'd also taught. Summer was wonderful but winter went on and on, with not enough to do – apart from some ice sailing and skating. The Russians came to Poland because there was more money, sometimes waiting for days to get across the frontier.

Frank Dombrowski was speaking in 1992, and now it's better or at least different. I've crossed the border by train and by bus and had no trouble, as a rich tourist from the west – and what Dombrowski said *has* happened: tourism is still the hope. Farming and forestry don't employ enough people because the farming companies that have moved in are highly mechanized, using seasonal rather than permanent labour. There's a huge spa hotel outside Mikołajki and the streets are lined with restaurants, most open (and empty) even in the winter snow. Venice seems not so far away on the bridge over a wide grey canal that links two lakes – but the channel that runs into the huge Spirdingsee or Polish Jezioro Śniardwy points to a distant wilderness, quite different to the Adriatic or its shores. Lorenz Grimoni thinks that East Prussia now offers one of the wildest parts of Europe.

The tourist trail re-shapes the past. Red-brick castles have become hotels and restaurants at Ryn and Nidzica or museums at Kętrzyn and Lidzbark Warmiński; fields have camping sites and woodland has been cleared for a theme park about the original Prussians (not their German conquerors). Signs in German point to Hitler's eastern headquarters – the Wolfsschanze or Wolf's Lair, where massive slabs of tumbled concrete form chambers of ghostly significance. Here the Poles have built one of the world's least inviting hotels, letting visitors walk after closing time through the hideous complex and think – there it is, sniff the air and catch it quickly: the stench of evil.

In fact Hitler loathed the damp East Prussian climate and flat landscape, yearning for the Bavarian Alps and the south. The Wolf's Lair was on the land of one of those aristocratic families that he despised, partly because most of them fell easily before him. About six or seven miles to the south-east, through fields and shelter belts of oak trees, on a broad peninsula between two lakes, is Steinort, now the Polish Sztynort, once the residence of the third family of that East Prussian cousinhood, the Lehndorffs.

Hans von Lehndorff, the house's last German owner, said that he was happy to have lost everything – the estate, the house, the isolated world, the wealth – in the upheaval that had been, in spite of its horror, 'one of God's blessings' and the start of a better life. But what he writes about his loss has a sense of recollected beauty, even celebration; like Marion Dönhoff he wanted to uncover a different country to the post-war ruin and shame.

Lehndorff didn't grow up at Steinort and was aged ten in 1920, the year of his first summer visit. He went by train to Angerburg before a two-hour journey in a horse-drawn wagon over muddy roads towards the house on the lake. It's still a Nordic landscape, the woods a mix of oaks and conifers, darkly thick, before the ancient oaks that line Steinort's one street and shelter the big house at the end. The approach to the symbol of ancestral power is still theatrical, although it leads to a smaller place than Schlobitten or Friedrichstein – to a French-château-like building of plaster over brick, now patched and boarded up, with side pavilions, looking out on ruined temples and tea houses scattered across an overgrown park. Now it's a tourist marina that brings life to Steinort (or Sztynort), not the Lehndorffs.

The family had come east with the Teutonic Knights, settling near Königsberg before buying Steinort at the start of the six-teenth century. Like the Dohnas and the Dönhoffs – with whom they intermarried – the Lehndorffs served the kings of Poland and the Hohenzollerns across shifting frontiers before Bismarck's wars brought incredible victories; a Lehndorff was briefly *préfet* of Amiens after the Prussians beat the French in 1870. When the young Hans came there, the house was chaotic; rickety beds sometimes collapsed during the night, windows were blocked by sprouting vegetation, water cascaded from primitive cisterns while Prussian royal portraits or the mangy heads of long-dead elks looked down from damp walls hung with faded Gobelins tapestries. Carol Lehndorff, Hans's bachelor cousin and Steinort's owner, welcomed guests from a first-floor balcony, holding a bil-liard cue, offering a glass of port and matches for the bedroom lamps. One guest who changed the tune of a clock that played melodies on the hour was thrown out by the host who could suddenly be autocratic, even censorious. Once Carol admonished Alexander Dohna for flirting with a woman.

Carol liked cards and obvious jokes; he invited the teachers from the school in Rastenburg (now Kętrzyn) to Steinort and locked them in a room so that the pupils could have the day off. When alone, he lived in two rooms on the warm south side of the house, contemplating his collection of Prussian coins. Gradually the porcelain became chipped and beetles crawled more daringly over the gilded empire furniture and the fine library. Only in summer did the place revive, sometimes with more than twenty guests, often those whom Carol had met on his winter travels. He didn't always come to meals; when he did preside, these could last a long time, with prodigious quantities of food and drink that occasionally made him so hot and agitated that he would ask the woman sitting next to him to wipe his brow.

Its eccentric owner's neglect seemed to burnish the myth of the great wilderness, taking it further outside time. Hans von Lehndorff, writing after the cataclysm, recalled an island near Steinort on the Mauersee, where a house and primeval woodland were completely removed from the modern world and the sportsmen had lunch during the summer duck shoots – an alcoholic feast without vegetables, for they upset Carol's stomach. To Lehndorff, Steinort was beautiful in the winter when you waited for deer or wild boar in the woods, cut through by the cold, or went to the ice-sailing regatta at Angerburg, where the sparkling ice seemed to burn into your eyes.

The boy grew up further west – where his father was director of the German national stud at Graditz, on the River Elbe. It could sometimes seem that horses ruled the family's life; so tedious had Hans's grandmother found the talk about them at meals that she once put oats into the bowls instead of soup. But the atmosphere of the large household – there were six children, five boys and one girl – was Lutheran, austere. Moreover the highest calling for a Prussian must be to serve the King, or the Emperor, as a soldier. After war broke out, Lehndorff's mother, at

Steinort: what remains.

Christmas 1914, dressed up her three oldest sons in little field-grey uniforms, only to destroy them when the slaughter grew worse. Hans was delicate, suffering from asthma and fevers, and his adored mother would come often to his childhood sick bed – a more yielding presence compared to the remote, respected father. The boy dreamed often, with immense vividness: terrifying nightmares about the house in flames and his mother being murdered by a crowd of violent men.

The Countess von Lehndorff was a daughter of the old conservative politician Elard von Oldenburg-Januschau. To go east by train across the Vistula and then in a horse-drawn cart to Januschau, seemed an enchantment to Hans – touching a subconscious part of him, like the nightmares of murder and fire but thrilling rather than fearful. His mother came from here, his father's family had been in East Prussia, in the great wilderness, for five hundred years; and after the victory at Tannenberg it seemed safe again, for ever. Hans von Lehndorff, as a small boy, shook Hindenburg's hand. He recalled, over thirty years later, an impression of the old man's deep humanity. The move east became permanent when, in 1922, his father was made director of the famous Trakehnen stud.

*

Yasnaya Polyana ('clear glade', the same name as Tolstoy's country house in central Russia) is a village about twenty or so miles from Kaliningrad. To reach it, you drive quite far down a rutted side-road enclosed by those lime trees that the Governor of Kaliningrad hates. I'm south of the main highway and west from Gusev which, as Gumbinnen, was one of the first German towns taken by the invaders in 1914 and 1944.

On this bright early autumn day a large coach and Mercedes and BMWs and Audis with German number plates are stretched along the side of a narrow road here, snaking into one of the fields. I see the diplomatic number plate of the car of the German Consul whom I had called on the day before. A few, smaller Russian vehicles are here but only a few.

Before 1945, Yasnaya Polyana was called Trakehnen and there's a meeting to celebrate the two hundred and seventieth anniversary of the famous stud, original home of the tough, elegant Trakehener horse. Hans von Lehndorff's father was director of the stud before the war and Hans passed some of his boyhood here. A white-painted arch still leads into what had been a tight, thoroughbred world but the fame of this place has become a memory. The centre of the Trakehner breed is now in Germany, some of the best examples having been taken west before the Red Army came.

Bunting flutters outside some of the old German buildings and little Russian flags are brilliantly clear in the sunlight. Before reaching the village, on the way from Gusev, you pass through undulating derelict land, interrupted by a few bands of trees or scrubby hedges. Johann van der Decken's farm, with its cultivated fields and planned cropping, could be in another country. But the landscape is the same – with few natural defences against a force wanting to destroy it.

Some of Yasnaya Polyana is of the old or restored red brick: the rest – including the stud's most prominent buildings – is of painted white stone, the windows edged in pale grey or blue. White picket fences make enclosures where thin horses stand, some saddled, perhaps for the visitors to ride, others covered with faded rugs. The grass is short only near the buildings and the largest of these, perhaps once the stud's offices, looks like a German country house: a protruding white centre block with a gable over the tiled roof and two lower flat wings. Now a school, it has a small museum with photographs of the life before 1945 – the fox hunting, Hans von Lehndorff's severe-looking father and the sleek Trakehner horses and foals in immaculate paddocks. Some distance away is a line of one-storey buildings, also painted white, where stud workers probably once lived. Now these sprout the occasional Russian satellite dish.

In front of the school, on the green lawn that has a few circular flower beds, some of the elderly visitors mix with the less expensively dressed locals. Other guests are in a long barn-like building nearby, listening to an elderly woman speaking German from a lectern, an interpreter repeating her words in Russian. Many of the women have silk scarves decorated with horse motifs like bridles and chains and wear chained bracelets or loose gold chains looped around their necks – and they are wrapped in quilted jackets for it is cold. The men, tanned and with shining silvery hair, are in Loden or tweed. Several wear name-tags; on one I see the words 'Dohna-Schlobitten'.

On the lawn, after the meeting, lunch will be served; and caterers are removing clingfilm from plates of cold food on long wooden tables. From an adjoining paddock, a horse leans over the white fence towards the plates, to be joined by another, both within reach of a pile of buns. Just in time, two of the caterers shift the table, preventing an incident that might have reinforced some of the western visitors' ideas of the place and led to talk later in the coach or the limousines – 'The horses got most of the lunch', then a shrug that implies, what do you expect in Kaliningrad? As if to remind the Germans of this new identity, there's another party going on in Yasnaya Polyana, outside the Elk Hotel, a red-brick building away from the old stud. Slow music comes from loudspeakers, three or four Russian couples dance sedately and a man sings in a deep, not quite tuneful voice.

To reach Trakehnen in 1922, after the Treaty of Versailles, you had to go through the Polish Corridor, giving rise to the sense of a territory under siege – and in April that year there was still snow on the ground. Hans von Lehndorff found himself in a traditional and efficient place, with oaks planted around the buildings, neat paths and avenues, only one metalled road (from the stud to the railway station) and a horse-drawn wagon that took the children to school. The East Prussian place names seemed strange – Jonasthal, Bajohrgallen, Kalpakin – but most important were the mares, stallions and foals, now a litany for a dead world: Pirat, Pirol, Parsival, Per Aspera, Panna, Feuertaufe, Polona, Traumkönigin, Tageskönigin, Paetitia, Polanka: then those of English blood – Priceless Cherry, Fiddle String. It was much wilder than Graditz.

They hunted the fox over country drained in the eighteenth century – each ditch and fence having a name, the scarlet huntsmen's coats startlingly bright across the flat land that was only sparsely wooded until Rominten forest. Rominten had the biggest red deer in Germany; once the preserve of the Emperor, it was, in the post-1918 republic, used by ministers and their guests but evidence of William II remained – the Norwegian wooden buildings put up by him, his chair shaped like a saddle. The Lehndorffs hoped that the monarchy might be restored, that the Weimar Republic would not last.

The great Weimar inflation of the early 1920s hit even Trakehnen, where the stud's land produced food for its employees. Hans von Lehndorff and his brothers kept guinea pigs and goats and shot hares and killed crows, sometimes selling these for millions of marks. Christmas became more modest although accompanied by the ritual of a big hare shoot in the snow.

Another big day was the tough obstacle race at the end of September to which people came from all over Germany; and during the sales of young horses more than a hundred guests would be entertained in the house. The coldest time was at the end of January and in February, when the air seemed to clutch at you 'like an animal with a thousand claws'. Hans von Lehndorff came to love the solitary thrill of stalking, looking for a deer's footprints, probing the forest and fields, searching for roe in April when the country revived after the long winter. The human world was more anxious and uncertain. Hans and his brothers visited their cousins – the Dohnas, the Dönhoffs or the Lehndorffs of Preyl. One evening he and Heinrich von Lehndorff were walking with their guns round a lake and saw lights over the water. Heinrich said he was sure it was a communist meeting and fired two shots in its direction. Aged fifteen, Heinrich had already been to a meeting of the newly formed Stahlhelm, a right-wing group, making a speech of fiery and intense patriotism.

At Januschau, when Hans went to see his mother's parents, they talked, of course, about the old times. There was no doubt in his grandfather's mind: before the First World War had been best – when the world was 'still in order'. The house at Januschau was typically Junker – ponies and horses in the paddocks, hunting trophies on the walls, not a vast palace but a neo-classical manor, set back from the village street. Oldenburg-Januschau had done well from protectionist policies that had helped agriculture east of the Elbe; when he was a member of the Reichstag he'd bought another estate in Lichterfelde, west of Berlin, so that he could have a country residence near the capital. But the couple didn't go easily into the post-1918 world. She was astringent and sceptical, apparently severe, terrifying in her photographs; he was a tough unashamed defender of his class and farming interests, but jovial, a great teller of anecdotes and specialist in rhyming telegrams (one was sent to Göring on the occasion of his engagement). The Januschaus sparred with each another. She complained about his meanness, asking why they got everything

– telephone, electric light, a car – twenty years after everyone else, to which he responded that this meant they would go bankrupt twenty years later as well. There were often three or four elderly female relations staying at Januschau. During the First World War and afterwards, in hungry times, these went back to their homes in Berlin or Hanover with berries from the woods.

After 1918, the old boisterous anti-democratic, monarchical politics of Elard von Oldenburg-Januschau faced something much harder. At first this had seemed controllable; Januschau sat near Joseph Goebbels in the Reichstag, patronizing and joking, teasing the National Socialist ('mein lieber Joseph') about his two-hour speeches. Goebbels's diary shows a certain awe of this throwback to imperial days. On 19 October 1930 he enthuses about Januschau's 'sensational' speech opposing the arrest of army officers for distributing Nazi propaganda and on 13 October the following year Januschau apparently embraced Goebbels, saying he was going to plead for the Nazis with Hindenburg. A couple of months later, Goebbels found the old man the most 'tolerable' of the reactionaries, although in August 1932 he feared that Januschau might influence Hindenburg in favour of the German Conservative Party. He felt confident enough, however, on 28 January 1933, just before Hitler became chancellor, to write of using Januschau to dispel Hindenburg's doubts about the Nazi leader. A strange postscript came in January 1940, when Hitler told Goebbels that he thought Winston Churchill was like the old Junker, 'bold' yet lacking in powers of 'reflection'.

The jokes were ending. Hans von Lehndorff, the grandson, saw this. After some months learning languages in Geneva, Paris and England, he went to study medicine in Königsberg and Munich, and, in 1931, in Berlin where old Januschau was back in the Reichstag. Like his grandfather, Hans had little admiration for Weimar. He met the charismatic philosopher Carl von Jordans – who was a conservative and opposed to Hitler – and, the evening before Hindenburg made Hitler chancellor, Hans and his brother, at the suggestion of the Jordans circle, went to the presidential palace where they saw an aide who said that the appointment of the Führer was for the best. Who could have known what was to happen, Hans von Lehndorff asks in his memoirs?

When the Reichstag burned down, Lehndorff thought no one would weep for it, sharing his grandfather's view that the parliament was 'die Quatschbude' (the nonsense stall). But the murderous Night of the Long Knives on 30 June, followed by the moves against the conservative Franz von Papen (Hitler's Vice-Chancellor) and his circle, showed the true face of the regime. Hans von Lehndorff went east to Januschau to ask his grandfather to speak to Hindenburg. The old man called Neudeck, to be told by an aide, 'Don't worry, the Führer has everything in hand.' Januschau answered, 'Yes, now they are dead, he has all in his hand.' The smooth Papen knuckled under, going as ambassador to Austria and scarcely remonstrating about the murder of his associates.

In the autumn of 1934, Hans von Lehndorff's father was pensioned off, his career over. The old Lehndorffs came to Berlin, to live in a second-floor flat. Hans's mother liked the capital and its cultural life even if this was darkened by National Socialism. While in Braunsberg – where her husband had gone after Trakehnen, to run another stud – she had shown her courage. After Hitler came to power, the Jewish dentist in Braunsberg found a sharp drop in the people coming to him for treatment because most of them feared the Nazis and wished to obey the new rules. The old Countess, however, refused to be cowed – and frequently and loudly expressed her loathing for Hitler in front of others in the waiting room, telling the dentist to let her know if ever he needed help. After the persecution became worse, he wrote to her in Berlin and she did not hesitate, having given her word; a letter duly arrived from a friend of the Lehndorffs in London offering the dentist shelter. By then it was hard to leave. The dentist did not write to the Countess again for fear of incriminating her. In the end he reached England through the help of a Jewish refugee group.

The Lehndorffs were in Berlin for Hitler's Olympics in 1936. Hans's mother got into trouble for too lukewarm a welcome of the Olympic torch but the authorities were impressed by her Mother Cross, a Nazi award for having had six children. Hans von Lehndorff had to admit that Berlin was fun at this time; he and his friends tried to celebrate as they would have done in the old imperial days. A year later he left Berlin for East Prussia, to work in the hospital at Insterburg, partly to escape the National Socialists' relentless takeover of the capital and also to return to what he thought of as his homeland. In East Prussia sometimes he was able to get away to Steinort which, after the death of the bachelor Carol in 1936, had passed to the eldest son of the Lehndorffs of Preyl, Heinrich.

His family speak of Heinrich as accepting, optimistic, not at all earnest – perhaps unpolitical. His younger brother had opposed the Nazis earlier and was arrested for eight days, then released before meeting his death on the eastern front, but Heinrich seemed to take life less seriously. When Hans visited him at Steinort, in October 1940, Heinrich talked of strange building works nearby: of aeroplanes going east. In November, officers were sent to find a field headquarters for Hitler – and chose the site near Rastenburg. By June 1941, the area had become a huge supply depot for the invasion of the Soviet Union. Heinrich von Lehndorff too went east with the Wehrmacht, to see horrors there that changed everything for him and led, indirectly, to his own end.

16: Journey to Irkutsk

Soon after the war, Marion Dönhoff was in London, with her friends the Astors, whom she'd known since before 1939. They went to the theatre in a large family party. The play was a comedy and she was particularly aware that night that any hope she might have of going back to Friedrichstein was dead. As facetious lines drove the silly plot forward – and the audience laughed politely – the courteous, gentle, safe, British evening seemed, for her, a desperately lonely one, even during the talk afterwards which was far removed from her own homeland's tragic end.

After 1945, she made a new world for herself, becoming not only one of the most admired women in the new Germany but a bright point in recent German history. However, even she wasn't exempt from swirling doubts and rumours as myths formed and dissolved. The extent of her work against Hitler was debated; her name was not on any of the lists of the conspirators found in July 1944 and, although interrogated, she hadn't been arrested. There was also ambivalence and difference of opinion about the motives (although not the courage) of many of the plotters, several of whom had been her close friends.

Those involved in the attempt to kill Hitler in July 1944 are often portrayed as knightly paladins – *chevaliers sans peur et sans reproche* – who took up their lances against a hideous modern power: brave people of elegance and honour whose drama still moves, partly through the power of martyrdom. Marion Dönhoff linked them to an old Prussia, of honour and duty, of the sacrifice of the self for the general good. Many of the conspirators were conservative nationalists who, having seen the disorder and humiliation of the Weimar years, had grown suspicious of parliamentary democracy. They had welcomed the Nazi revival of national pride, the tough anti-communism and early diplomatic and military successes. Many had held high civil or military rank in the Hitler state and tolerated the pre-war measures against the Jews. In the interrogations after the arrests in July 1944, some said that they had been sympathetic to Hitler at the start of his regime, even fundamentally anti-Semitic. It was, they claimed, the Nazis who had corrupted their own ideals, by brutality and adventurism.

Claus von Stauffenberg, the planter of the bomb, had thought before 1939 that it was right to curb excessive Jewish influence. He and his brother belonged to the idealistic, self-consciously exclusive circle of the poet Stefan George, an opaque advocate of Teutonic exceptionalism and of a spiritually revitalized Europe under German leadership. Out of discipleship and cliques can come contempt for those outside the circle. In 1939, when Stauffenberg took part as a brave officer in the brutal conquest of Poland, he described Polish civilians as 'an unbelievable rabble, very many Jews and very much mixed population. A people which surely is comfortable under the knout.' His words are reminiscent of Alfred Knox's anti-Semitism in August 1914. Later he found out about the mass murders by the SS and the Gestapo of Polish intellectuals and Jews, of the mentally backward. By the summer of 1942, Stauffenberg had turned against Hitler.

It was the atrocities on the eastern front that persuaded many of the July conspirators that they must get rid of Hitler. Among Marion Dönhoff's sources were her cousin Heinrich von Lehndorff from whom she heard of the brutal destruction in Ukraine and western Russia, also of the SS murder squads. Like her friend Helmut Schmidt, she said that not until after the war did she know about Auschwitz and the death camps. Heinrich von Lehndorff, the heir to Steinort, had been Marion's ally since childhood, someone whom she loved, before and after his marriage. He shared with her and with the others of their small, privileged

circle what she saw as Prussian virtues: the acceptance of responsibility, a seriousness of purpose, frugality even in their grand
houses, a contempt for display.

Etched into all this was military duty and tradition. Early in
1939, in a Königsberg hotel, the cousins gathered to say farewell to
Heinrich von Lehndorff's younger brother, who had been summoned at the age of twenty-three to rejoin his infantry regiment. To
Marion Dönhoff, the scene became a romantic memory: the serious boy, whom she thought classically beautiful, his eyes brighter
than she had seen them since childhood, calling out as he left, 'We
will meet again on the barricades.' By then none of them doubted
that war was coming. Two months after the invasion of Russia, the
young Lehndorff was killed on the eastern front. Marion's ally
Heinrich was hanged after the failed bomb plot in 1944.

I said to her when we met that the land must have been full of
ghosts when she went across it in August 1989, for the first time
since the war. She shrugged, turning back to the beautiful linen-
backed map on which she was showing me the route of her
journey; it was better to stick to the facts. I wondered if the dislocation could have been as great as that between her childhood
world and the rulers of Hitler's Germany. How intensely different
the Dönhoffs' life had been from the beginnings of the Nazi
movement in the smoke-choked, sweaty beer halls of Munich.
By 1989, both had gone: the resentful hysteria of one and the
beautiful exclusion of the other. The journey with Kant's statue
would reveal a new land.

Even the way east was different. Before 1945, Marion Dönhoff could drive the three hundred and thirty miles from
Königsberg to Berlin in a day, leaving German territory only to
cross the Polish Corridor. In 1989, the Soviets blocked this direct
route, even if Kant was a passenger. So she and her nephew Hermann had to take his little Citroën through Warsaw and Brest and
Vilnius (Dönhoff called it by its pre-war Polish name, Wilna), one
thousand instead of three hundred and thirty miles: a two-day
trip to Kaliningrad.

Communist central Europe unveiled itself outside the windows of the *deux chevaux*: treeless roads; sparse traffic; well-cultivated fields (in the centre and south of Poland, agriculture hadn't been collectivized); the Soviet frontier at Brest; Lithuania with its tree-lined villages, timber houses, brightly painted doors and gardens overflowing with sunflowers and geraniums in the summer heat. It was a replay of the pre-war world: a farmer walking with a single cow, and cattle grazing beside the empty highway: then the sign for Wirballen, now Lithuanian but still with its old German name, and East Prussia's old border, now the gateway to the Russian enclave of Kaliningrad.

For Marion Dönhoff there had been a preparation for all this. In September 1962 she had gone, as a journalist, to Poland, finding herself under eastern European skies for the first time since 1945, in a cold, wet, early autumn. Then too she had felt the past, with hay piled on wooden stooks, geese on the roads, horses working on the farms. It was extraordinarily familiar, as if part of her life had been resurrected, with a new backdrop – the atrocities committed by the Germans. As hosts, the Poles were, she found, the most courteous and chivalrous people in the world. Only when pressed did they talk of their suffering in the Warsaw uprising, of relations murdered in the camps: one aged professor in Warsaw apologized for his wife's poor German because she didn't have enough time to learn the language while a prisoner in Auschwitz. Only once, in her subsequent piece in *Die Zeit*, did Dönhoff explode – over a Polish Foreign Ministry paper that exaggerated the number of Poles who had lived in the former German territories before 1945. What remained unavoidable in 1962 was the grimness of communism.

So in August 1989, Marion Dönhoff was prepared for the new Soviet world. Almost immediately, no doubt partly in her imagination, the landscape seemed to change, bringing a revival of a sense of solitude through its emptiness yet also the feeling that this was where she belonged. The alleys of trees began along roads unimproved since the Russian conquest: the thick dark trunks smothering the little Citroën between lines of limes, ashes and oaks or a shadowy stretch of birches that seemed dream-like in the blurred tumbledown villages and neglected fields at twilight. Around eleven o'clock in the evening, Hermann and the Countess reached the edge of Kaliningrad. She had no notion of where to go; the city seemed scarcely recognizable, like an old torn poster advertising Soviet life. At the centre, opposite an empty tower block, stood the Hotel Kaliningrad, a bleak Intourist place across from the site of the old royal castle. There'd been a muddle; the hotel had no record of their reservations. After some frantic telephoning, a taxi arrived to take the visitors to a guest house in the suburbs. She and Hermann paid the driver with two packets of Marlboro cigarettes.

Much of suburban Königsberg remains. Dönhoff felt that she could be in Dahlem, a green district of Berlin. But in the centre – despite the ruins of the cathedral, the forts, the nineteenth-century gates and old government buildings – she thought of Irkutsk, deep in Siberia. Although the House of Soviets seemed to her to be the ugliest building she had ever seen, Dönhoff praised the rapid reconstruction later in *Die Zeit*, remembering the annihilating raids of August 1944. The Countess thought it unforgivable what the British had done, not only to Königsberg but later – when German defeat was inevitable – to Dresden and to Potsdam. She admired Kaliningrad's large-scale urban planning and the many memorials to the war dead. Surely the statues of Red Army soldiers, their defiant generals and the names of men and units engraved on slabs of stone meant a wish for peace.

She wanted to see the remains of Friedrichstein. A Russian vis-itor to Germany had given her a tile from the site, from a stall in the old stables – all she had seen since the end of her childhood home, the vast Dönhoff shrine. It had been, she told me, the most beautiful of all the East Prussian great houses. In fact, the destruc-tion hadn't been the complete, symbolic smashing of an old world that she implies in her memoirs. In January 1945, after Marion and her brother Dieter had fled, drunken Red Army troops had burned much of the top floor and the roof but a recognizable shell remained. Rumours spread that it had been a fascist palace, used by Göring, and the place became a target. By 1950, the windows and doors had been gone; in 1957 stones and bricks went for housing at a nearby school for military engineers, once a German panzer training ground. By the end of the decade little was left, after this gradual disintegration.

Kaliningrad was only a dozen miles away from the old Friedrichstein. The writer and post-war pioneer of links to the old Königsberg, Yuri Ivanov, one of the Russians who saw Marion Dönhoff in 1989, recalls the small grey-haired woman, a red shawl about her neck, a hand held out in friendly greeting, obviously tired after her trip in what Yuri called the sardine box, with Kant in the back. After leading her part of the way in his car, Ivanov felt that she must see Friedrichstein alone. The road, away from the rebuilt city, soon became familiar – through empty fields and scrappy woodland before you turned left at what had once been Löwenhagen (now Komsomolsk) where the Dönhoffs had worshipped in the now destroyed church.

Her breath seemed constricted; would the old avenue of trees be standing? Yes, although some had died, which was scarcely surprising, and the leaves were already turning after the short north-eastern summer. They reached the lake and a grave, still with the stone to her brother Heinrich who had been killed in Russia, with its inscription 'Der Tod ist das Tor zum Leben': death is the door to life. But Friedrichstein (to the Russians, Kamenka), with its plain neo-classical exterior and its baroque rooms, had vanished. Of the outbuildings – the old mill, the stables, the brewery – there were either overgrown walls or nothing; it was the conquest of civilization, Dönhoff thought, by a wild growth. Of the palace, the most obvious survival seemed to be a small wooden surround of a bell that had once rung each day at noon.

This obliteration must have darkened the next day's events when she handed over the statue of Kant. In the Kaliningrad city

hall, Yuri Ivanov declared that the philosopher belonged not to
the Russians or the Germans but to all of humanity. Dönhoff
noted how Kant's tomb near the cathedral and the statue of
Schiller by the city's theatre were honoured by the Russians – a
welcome sign of reconciliation. What might happen to Kaliningrad, she wondered later? The answer was already in the air:
the creation of a duty-free zone, the encouragement of joint ven-
tures with the west, the development of the port as an entry to
north-western Russia. In 1989, however, the old bureaucracy still
ruled. Marion Dönhoff and Hermann had hoped that they might
save many miles on their return journey by crossing directly from
the Kaliningrad district into northern Poland. The local officials
pleaded with Moscow but permission was refused. So the empty
roads began again, exhausting for Hermann with his long legs in
the small car (his aunt often had to put her left foot on the accel-
erator pedal from the passenger's seat to relieve his cramp).

The frontier had long queues of cars and lorries, as did the
rare petrol stations in Poland – which gave her time to reflect on
the visit. She recalled the extraordinary kindness of the Russians
and wondered about Friedrichstein's reality. Was it the wreckage
that she'd seen or the dream world of the past? The eighteenth-
century house, its history and its end had given a memory and a
drama that stayed in her writing. She might have reflected too
that when places are destroyed those who were once a part of
them can rebuild them as they wish – for themselves or for others.
With the end in 1945 came a new freedom, potentially without
limit, what Kant had seen as dangerous in spite of the immense
value of being free.

Devastation – the end of most of what she had loved –
brought Marion Dönhoff into journalism. When she looked back
in old age to 1946 – the year she had gone to Hamburg to work
on the new *Die Zeit* – she saw that time as the most exciting of
her life. To be with the four founders of the paper, although the
venture had no money and Germany's future was uncertain,
seemed to her to be a life without limit, partly because the ruins

and the well-meaning victors made room for almost anything. It had taken her a day, a night and then another half-day to reach Hamburg from where she was staying with relations in Lower Saxony – a lift for twelve miles on a lorry and the rest of the journey on foot.

Dönhoff's new colleagues had asked for her. They'd seen an explosive memorandum of protest that she had written to the British occupying forces; she had anti-Nazi credentials; her doctorate was impressive, as were her imagined establishment contacts. Some on the paper were doubtful about her Junker ancestry (reminiscent of a bad, old Germany). Her title also seemed inconsistent with what they wanted to be. But risk was part of the project which was probably doomed; they might all be out of work in a year. What moved them was a sense of responsibility or disgust (some of them were Jewish) for the Hitler years – and a wish to make a new, decent liberal country. A colleague wrote of Marion Dönhoff as being a symbol of these hopes – young, passionate and amateurish like many of the others. Her writing was strewn with commas, she lived in small rented rooms and often went hungry. A veteran journalist mocked *Die Zeit* as a group of friends talking loftily about God and the world, out of touch with reality. This shocked her – before she saw that this was how they should be.

Her self-confidence – and self-righteousness – can be seen in what she wrote about the poor distribution of food and clumsy censorship by the British occupying forces. She decried the victors' justice at Nuremberg, believing that Germans who had opposed the Nazis should sit on the war crimes tribunal as well. Her authority and moral power grew as she settled into her new world. Later there were rows, even temporary exile to London where she worked on the *Observer*, then edited by her friend David Astor. The force was there, if she was right or wrong: an echo of the old Prussia of Frederick the Great and the nineteenth-century reformers. What was reasonable and best should be obvious, clear to everyone, not just to her.

To achieve anything like this, as a woman, was rare. The irony is that the Countess remained quite old-fashioned. She preferred male company, took little interest in feminism and liked being the only woman in the room. Even in old age she could be flirtatious. Young men – her nephews, great-nephews or younger journalists at *Die Zeit* (known as her 'Bubis') – were close to her, alongside grand friends like Willy Brandt, Helmut Schmidt and Henry Kissinger.

The nickname – the Red Countess – was still used by her opponents. Perhaps because of the chaos she had seen and through a wish to be in touch with her old homeland, Marion Dönhoff, although anti-communist, spoke against the build-up of arms and a confrontation with the Soviet Union. She was suspicious of the Americans, particularly of Nixon and of Reagan. When defiance burst out of the Soviet empire in the 1980s – from Lech Wałęsa's Solidarity in Poland or Pope John Paul II – she was sceptical of these. It was better to work for detente, for gradual change, and not risk angry confrontation, perhaps another war even worse than her memories of the last. She supported the communist General Jaruzelski's imposition of martial law in Poland, believing that it may have prevented a Russian invasion. For this Marion Dönhoff was criticized. Perhaps, it was said, her most useful role had been as a chronicler of her own extraordinary past.

*

Schlobitten, Januschau, Steinort, Friedrichstein – the lost houses of East Prussia – represented refinement of the fortresses of the Teutonic Knights into outposts of courtliness or political power before their entrapment between two revolutions: those of Hitler's Germany and Stalin's Soviet Union. Eventually there was only one possibility – flight and an end to the eastward movement that had begun some eight centuries before.

I met Olga in 1992 when she had just left university. She was working then for a group of British farmers who wanted to invest in the Kaliningrad region; now she's with the European Union office in the city and sometimes guides foreign visitors. Today she drives me out of Kaliningrad through early-winter drizzle, the traffic bad in the rush hour as we go in search of what has survived.

We go right at the Dohna tower and the Amber Museum, away from one of the city's many war memorials – a statue of Vassilevsky, the commander of the Red Army's last assault on Königsberg – to a stretch of the old German wall, past a turreted gate. Through the trees to our right is the low red-brick bungalow of the German–Russian Friendship House; you can just see the bright-yellow sculptures of figures sitting on a bench – apparently two drunks leaning towards one another, one playing an accordion, the other the balalaika, Disney-like symbols of reconciliation.

We head past the car dealers' glass showrooms to the new ring road, for which all the crushed stone was imported from Sweden. Alongside us, the limes and chestnuts form a broken avenue, still with some leaves left. Before his dismissal by Putin, Governor Georgy Boos had wanted all these trees to come down for they stop progress (or road widening) and are foreign. Attempting to give a certain idealism to the destruction, he's said to have compared their deaths to those German soldiers killed in the Great Patriotic War.

Yes, Olga says, the Brezhnev years – when the castle was destroyed and the cathedral nearly went – were stagnant but a relief (if you stayed in line) after earlier hardship. She runs through the good points: handicapped people were better cared for (although hidden because all Soviet citizens should be seen to be strong), the old better looked after; there was less financial corruption, alcoholism was controlled and treated. But then she could never have had this life where her daughter and she travel to Europe and to the United States. Recently she came to London for several weeks to stay with a friend in an eighteenth-century house in Spitalfields.

We reach scrubby land and a broad cultivated field where the rainy horizon is blurred and some distant clumps of trees loom like enormous dark cages. We cross what seems like a border through an old gateway into a thin, straight alley where limes form a high perforated tunnel. At the end, on the right, are some German houses and a glimpse of a large lake before a red-brick building and a clearing, perhaps where the mansion may have been. Now there's only what look like two adjoining barns, one of familiar Prussian red brick, the other covered in grey white plaster.

A low, more recent construction is at right angles behind this, with two or three neat gardens in front of it. In one of the gardens, a man briefly turns off his leaf-blowing machine to say that the only person who knows about the place's history has moved to Kaliningrad. I see a large stone with a creeper trailing across it, beside a garden seat where he's made what looks like a rockery. On the stone, beneath the plant's tendrils, are the carved words 'Heinrich Graf Dönhoff' then the dates of his birth and death (1899 and 1942) and the words, 'Der Tod ist das Tor zum Leben' (death is the gateway to life) – Marion's eldest brother who was killed in a plane crash on the eastern front.

Now the place is no longer a private realm, one family's cherished paradise, but free for anyone to come and go as he or she pleases. In the woods that cover much of the old landscaped park and garden we see empty bottles and burned litter – remnants of summer evenings – and a notice saying beware of the arrows shot in the practice sessions of a local archery club. Friedrichstein exists only in old photographs. In these you can see the park and gardens, the grand rooms and the study of Marion Dönhoff's father that was changed at the end of the 1930s into an apartment for a forester. The study looks Spartan, with functional furniture and hunting trophies on the walls – and, in one photograph, beside a stag's head, a drawing of Adolf Hitler. In the 1980s when Yuri Ivanov came with Rudolf Jacquemien to look for the statue of Kant, there seems still to have been the church tower at Komsomolsk, all that remained of the place where the Dönhoffs had worshipped together, a reason given by Marion for why the children of her brother Heinrich and his Roman Catholic wife couldn't inherit. Someone in Komsomolsk says that the whole church was demolished and the brick and stone used for building elsewhere.

17: 'The Terrible and Great Way'

The poet Agnes Miegel was at the great 1955 Königsberg reunion in Duisburg – a neat, housewifely woman in an overcoat and tight dark hat, her appearance at odds with her powerful work. Miegel had enshrined the East Prussian story in verse and prose; her own flight across the Baltic to a Danish refugee camp in 1945 was what many of those at Duisburg would have experienced. But there's one Miegel poem – what an admirer calls 'the great error' – that makes Lorenz Grimoni agitated when he tries to explain it.

'Look,' he says to me, picking up his pencil and seizing another piece of paper, 'here is how it was.' He draws a series of circles, a rough map. 'Here is East Prussia after 1919.' One circle. 'Here is Bolshevik Russia.' Another bigger circle, to the south and east. 'Here is the new Poland.' A big circle to the south. 'Here are the new Baltic States.' A smaller circle to the north-east. 'You see – surrounded. Cut off!'

The circles aren't complete so he quickly draws another line, making it dark and deep – like the chart of his journey west in 1945 – to show the Polish Corridor. 'Yes,' he says, 'Agnes Miegel was brown.' This means National Socialist. 'But she lived on the frontier.'

Reading Agnes Miegel (who is now remembered by few people in Germany) you sense a fragility that yearned for strength, even in her popular journalism. These friendly essays – written for Königsberg papers between the wars – are different to her ballads and stories that are set in a wild, often violent past. If only she hadn't written the poem; it led to a ban on her publishing anything for several years after the war. When Agnes Miegel came back into print, one theme was how grateful she was to have known her homeland before its end. Born in 1879 in Königsberg, she wrote of the vast skies of her childhood, of the myths and history of the German east, also of an undisturbed, stiflingly cosy bourgeois world.

Agnes Miegel was the only daughter of a successful businessman. Her mother's family were farmers who had left Salzburg for East Prussia in the eighteenth century because of their Protestant faith. This combination made her, she felt, a good representative of the province. It was a cultured household – and years later she remembered what had seemed even more important: home, the garden with her own flower bed, the evening cooking, the singing of the gardener's wife, the brightly lit and full shops; the only intrusion, a voice calling her to what she thought of as the lonely, dark way of art. After leaving school she worked in Weimar, Berlin and England (in Bristol) as a children's nurse and teacher – before returning to Königsberg to look after her sick parents. Most of her life she suffered from bad health.

The poet Börries von Münchhausen considered Agnes Miegel the greatest living poet of ballads and took her into his Göttingen literary circle. She seems to have had no lasting, loving relationship although she loved Münchhausen. In 1913, the year her mother died, she won the Kleist Prize and by 1917, the year of her father's death, she was already well known. Her 1920s sketches of East Prussian life were popular, perhaps because they show a cosy and kind world at a time of threat. With these came the more powerful poems, ballads and tales of the Prussian past. In 1924, during the celebrations of the two-hundredth birthday of Kant, the University of Königsberg gave her an honorary degree. In 1936 she won the Herder Prize; in 1945, the Goethe Prize in Frankfurt. At the end of the war, Agnes Miegel was one of the most famous poets in Germany.

She had written of a premonition of destruction and often her work is dark and tragic. Miegel's most famous poem, 'Die Frauen von Nidden' (The Women of Nidden), is based on what was

thought to be a true story about people on the Curonian Spit (or
Kurische Nehrung). These believed that as God had protected
them from the huge shifting dunes, so the plague would be kept
away by the lagoon that separated the Spit from the mainland.
But, carried by elk, the killer disease reached the Spit, leaving only
a few women alive who pray that they may attain peace by being
buried by the giant dunes. At the poem's end, their prayers are
answered.

The *Ostpreussische Zeitung* pieces, written between 1923 and
1926, the year she had her great success as a novelist with *Stories
from Old Prussia*, must have appealed to the paper's readers –
mostly conservative nationalists and property owners. They show
the dark times after the First World War and find comfort in the
friendliness of housewives and stall-holders and shopkeepers,
the silver River Pregel, the spring sky, the country people and
clouds of pigeons and doves. She writes of the wind from the east
– not from the ocean or from the Alps but from the endless land
of the Steppes – and scorns people who live west of the Vistula
who could never appreciate the relief of an East Prussian spring.
Gloom about the new materialism, the world of cars and fashion
and her humiliated land haunts her. In Hamburg with her blond,
brown little godson Jochen, she sees a ship flying the German
flag and feels a surge of pride through the humiliation of defeat.
Germany, she writes, is like no other country. It must go its
own 'terrible and great way', the Titan's destiny.

Agnes Miegel joined the National Socialist Women's Organization in 1937 and the Nazi Party in 1940. To her, Hitler was the
new Hindenburg, the defender of East Prussia. She had written a
poem to the old Field Marshal and did the same for the Führer of
the new Reich, including both of these in *Ostland*, published in
1940, the volume that she came to regret deeply. Many of the
poems were part of the propaganda that she and others favoured
by the Nazis were encouraged to produce. One is addressed to
Hindenburg, remembering the Tannenberg victory; another calls
for the rest of Germany to show support for East Prussia during

Agnes Miegel.

the plebiscites of July 1920; 'Copernicus' claims that the great scientist was definitely German, not Polish; the loss of Memel after 1919 is lamented; she rejoices in the 1939 recovery of Danzig; and 'To Germany's Youth, Autumn 1939' is a call to arms. Agnes Miegel shows an anxious, threatened East Prussia – civilization's last redoubt, a warrior land.

The poem to the Führer, with which *Ostland* begins, had been written not, she says, with 'youth's enthusiasm' but with mature judgement, with a joy that all had been renewed and a wish to serve him ('overpoweringly, humble thanks fill me'), to sacrifice herself, conscious that past troubles have been:

'Wiped away like the tears from the face of a widow
By your hands! . . . '

Perhaps it was innocence that led to such capitulation, perhaps also a subliminal wish to be not only protected but overwhelmed.

After 1945 she had to wait before her work could appear again. Now the poetry and the essays were mostly nostalgic, glimpses of a good past, reassuring to those who had been expelled and blaming the loss of her old home not so much on German guilt as on mysterious, dark fate. The title of her first post-war book of poems, published in 1949, was *But You Remain in Me*. It had glimpses of destruction, as in 'Autumn 1945':

> 'Splintered stumps gaped
> Over at the collapsed ruins
> Wild dogs hunt in packs
> Through blackened barns . . . ';

and that lost but longed-for East Prussian cosiness, recalled in 'Christmas 1948':

> 'What were you Christmas to my child's heart? . . .
> . . . I am but a guest
> in a country still German . . .
> Answer me in this night wind,
> Coming from the homeland as hushed weeping . . . '

Photographs show her as a beautiful young woman. Did she ever have sexual experiences? Lorenz Grimoni glares at me, grasping his pencil like a dagger to defend her, so I don't ask him. In Berlin, I ask a Polish friend who's written about East Prussia but he's never heard of anything. Could there be something in the Agnes Miegel archive in Marburg, he wonders?

Her poetry is passionate, etched (especially after 1945) with memory although she said she felt no bitterness. She began to win prizes again – in 1958 the East German cultural award, in 1959 the prize of the Bavarian Academy of Art (many refugees from the east had settled in Bavaria), in 1962 the prize of the West Prussian Landsmannschaft, an organization for the 'expelled'.

In her new home in Bad Nenndorf, she said how hard it was to dispute lies, implying that these had been spread about her past; her friends believed that she was entitled to some mistakes. The Christian faith stayed with her: the sense also that she'd been lucky in life until 1945 when what she thought of as her good world had ended in shame. Lulu von Strauss und Torney, her great friend, had married Eugen Dietrichs, a collaborator of the British racist and Teutonophile Houston Stewart Chamberlain. Börries von Münchhausen killed himself after the defeat of his idol, Adolf Hitler.

The stain remains, darkening attempts at revival. At an Agnes Miegel day in Bad Nenndorf in 2005, only sixty people came to hear a Berlin theatre troupe put on dramatized readings of her oriental fairy stories *Tales of Ali the Poet* – the actors dressed in fezzes and brocaded robes, puffing at hookahs. The day's organizers had hoped for more. One lecturer spoke of the power of Agnes Miegel's work beyond that one fatal poem: for instance the 1931 story 'Homecoming' – about a Berlin doctor returning to his old home in Königsberg to see his dying grandmother: and about how the city's bridges, towers, cemeteries and gardens blur between memory, fantasy and reality into an imagined paradise. Was this a premonition that the place would soon live only in the imagination of those who had been expelled from it? Agnes Miegel, her admirers believe, had mystical power.

How good it is, the old Königsbergers think, that today there is an Agnes Miegel Society in Kaliningrad – extraordinary when you recall some of her work: its exaltation of force and a glorious German past. In the winter of 2005, a group of Miegel admirers went by bus from Duisburg to Kaliningrad, thinking of her line about her heart rising 'like a lark, upwards, upwards to the old homeland.' They were met by Russian fellow enthusiasts; readings took place in German and Russian and a wreath was laid under the bronze tablet on her old home. Among the poems read by a Russian writer was 'At the Garden Hedge' where the poet meets a Russian mother who lost her son in the First

World War. 'Bread', the Russian said, was his favourite Miegel poem; the visitors were impressed that he liked these lines about the joy of eating German bread again after the flight to Denmark. The Russians have even named a school after her in Kaliningrad.

Other exiles polished their memories until the old landmarks – the Curonian Spit, the Frisches Haff (the lagoon), the dunes and the amber, the woods and the lakes, Rominten Heath, the horses at Trakehnen, the elk and the deer, Königsberg and Marienburg – shone like gold. But the road back to a new life was hard at first for Agnes Miegel. That poem was always there, with the grim finality of publication, even if she kept it out of all new collections of her work. Her resonance and power, rooted often in myth, did find readers, not only among the exiles. Schools and streets were named after her in several German cities, her head was put on a postage stamp in 1979, to mark the centenary of her birth. The names of the schools and the streets were sometimes changed, however, when a watchful local or a campaigning councillor brought Miegel's past to the surface again. That poem of 1938 to Hitler – like Carl Diesch's article on Heine or Konrad Lorenz's utterances on eugenics or the extracts from the published transcripts of the interrogations of the July 1944 conspirators – shows how widely the Nazi stain could spread.

*

Order was what Agnes Miegel cherished. But it wasn't only in Germany that politicians stressed the need for order as a guard against revolution. The chaos that he'd seen in Russia – and the need to fight it – featured very strongly in Alfred Knox's political life. At Westminster, as a newly elected member of parliament, he castigated the 'immoral' trade agreement with Russia of 1921 and 'the Soviet sore' – and on 5 February 1930 quoted Mussolini on Soviet Russia, 'It is a system that supported dictatorship on a pile of corpses.' As an imperialist who had served in India, he, like Winston Churchill, favoured rigorous British control of the sub-continent. Indian home rule must lead to 'a communist state in India within our lifetime'.

At first, Sir Alfred Knox was suspicious of the new National Socialist German state, fearing any kind of German rearmament. Five months after Hitler had come to power, Knox called for the British government to threaten to cancel trade agreements with Germany, and two years later asked a question about Switzerland supplying arms to Nazi Germany. He advocated British re-armament and favoured Franco's forces in the Spanish Civil War, admiring their fight against communism. 'Wake up, England,' Knox called on 11 December 1936, from the 'dream' of a peaceful world brought about by the League of Nations. It was his loathing of the Soviet Union that led him to become more tolerant of the German revolution. By June 1937, he was defending the speech given by Nevile Henderson, Britain's Ambassador to Germany, which some called 'a panegyric on National Socialism' but which Knox described as 'a real contribution to the cause of peace'. Knox thought that the new Germany was the only European nation actively fighting the Bolshevik threat.

Defence worried Knox – this and his country's moral decline. On 8 March 1939, he contrasted Britain unfavourably with Germany. 'The motto there is "the interests of the State are more important than your private interests", and they act up to that motto,' he said. 'Whatever one may think of their policy there is a general spirit of self-sacrifice among the youth of that nation. The Young Folk from 10 to 14 years of age carry out drills and undergo semi-military instruction. The Hitler Youth carry this training on from 14 to 18 years. In the twentieth year every man in Germany, whatever his rank or class or wealth, has to go to a labour camp for six months. There he gets good discipline and good healthy food, and it hardens him in mind and body. After that he goes for two years' military service. How can we compete with that process?'

Later that month, however, Knox's patriotism was roused. In contradiction of the spirit of Munich, he called for an economic blockade of Germany, and once the war had started, demanded the arrest of communist as well as fascist sympathizers. In 1944 he watched with horror as Stalin began to take over Poland and the Red Army rampaged through central Europe. Couldn't British military representatives be sent to the eastern front, Knox asked, to report the truth about this brutal campaign? Always he remained deeply suspicious of Soviet Russia.

In fact the old firebrand had been much less enthusiastic about National Socialism than several other British members of parliament. The pre-war career of Sir Arnold Wilson – a figure also steeped in late-Victorian imperialism – shows a much deeper yearning to imitate the new Germany. Born in 1884, the son of a clergyman who was also a headmaster, Wilson grew up in the atmosphere of the Victorian public school – which owed much to the Prussian system – where character was thought to be as vital as intellectual grounding. A brilliant and brave man, he passed out top at Sandhurst and became an officer in the Indian Army, showing extraordinary skill in languages and great resourcefulness on dangerous missions in remote parts of Persia.

During the First World War, Wilson was decorated for courage. Britain was given the mandate to govern the former Ottoman territory of Mesopotamia at the peace conference and Wilson was again promoted, becoming responsible for this vast new land, to be called Iraq. But his forceful way of putting down an Iraqi rebellion was criticized and he resigned, briefly joining the Anglo-Persian Oil Company before returning to Britain.

Wilson settled in Hertfordshire and, in June 1933, was elected as the local constituency's Conservative member of parliament. Among his preoccupations as a politician were – like many scientists and public figures of the time – eugenics (or controlled breeding to improve a population's capability) and what he saw as a worrying decline in the birth rate of the 'civilized' nations. Here the British could, Wilson thought, learn from fascist Germany and Italy – even from Soviet Russia and its rapid increase in population. In May 1934, some sixteen months after Hitler

had come to power, he began a fact-finding journey through
Europe, visiting Germany first. On similar trips round Britain, he
had often been told that the country needed a Hitler or a Mussolini – which he'd always denied, saying that democracy, with all
its faults, was best.

Wilson loathed what he had heard of the National Socialist
policy towards the Jews and the Churches (he was a devout
Anglican). But he became fascinated by the vigour and popularity
of the new regime. Hitler's ability to win people's passionate
support, shown in the astonishing amount of work they did
(sometimes voluntarily) for their revived country, seemed impressive compared to a torpid, peevish Britain. The bright early-
summer days seemed to symbolize the decline in crime, the clean
streets and the healthy young people in the work camps (the
Arbeitslager) or in public places. In Berlin, Wilson met Hitler
(who impressed him by his aura of quiet strength) and stayed
with Joachim von Ribbentrop, the Führer's foreign-policy adviser.
But he found the atmosphere of the prison at Dachau dark and
repellent and challenged his hosts on their treatment of the Jews,
the churches and political opposition. He was told that a gentler
country would emerge when the crisis had passed, although the
reassurances about the Jews were vague, often combined with an
assertion that it was necessary to be hard.

Arnold Wilson believed that a powerful Germany, including
what was left of Austria, was unavoidable; that its stability and
the maintenance of order in the centre of Europe were vital for
peace; that Hitler was strong and popular enough to bring about
these conditions. But he found it difficult to tell if the new state's
leaders were responsible or just a collection of gangsters, especially when, during his visit, Hitler arranged the murder of his old
colleague Ernst Röhm, the SA leader, and others in the Night of
the Long Knives.

Königsberg was the last German city on his tour. To Wilson,
East Prussia, cut off from the rest of the country since 1919 by
the Polish Corridor, had the air of a German colony although its

very isolation made the province a place for grand statements of national pride such as those given by Hindenburg, Hitler and, before 1914, the last Emperor. In Königsberg, Wilson spoke at the university, criticizing National Socialist anti-Jewish policies and the campaign against the Churches while commending the patriotism and unselfish national unity among the young. He went round the sights – the museum, the cathedral, the Wallenrodt Library, the castle and the tomb of Kant. One student said that they had been taught from childhood that society had claims on them equal even to those of their families. Britain was too complex, too anarchic, too much moved by tradition, a place of 'untidy minds, untidy cities, and untidy laws'. National Socialism was about simplification. Wilson was tackled by the Nazi Gauleiter Erich Koch and others about the new frontiers imposed by the Treaty of Versailles. The most dramatic moment came on the beach at Cranz when he was among a large crowd listening to the transmission of Hitler's speech to the Reichstag about the murder of Röhm. For nearly an hour and a half, people stood, scarcely moving during the harangue, showing at the end that they enthusiastically accepted what their Führer said.

A year later, in May 1935, Wilson was again in Königsberg, speaking at the university about the Jubilee celebrations of King George V and Queen Mary; to his audience, it must have been an insight into something of almost unbelievable quaintness and serenity. At a lunch afterwards, General Walther von Brauchitsch, then the commander in East Prussia, and Gauleiter Koch argued that individualism had had its day, that nationality was a person's most important attribute – 'races, nations and peoples, when well-led, made history, not individuals'. The complex German soul needed a point of coalescence. Koch and Brauchitsch thought that Kant had understood this (a strange reading of his philosophy) yet not as well as Fichte; Goethe had not grasped it at all.

Back in London, sitting in the House of Commons library, Wilson read Kant's essay on perpetual peace. He noted the philosopher's strong disapproval of one state taking over another by armed conquest or negotiation: and his belief that standing armies should eventually be abolished, that no war should be too brutal to prevent the quick restoration of a defeated state's confidence, that wars of extermination were absolutely wrong. To bring perpetual peace, Kant recommended that each state should be a republic within a federation of free states; that the rights of men, as citizens of the world, should be reflected in universal hospitality. Man had, Kant thought, a natural predisposition towards harmony.

The quest for morality in politics – glimpsed, he had hoped, in the new German idealism and pride – was typical of Wilson. He went on seeking some accord with fascism by supporting Chamberlain's policy of appeasement and backing General Franco in Spain. But, like Knox, when war came in September 1939, his patriotism rose again. Aged fifty-five, he volunteered for the RAF, becoming a pilot and, later, a rear gunner. Arnold Wilson was killed in May 1940 when his bomber was shot down over northern France.

An earlier – and more ostensibly liberal – British visitor to Königsberg was Philip Conwell-Evans, who had worked as private secretary to a recent Labour minister and in 1932 published a book on British responsibility for the First World War. Perhaps because of this, he was asked to give lectures at Königsberg University in 1933 and 1934. Reporting on his time there, Conwell-Evans began, like Wilson, by condemning the National Socialist treatment of the Jews. He compared this to Louis XIV's revocation of the Edict of Nantes that had victimized the French Protestants (and led to an exodus of many to Prussia), although 'this is not to ignore the fact that Germany has a Jewish problem'. Regrettable also, Conwell-Evans thought, were the arbitrary detentions and the 'third rate' leaders who owed their position to loyalty to Hitler. Yet he believed that the street brawls and the thuggishness had been the work of 'a very small minority of roughs' – and that Britons should curb any righteous indignation. Britain's blockade of Germany had, after all, gone on for four months after the armistice, an act of cruelty that had caused much suffering.

Königsberg, Conwell-Evans said, was unique: a town of some three hundred thousand people, with the famous university where Kant had taught, founded in 1544 – and a town, since 1918, just over the frontier from the new Poland, the Baltic States and the Soviet Union. He found the atmosphere more liberal than in other parts of the German east, like Pomerania or Silesia – perhaps the legacy of Kant. Ninety-nine per cent of his students were members of the Nazi Party but Conwell-Evans, who had a doctorate from Oxford, had never met such a courteous and grateful group. For example, on an outing to the country, during a five-mile walk, they didn't sing the usual National Socialist songs because of the possibility of offending some Jews in the party. The burning of the books in one of the city squares was also thoughtfully done, with some copies of works by Marx and Engels and other socialist writers kept back for use in research. To Conwell-Evans the flames were an old German tradition, reaching back to Luther and supporters of Fichte. Would British students do this, he was asked? He believed not; they had too great a sense of humour.

The great causes of pain, Conwell-Evans thought, were the treatment of Germany as an international pariah, particularly the war 'guilt' clause in the Treaty of Versailles, followed by the terrifying inflation; the sense of defencelessness within a ring of armed states; the French invasion of the Ruhr; the taking of Upper Silesia by the Poles and Memel by the Lithuanians in defiance of the League of Nations; the occupation of the Rhineland by black French troops. National Socialism had staved off a communist revolution and brought stability out of the babble of parties in the Weimar republic. Königsberg students, according to Conwell-Evans, respected the new Poland. At youth camps, young German Nazis joined young Poles from the nationalistic Piłsudski Youth, each singing each other's national songs, and at the university, many were learning Polish. The students felt that East Prussia should be repopulated with people brought in from western Germany. They denied any wish to assimilate other countries, except, of course, Austria.

Conwell-Evans emphasized the fear in East Prussia of Poland where, he claimed, there was open talk of conquering the province. Was it surprising, Conwell-Evans said, that youth organizations equipped themselves for defence? British public-school cadet forces seemed far more aggressive. The SA and the SS had done much to stop crime and to give purpose to the young unemployed. These organizations were democratic; all classes joined and took part in the work camps. The constant processions and carrying of flags were merely a reflection of a German, particularly a south German, tradition. Germany was at the mercy of its neighbours: France, Poland, the Soviet Union. The way to win its 'confidence and ready co-operation' was to treat it as an equal.

Conwell-Evans, during the 1930s, became a secretive but determined advocate of closer relations with the new Germany, arranging for British officials and politicians to meet National Socialist leaders like Ribbentrop, to whom he was close. In 1938, however, he had a flash of perception and changed his view utterly. Henceforth Conwell-Evans used his links to warn the British Foreign Office about the terrifying regime that he had once admired.

18: The Prussian Sahara

You had to think of the coming and going across the land, a Polish friend tells me in Warsaw. How could you freeze natural movements that had lasted for centuries? The only way had been through unnatural cruelty.

The poet Johannes Bobrowski knew this. He looked back to Sarmatia, a partly mythical world that had stretched from the Vistula and the Danube to the Volga and the Caucasus until the Goths arrived at the start of the Christian era – a region where nomads and hunters had wandered across a vast landscape, worshipping its trees, forests and rivers. Born in Tilsit in 1917, the son of a German railway official, Bobrowski caught the last whisper of this mixed culture in the Jews, Lithuanians, Poles and Germans that he saw during his childhood visits to his grandparents' farm just over the border from East Prussia, in Lithuania.

Already he could hear the distant 'silver rattle of fear'. What shocked him into writing about it was his time as a German soldier on the eastern front in the summer and autumn of 1941. In Kaunas, the SS and the Lithuanians slaughtered Jews; in Novgorod the German invaders came with mechanical violence and contempt for centuries of culture and history. On the shores of Lake Ilmen, Bobrowski and his comrades found a landscape where after their departure 'The wolf crossed the clearing. / Listens for the bells of winter./ Howls for the enormous/ Cloud of snow' in a reassertion of a huge natural world that seemed to absorb even this cruel destruction. To Bobrowski, 1941 seemed a repeat of the Teutonic Knights whose victims he recalled in his 'Pruzzian Elegy':

> 'People
> Of smouldering groves,
> Of burning huts, green corn
> Trampled, blood-stained rivers –
> People,
> Sacrificed to the singeing
> Lightning-stroke . . .'

You can trace the shifting cultural identities that Bobrowski cherished – through the names on old and new maps. Some towns and villages in the Kaliningrad district (or Oblast) have three possible names: Polessk, for instance, was once the German Labiau but also the Lithuanian Labguva; Sovetsk could be the Lithuanian Tilžė in addition to the old German Tilsit. To Lithuanians, Kaliningrad is Karaliaučius as well as Königsberg. In the west, near the present Lithuanian border, there was Little Lithuania, on the edge of what was then Germany and Russia. Here you find the town of Chistye Prudy, once the German Tolminkehmen or the Lithuanian Tolminkiemis.

How confusing all this is, the Russian writer Yuri Ivanov thought, wondering if he or anyone could unravel the region's identity. Would it drive him mad? He was in a bus, heading out of Kaliningrad with a group of Russian and Lithuanian writers, scholars and artists who sang and joked as they went through the spring landscape. The gathering was partly to celebrate Kristijonas Donelaitis, the great eighteenth-century poet who had lived in Chistye Prudy as a pastor, preaching in German and Lithuanian. While under Prussian rule, Donelaitis had prompted Lithuania's literary renaissance. His most famous poem evokes the abrupt changes of the Baltic seasons as a violent disruption of fantasy:

> 'The sun came up further and woke the world
> Mocked the work of the cold winter and threw it into ruin.
> Melted the ice and the fantasy built by frost . . .'

Prussia's absorption into the new Germany, Ludendorff's

Ober-Ost, Hitler and the Soviet empire changed the tolerance that had let Donelaitis preach in German and Lithuanian. In 1994, Lithuanian nationalists blew up the Vilnius to Kaliningrad railway line and some in the new Lithuania wondered about absorbing the then decaying Russian enclave, a dream as unreal as Marion Dönhoff's idea of a joint ownership by the new Russia, Germany and Poland. Either of these schemes would have led to another influx and exodus of people, a further blurring of identity. This is a part of Europe where boundaries are vague, where names deceive. 'My Lithuania!' Adam Mickiewicz writes, at the start of the long poem that became a nineteenth-century battle cry of Polish nationalism.

Such confusion shows how history can scatter identity. North-east from Little Lithuania, on the coast, across the border from the Kaliningrad region of Russia, is the Lithuanian port of Klaipėda, once the German Memel. East Prussian, or German, until the end of the First World War – and featuring in the national anthem as the most eastern part of the Reich – Memel became an international city in the peace treaty of 1919. But in 1923, Memel was seized by the new Lithuania. The town's German majority waited, not always patiently, for it to become German again.

In September 1938, when war seemed imminent, an Englishman set out along the shores of the Baltic on his trusty bicycle which he had named 'George'. Bernard Newman was a writer who had worked in intelligence during the First World War and written fiction and fact about espionage. His other line was travel books, the sort where the English clumsy clot somehow gets where he wants to go and, as if by mistake, uncovers much about the place. Their titles give the flavour: *Albania Back-door*, *Ride to Russia*, *Pedalling Poland*.

Newman found a Baltic German in a bar in a small town in the Lithuanian lake district: one who'd been a colonel in the imperial Russian army. This former landowner, who had lost his estates in the land reform after Lithuanian independence, said that Germany was the natural dominant power in Europe – much more than the Russians. England was 'shot to pieces', no one could stand up to the invincible German nation represented by Hitler who would take the port of Memel when he pleased, then give the Baltic Germans back what had been stolen from them. Lithuania was fit only to be a province: not a country. A part of the trouble in Europe was little states playing at being big countries. It was the Tsar of Russia and the King of England who had planned the First World War, because of their jealousy of the German Emperor. As the tirade collapsed into incoherence, Newman wondered if it was the last gasp of the Baltic barons or part of the opening salvo of another conflict.

Pedalling south, Newman reached the old pre-1918 frontier between Germany and Russia, in the region of Memel-land, once East Prussian, now in Lithuania. He noticed a change as Prussian red-brick cottages replaced Lithuanian timber shacks. At the old Memel, since 1923 the Lithuanian Klaipėda, he found a clean, unexciting town – once a sleepy German timber port but now made into a place of immense significance by the Lithuanians, who had spent millions on it. The atmosphere in Klaipėda, Newman thought, was overwhelmingly German, with a large German majority. Demonstrations were forbidden, but he saw youths in plain clothes marching in a street and other Germans told him they would not rest until Memel was back in the Reich; the omniscient Führer would settle everything in good time. Newman saw the forbidden swastika inside several houses, like a symbol of some secretly worshipped God. Lithuania had no allies. Poland, her powerful neighbour, had become estranged over the question of Wilno (the present Vilnius) which had been taken by the Poles in the war against Bolshevik Russia in 1920.

Newman caught the ferry to the Kurische Nehrung, the long spit that stretches between a lagoon and the Baltic. Fascinated by the great shifting dunes that had been steadied a hundred years ago by the planting of sand-growing grasses and pine trees, he saw coastal birds and an elk at peace and bathed in the mildly salty sea water. Ninety per cent of the people in Klaipėda were German. In the fertile hinterland, east of the port, among prosperous farms, it was different; here the owners of land and large properties were mostly German but the poorer inhabitants were generally Lithuanians – in fact the numbers of the two peoples were almost equal. Newman pedalled on, crossing the Queen Luise Bridge over the Nieman into East Prussia, to find the town of Tilsit festooned with swastikas and echoing to Heil Hitlers in the anxious patriotism of a borderland.

In March 1939, Hitler obliged the Memel Germans. In the last of his pre-war triumphs, after a journey by sea, during which he was painfully sick, the Führer passed through hysterical crowds to the town square where he spoke from the balcony of the little opera house. The rest of Europe did nothing to stop this. It was undeniable that the seizing by the Lithuanians of Memel from the League of Nations in 1923 had been as illegal as this coup some sixteen years later.

*

Today the bus from Riga to Klaipėda takes four hours, through forested country opening sometimes into long meadows or brightly painted, wooden villages where cows and geese graze by the road and you expect to see a horse and cart. At the journey's end, as the bus goes through the suburbs, past Klaipėda's Soviet-era housing which reaches far above old Memel's German red-brick buildings, rain starts to come in from the Baltic.

In a Klaipėda restaurant, waitresses wear what look like monks' habits, divided revealingly at the side. They glide through a dim room whose vaulted ceiling is probably meant to evoke medieval feasting but also has the air of a dungeon, appropriate to these turbulent borderlands. Crosses have been stitched on to the waitresses' gowns and other banners and cushions, perhaps showing Christianity's triumph; Lithuania was the last pagan country in Europe until it joined the Polish–Lithuanian Commonwealth in the fifteenth century. The restaurant's fluting, soft background music, like the slow seeping of a soapy fluid, could represent this late drift towards western Europe. Yet there are no churches in Klaipėda's old town – for the Soviets destroyed them all. As if to recall this past vulnerability, the European Union flag flies near the restaurant, to show that Lithuania is no longer alone.

Klaipėda is empty at night. Among the cobbled streets, pizza parlours, bars and old red-brick and half-timbered German houses and concrete apartment blocks, you sense the struggle to make Prussian Memel and Soviet Klaipėda into a Lithuanian place. But the past is oppressive and the ghosts remain. The little neo-classical opera house – where Wagner conducted and Hitler spoke – forms one side of the old town square behind a fountain with a sugary statue of the teenage girl who captivated Simon Dach, the seventeenth-century German poet from Memel. Across the bridge, you can look up at the heavily curving limbs of the caryatids sculpted on the art nouveau façades of Liepų Street's smart late-nineteenth-century houses; as in Sovetsk (Tilsit), the German years are above as well as below, on the balconies and the pillars and in the soil.

Back across the river, black-clothed, armed guards stand outside a casino: an undoubtedly contemporary scene; but away from the tourist parts, a foreign land surfaces again in the memorial to Lithuanians deported to Soviet Siberia – their names engraved on metal plates below the figure of a sitting man curled up in pain. This is now a softer place. People should come to see Klaipėda's version of the *Cutty Sark*, a tall, three-masted sailing ship berthed on the River Danė. While looking at the statue in one of the squares of Martynas Mažvydas, they should reach back to 1547 – when Mažvydas's Protestant catechism, the first book to be published in the Lithuanian language, was printed in Prussian Königsberg.

It was twentieth-century nationalism that brought symbolic demolition and new building, then demolition again, to Memel or Klaipėda. In 1807, the Prussian King Frederick William III and the beautiful Queen Luise fled to Memel, their most eastern city, to escape Napoleon. In 1907, a century later, a huge bombastic monument called Borussia (the Latin word for Prussia), flanked by bronze busts of Prussian military and political leaders, was put up near where the tragic King and Queen had stayed. In 1923, in the new Lithuanian Memel, Borussia was removed; then restored in 1939, after Hitler's coup, then carried away by the new Soviet rulers in 1945 to be replaced by a statue of Lenin that was taken down when Lithuania became independent.

Outside one of the hotels – an Intourist-era tower block glowering behind flickering advertisements for its gym and solarium – the Klaipėda Motorcycle Club is assembling: a few middle-aged men and women in black leathers. Some have dark glasses although it is raining and they walk slowly, perhaps to avoid collision in the gloom; all carry big helmets, a contemporary version of medieval armour. The bikes are lined up by the kerb where the riders mount them, seeming like temporary warriors in the tranquil evening of what has been a violent place but is now disturbed only by these harmless engines. Bystanders watch the power; the noise stops; in the silence, a rider turns to ask what happens next. 'We must go' is the answer – and some thirty bikes leave in a ragged group, aiming for symmetry but soon pushed into a disjointed line by other traffic. A few yards on, they stop at a set of lights, subdued and controlled, the odd rev a little sad perhaps but reassuringly useless in the dusk.

Klaipėda is one of the gateways to the Curonian Spit – the Kurische Nehrung in German or Kuršių Nerija in Lithuanian. You take a ferry across the lagoon, then a bus down the road at the centre of the peninsula, with pine woods on either side of you – and, through them, the sea to the north and the lagoon to the south. In late autumn the place is quite empty and the buses few and far between; in summer, visitors crowd onto a much more regular service, getting off to make for the long Baltic beaches to sunbathe or swim although there are varying opinions about the cleanliness. Certainly the green lagoon, topped in places by

Thomas Mann outside the Nidden house with four of his children.

patches of brownish foam, is thickly polluted and it's hard to see how anyone could want, or survive, even a quick dip. It's a place for escape into a dramatic landscape that's at its most extreme when you get further south, to the dunes near the village of Nida (whose German name was Nidden) that stretch across the Russian border. This is 'the Prussian Sahara' that entranced the German novelist Thomas Mann.

Mann gave a talk to the Munich Rotary Club on 1 December 1931, entitled 'My Summer House'. Visual appreciation came late to him – perhaps the reason, he said, that he could not adequately describe the primitive and fascinating appearance of the Spit that the early nineteenth-century traveller Alexander von Humboldt placed on a par with Italy as somewhere one had to visit. So besotted was Mann on his first visit that he decided to build a house there – an idea that he and his wife Katia had previously had at Aswan in Egypt and St Moritz in Switzerland. He mentioned the southern aspect – the deep blue of the lagoon, the white sails of the fishing boats, the brilliant sky, the pine trees (as in the Mediterranean) and even (on a clear day) a sense of the North African coast. The lagoon could be rough and dangerous, especially in autumn; there was the occasional very fierce storm in summer. The locals were not beautiful, Mann said, but they were kind and rare – Slav in looks, with blue eyes and strong cheek bones, toughened by a hard life, speaking Russian-accented German, Lithuanian and what was called Kurische which, to Mann, had overtones of Sanskrit. The dunes were much greater than the dunes at Sylt: elemental not so much at their summits (although the views seem limitless) as in the ravines where there was only sand and the sky.

Mann stressed the sense of being on the edge. Elk roamed, he said, through the woods where the birch and conifers evoked Turgenev's Russia, giving you the feeling that the two parts of Europe – west and east – were colliding. But perhaps the sea was the climax to what seemed to be an endless beach: the northern sea as Mann, who grew up beside the Baltic at Lübeck, had never known it, with towering waves and a west wind, strong and primitive, and a dangerous pulling tide. At the end of the talk, Mann urged his audience to come to Nidden, a place, he admitted, of drama rather than of ingratiating beauty. Nowhere else in Europe did he feel so far from Europe.

Thomas Mann's new house at Nidden was another sign of the village's position as a gathering point for artists; it was said that you could hear the talk of the Berlin literary cafés among the dunes and *Buddenbrooks* was on sale in the little shops. But Mann was hardly seen in the town, toiling each morning over his massive novel *Joseph and his Brothers* or on speeches to be given at The Hague and Geneva. He was not only a writer who had won the Nobel Prize in 1929 but a political and social critic whose conservative and nationalistic *Reflections of an Unpolitical Man* had come out during the First World War. He had thought that Hindenburg should be made the wartime chancellor of Germany.

Thomas Mann's extraordinary discovery of what, until 1919, had been entirely a part of his native Germany began in 1929, two years before his Munich talk. It's hard now, perhaps, to appreciate the stature (in his own eyes as well as those of the world) of the German novelist or how interested people were in what he had to say. In August 1929, he descended from the mountain of his eminence to give an interview to the *Königsberger Allgemeine Zeitung*. He spoke of East Prussia, of the landscape and of the sea, of the woods and the ravines, how they seemed to fulfil 'an old yearning': how he wished to build a calm refuge there, for contemplation and proximity to nature. This most eastern part of Germany had thrilled him, perhaps partly through its bridge to the Slav world; here he thought of Tolstoy, in the 'unbelievable landscape of dunes', 'splendid woods', wild sea and idyllic beaches. Asked who he thought should win the Nobel Prize for Literature in 1930, Mann answered André Gide (a homosexual) or Sigmund Freud (a Jew), indicating how distant he was from National Socialism. The Fatherland would soon change irrevocably for him, not least here, in the east.

His first trip to East Prussia had arisen out of an invitation to speak to the Königsberg Goethe Society; he and his wife Katia also brought their youngest children for a four-week holiday by the sea. The Lithuanian Consul advised them to visit the village of Nidden, which since the war had been on the Lithuanian side of the frontier that divided the Curonian Spit. At Nidden, they stayed at Hermann Blode's inn, a haunt of writers and artists like Freud, Lorenz, the architect Erich Mendelsohn, the painter Lovis Corinth. Mann, intrigued, already knew of the Spit through the writings of Alexander von Humboldt. He had read Agnes Miegel's mesmeric poem, 'Die Frau von Nidden', about mythical death and burial.

Shown a site on a nearby hill by Blode's successor, Ernst Mollenhauer, Mann decided to build a house there – a crazy idea, he admitted, for it might attract people to the village; the novelist knew the power of his name. Mollenhauer advised on an architect from Memel who thought the house should be simple, like a fisherman's dwelling. Back in Königsberg, Mann fantasized about an elk's antlers on its walls and thought that the clear, still lagoon resembled the sea at Portofino in his beloved Italy. Germany seemed far away, even though the gliding school at Rossitten was quite near. Sometimes the silent gliders drifted above them and occasionally on walks you could hear the shouts from a militaristic sporting camp over the border. On the Nidden beaches, some of the boys wore swastikas on their shirts and jerseys.

The cost of the eleven-room house, with a veranda and a terrace, was met out of the Nobel Prize money and his books' increased sales. On 16 July 1930, the Manns saw it for the first time, arriving by boat from Cranz on a wet, cold day that displayed the northern European rather than the North African side of the 'Prussian Sahara'. In photographs, Thomas Mann wears a heavy, belted mackintosh and a floppy trilby-type hat, apparently irritated and tired in one close-up, then more genial as he looks straight at the camera from the front seat of the carriage that has come to meet them. The journey had shown Nidden's remoteness from the two centres of Mann's life – Munich, where he lived, and Berlin, Germany's intellectual heart.

A large crowd welcomed the Nobel Prize-winner who, with his family, was driven to the Blode inn and then to the new house. A ninety-nine-year lease of the land had been arranged. The structure was a wooden building painted dark ochre with bright 'Nidden blue' shutters and pediments, the roof partly thatched and the gables crossed above in a heathen motif of carved horses' heads; it had a comfortable panelled interior. Mann's writing room was above the front door, with a view over the lagoon. From his room he could see a pine tree, some reeds and then the water: sometimes still and blue, like southern sea, or grey and rippling, or a greasy brown streaked with yellow light. On the terrace outside, he felt he was on a ship. Mann could be undisturbed here, protected from his panic about people, from the local interest in what became known as 'Uncle Tom's Cabin'.

Thomas Mann had a façade of dignity and stiffness and was seen by many, not least his own children, as cold. He hid what he called 'the hounds in the basement' – his self-doubt, anxiety and homosexual feelings – within an iron structure of work and the bourgeois life into which he had been born as the child of a rich Baltic business family. The Mann household in Munich reflected not only prosperity, with servants, a chauffeur (who became a spy for the Nazis) and secretaries, but also his own agonizing solitude. Sharing Nietzsche's romantic idea that artists were sick, too weak for the world, Mann saw them as condemned to suffering and isolation. He had, however, tried to break this, to him, enforced detachment with a strong patriotic belief in what he thought of as uniquely German possibilities and ideals – different to British commercialism and the cool rational French: a version of Agnes Miegel's 'terrible and great way'. The defeat of 1918 – and the chaos that followed – led to a crumbling in his mind of this conservative nationalism. In East Prussia, at his new holiday home, he saw yet more evidence that life for him in his beloved Fatherland was ending.

Mornings at Nidden were set aside for work. Mann told a Königsberg journalist that he wrote slowly, only one and a half narrow sides of quarto paper each morning: that his huge books – *Buddenbrooks* or *The Magic Mountain* – came from small ideas that grew uncontrollably, bursting out of the format of shorter masterpieces like *Tonio Kröger* and *Death in Venice*. So his routine became as firm as it had been in Munich: a short walk in the pine woods before breakfast: then several hours of work at his desk before joining his family on the beach.

Mann was no great swimmer. A photograph shows him with arms rigidly crossed, a cigarette drooping from grimly clenched lips, eyes joylessly fixed on the distance, his body swathed in a thick plaid robe that covered every possible part of it, his hair oiled and only slightly ruffled. After a plunge in the often rough Baltic, he would sit in a heavy beach chair, the only one of its kind that summer in Nidden, sometimes in more formal coastal wear

Mann on the beach.

of a blue blazer with brass buttons, pale grey trousers, white shoes and peaked yachting cap. Mann liked to admire the almost naked bodies of the good-looking young men, imagining how the absurd Nazis would cherish their physique. On his knee was a pad, because work always came with him. After lunch he took a short nap before the dictation of letters to his wife; in his children's early memories, the sound of the typewriter offered a soothing breach in the silence of the house. In the evenings Mann ('the magician') read aloud to his family or played cards with them, listened to music or to shocking radio reports about the economic crisis – or read his latest work to Katia.

In August 1930, the Manns astounded the village with a firework display to celebrate the eightieth birthday of Katia's father, a Jewish professor of mathematics from Munich; it was her Jewish origins that made the general political scene more threatening for them. In September, Thomas Mann went by horse-drawn coach across the border to the village of Rossitten, to vote in the German elections: the only time he left Nidden that summer. In October, in Berlin, he made a speech, urging the abandonment of extremism; in Rossitten, the Nazi candidate won. Mann still thought that the good sense of most Germans would prevail but he began to regret his wartime praise of the cold, contemptuous Frederick the Great, his use of Kant's 'practical reason' to condemn scepticism during the mass emotion of 1914 and his sympathy with Fichte's glorification of Germany's long, lonely struggle.

The Manns came back to Nidden for the summer of 1931. Again the daily routine was as rigid as Kant's; again the novelist was moved, as painters like Lovis Corinth were, by the brilliant Nidden blue – of the sky, of the painted shutters and pediments, of the clear lagoon. He walked over the great dunes, survivors of some epic upheaval, with their reminder of buried villages and the camps where French prisoners had died in the Baltic winter during the Franco-Prussian War. Increasingly Mann felt that he had to fight the new barbarism; now the blond Adonises on the beach seemed like potential murderers. In Königsberg, on their return journey west – to the Reich, as East Prussians called the other side of the Polish Corridor – in the late summer of 1931, the Manns saw the barbarity of Nazi gangs, emphasized the next year when, after the elections of 31 July 1932, SA thugs murdered socialists and communists in the city. From Nidden, Mann wrote about this for a Berlin newspaper, which – fearing Nazi revenge – toned down his words about 'the mish-mash of hysteria and mouldering romanticism' and 'half-idiotic slavering of so-called Führers'.

The Nazis loathed Thomas Mann. Goebbels ranted against this 'mongrel of Indian, negro and Moorish blood' in reference to the novelist's Brazilian mother. In Nidden, Mann met threatening men on his woodland walks, the house was stoned and a partly burned copy of *Buddenbrooks* left outside it. In September 1932, he left, having kept engagements to read at Königsberg and at Elbing, further west in East Prussia. It was the start of his departure from Germany, hastened by the growing anti-Semitism after Hitler came to power in January 1933. That summer, while in Zurich, Mann decided to stay in exile, leaving for the United States in 1938 and becoming an American citizen in 1944.

In California, he burned his Nidden diaries and notebooks. The last volume of the immense novel *Joseph and his Brothers* was published in 1943. In exile, the patriot of the First World War thought that no remorse or contrition could be enough 'after the vicious presumption, the wild frenzy of superiority and chimeras of power this people has shown in its intoxication' while acknowledging that 'it has been a singular fate, half painful, half honourable, to have been born a German'. Mann did not return to Germany until 1949, still thinking that the apparently remorseless national self-pity was to be feared. He moved to Zurich, dying there in 1955.

Göring used the novelist's Nidden house on hunting trips, building a bigger residence nearby; Speer visited it while he was on the Spit. Mollenhauer of Blode's inn tried to protect the pictures Mann had left behind but the Red Army destroyed them, leaving the house a skeleton. In 1967, some writers persuaded the communist Lithuanian authorities that Mann had been anti-fascist; the house was partly restored and, eight years later, on Thomas Mann's hundredth birthday, celebrations there involved the East German Culture Minister and an exhibition that included films of the novelist's post-war visits to eastern communist Germany – which he preferred to the Federal Republic where (he said) too many ex-Nazis remained unpunished. A commemorative tablet had words in Lithuanian and Russian, none in German. In 1995 and 1996, in a free Lithuania, a complete restoration took place. Now there are concerts and readings in summer and links to the other Mann monuments – his old home 'Buddenbrookhaus' in Lübeck (where his love of the Baltic began) and the archive in Zurich.

Thomas Mann had been brave. After 1931, when many were preparing to make the best of Hitler, he went on defending Weimar democracy; the Nazis took away his citizenship and burned his books. What Mann thought of, with some shame, as his bourgeois discretion and constraint, his detached and elegant irony – that coldness of the endlessly observing artist – were overcome by his courage. At the end of *The Magic Mountain*, Hans Castorp sees the disintegration in the trenches of pre-1914 Europe, of the world of *Death in Venice*. Within twenty years of the book's publication, a new, worse barbarism seemed to be symbolized at Nidden by Göring and Speer, and then by the Red Army. Miraculously, Mann's house, the symbol of a great writer's discovery of a wild land and momentary peace, has survived.

*

As in Mann's day, there are horses on the Spit – some thin ones in a clearing in the woods by Smiltynė, the village near where the ferry gets in from Klaipėda. I ask in the tourist office how many people come each year and the girl thinks about ten thousand. Of course it's quite deserted now, she says, near the end of autumn but the summer crowds are big – some foreigners (almost all Germans) but many Lithuanians. Did I know that the weather was going to get better? As she speaks, the sun appears. I must keep an eye out for the elk, she says. She has seen several during the last week. Nida (or the German Nidden) is the place to stay, she says. There are some nice hotels in Nida – and I ought to try to catch the Lithuanian folk-dancing in Juodkrantė, another village. They will be dancing on the green in front of the tourist office – a nice gathering with people in national costume, stalls and food: local specialities, very local. I must be certain to take in the pretty wooden fishermen's houses. Fishing is still the main activity on the Spit – fishing and tourism.

Today the people coming off the ferry are mostly local, some with fishing rods to try their luck in the lagoon, other families bound for the sea-life museum in the old Prussian red-brick fortress that guards the entrance from the lagoon to the Baltic. It's a long wait for the bus to Nida, which is parked by the ferry terminal with the doors shut and the driver inside smoking and reading a newspaper, then sleeping for at least an hour.

After we move off down the Spit, the gap widens gradually between the mainland and the peninsula so that when the bus reaches Nida's painted wooden houses, the Lithuanian and Russian coastline is dim through a haze. Nida is still a holiday place of sailing boats, cafés and restaurants and bright wooden signs and weather vanes, with only a few Soviet-era additions.

Wartime destruction reduced the Hermann Blode inn to one wing from which guests wander across to the crisply kept thatched Mann house that is just across from it. Blode, who died in 1934, is buried in the graveyard of the nineteenth-century German red-brick church – and Nida became the German Nidden again in 1939 when Memel returned to the Reich. Erich Koch, East Prussia's Gauleiter, wanted to set up a Strength Through Joy youth camp there. Albert Speer, who had stayed at the inn, helped to stop this and the place was quiet until the summer of 1944 when the Red Army guns broke the tranquillity and the inn filled up with refugees. As the Soviets took Preila (the German Preil), the next village, Ernst Mollenhauer, Blode's successor, fled. His collection of pictures – by artists like Lovis Corinth and Max Pechstein who had often paid Blode with their work– was fed into the flames of a makeshift Russian sauna.

The Spit is still an enchanting memory. Michael Wieck, the retired leader of the Stuttgart Chamber Orchestra, remembers his childhood trips there from pre-war Königsberg – when they left the North Station in a wheezing steam train that went across the Samland to Cranz before boarding the ferry to Nidden. No cars or vehicles were allowed on the Spit – only horse-drawn carts. The clear lagoon rippled on one side, the Baltic heaved on the other and between the two were the dunes and pine woods, the wind sometimes flinging the sand with such force that it stung your bare legs. The Wiecks (both Michael's parents were musicians) and other artists stayed at Blode's guest house. But even in this remote place, Nazi songs began to be sung, the fishermen became infected and the local tinker was called a 'Yid'. This threatened his family for Michael is a Jew.

19: 'My dear Jews'

Michael Wieck is Jewish through his mother. Her father had been a Prussian master builder – an engineer and a cultured man who had entertained a distant cousin, Clara Schumann, and the composer Brahms and the violinist Joachim at his house in Berlin. The Wiecks, however, were gentiles. Some of Michael's relations died in Auschwitz, others were fellow-travellers of the Third Reich.

Königsberg's German Jewish community goes back to 1540, to two doctors; by 1716 there were thirty-eight Jewish families, the population rising to some five thousand in 1880 (or approximately 1.8 per cent of Königsberg's citizens). Immigrants from the Russian persecutions continued to come until 1914 even though border controls were tightened. The so-called Ostjuden were looked down on, not least by western Jews, and the influx led to tension. To be a Jew in East Prussia was, like everywhere in Europe, to be set apart.

Before 1914, however, Jews could feel cherished in Königsberg. At the inauguration of the city's new synagogue in 1896, the Mayor, alongside the Governor of East Prussia, Count Wilhelm von Bismarck (son of the Iron Chancellor), and several Christian priests, spoke of his gratitude for 'the active and devoted work of our Israelite fellow citizens, not only for the communal administration but in general for every public concern'. He praised the Jewish love of the family, appreciation of arts and sciences, obedience to the laws and to the Emperor; 'only blind fanatics', the Mayor declared, would want to persecute such a people. There was anti-Semitism in clubs or in student fraternity houses; as in the rest of Germany, Jews were excluded from senior posts in universities, the civil service and the army, and in East Prussia's rural hinterland the atmosphere was less friendly. But pre-1914 Königsberg has been described as being 'as close to real pluralism as a Prussian city could get'.

Felix Grayeff was born in 1906 into a Königsberg Jewish family who were involved in the highly profitable corn trade. Grayeff remembered a thriving place, with a symphony orchestra, an opera house, three theatres and three daily papers, the most celebrated of which, the liberal *Hartungsche Zeitung*, had been read by Kant – and approximately three thousand Jews: some first- or second-generation immigrants from Lithuania or Ukraine (and from Russian persecution) and others whose families had been there for centuries. One of Grayeff's earliest memories is from 1910, of the thunderous welcome for the Emperor and Empress in Königsberg. The boy was told that the Russian Tsar couldn't move freely among his subjects without danger of assassination whereas William was so loved he did not even need special police protection.

Felix Grayeff's education was thoroughly German or Prussian, modernized so that French was the first foreign language instead of Latin. Emphasis was on rigorous classroom work, with what Grayeff saw later as nationalist indoctrination, similar to the idea of imperial mission that filled the heads of his young British contemporaries. Civilization (brilliant repartee, paradox, elegance, constant questioning, disrespect for authority) was what Germany's rivals, Britain and France (particularly France), prized, the teachers said; the German way, however, was *Kultur*, an experience of – and a reverence for – what was profound in thought, feeling and knowledge. A way of reaching this was through the great past – and through the geniuses who had formed it: Kant in philosophy, Goethe in poetry. The German language was, the teachers declared, the most expressive and the most serious, the most flexible of all modern languages, second only to ancient Greek. A thorough gathering of facts must, it was thought, bring impartiality and good judgement to any decision.

Kant was at the heart of this – his categorical imperative and his emphasis on duty. Always speak the truth; never let a lie defile you: this was drilled into the young Felix. Out of it all came bluntness, perhaps discourtesy; but the line from Goethe's Faust should be the guide; 'In German one lies when one is polite.' History, however, was different – and here Felix Grayeff's teachers showed a contradiction. The cunning of Bismarck and of Frederick the Great should be admired, even if it differed from the high standards expected in private life. Foreign statesmen like Richelieu and the Elder Pitt were praised for their ruthless use of power.

The Grayeffs were intensely patriotic. A year or two before the First World War, his uncle asked the young Felix to imagine that the Emperor was nearby and that someone tried to kill him. Would the boy throw himself in front of the assassin? The uncle said that he would not hesitate to sacrifice his own life for the Emperor. On the first day of the war, this man, although thirty-five, volunteered for the army, to be killed a year later. During the campaigns in the east, the German army encouraged Jewish Russians to desert from the Tsar's forces, distributing leaflets in Yiddish, beginning 'My dear Jews', that offered release from Russian anti-Semitism.

After 1918, Königsberg's Jews lived in the shadow of economic crisis and political threat. Michael Wieck believes that only four Jews forced to wear the Star of David in Königsberg survived the Second World War, the persecution and the Russian occupation, for Jews were murdered not only under Hitler but by Stalin's Soviet regime as well. Two men seem to him to be particularly bleak representatives of that dark past, partly because they went on to great acclaim, one as a scientist, the other as a soldier who was thought to have saved German lives: Konrad Lorenz (the Nobel prize-winning zoologist) and Otto Lasch (the German commander of Königsberg at the end of the Second World War). He cannot forget some words written by Konrad Lorenz in 1940, when he was a professor at Königsberg, that seem to justify fascist policies of selection and extermination and 'an even more

The Königsberg synagogue.

rigorous eradication of those who are ethically inferior than is the case at present' – the need to rely 'on the healthy sentiments of the best among us and entrust them with the selection that determines whether our race thrives or decays . . .'

Wieck's mother was the violist and his gentile father was the second violin in the Königsberg String Quartet. They had separate apartments to allow each to practise without hearing the other. Simple love came from his mother's sister, his spinster aunt Fanny, who was not intelligent but warm and soft and beautifully gentle. As a thirteen-year-old boy, Michael went with Fanny and his Jewish school teacher to the train station where his aunt sat exhausted with her suitcase – red faced, eyes imploring. The teacher told him to leave before the train took them off, perhaps to Chełmno, where the first mass gassing took place, or to Auschwitz.

Made to feel inferior at school as a Jew, he had to stand in

the back row when Hitler was welcomed hysterically to Königsberg; after this he transferred to the easier atmosphere of a
Jewish private school. Throughout Michael Wieck's childhood,
however, the city seemed a fairytale place, with its castle, narrow
streets, great squares, heavy fortified gates, high medieval walls
and the dark warehouses along the River Pregel, even if intima-
tions of horror began when the Nazi Jungvolk (the junior section
of the Hitler Youth) waited for the Jewish children. It was a tense
but exciting time. War threatened, yet young love and intense
emotionalism could be overwhelming, as during a performance
of Carl Maria von Weber's *Der Freischütz* at the Königsberg
opera: in the Wolf's Glen scene a terror of death came over him
followed by an extraordinary acceptance of it. It was, Wieck
thinks, a hint, he thinks of what the end might be – the horror,
and then peace.

In October 1938, after Kristallnacht, and the burning of the
synagogues, Michael Wieck's teacher described how the Torah
scrolls had been ripped apart and thrown out into the street. His
sister Miriam was sent by his parents through a Quaker programme to a boarding school in Edinburgh; he didn't see her for
ten years. Michael's father had an invitation from relations to go
to Sweden which would have saved them all – but Herr Wieck
couldn't face the dislocating change. With war – and the string of
early victories – all Germany seemed drunk, rocketed into some
sublime place. The Jews were pressed further down, their food
rations cut and only certain shops remained open to them; they
could not go out after eight o'clock in the evening and were
drafted into dangerous jobs. Wieck's mother, the viola player, was
made to work ten hours a day in a chemical factory.

The invasion of Russia began in June 1941. In July, Michael
Wieck had his bar mitzvah, in the small Orthodox synagogue that
had been badly damaged but not, unlike the larger liberal one,
destroyed. The Wiecks were visited by Michael's half-brother,
Peter, his father's son by a first marriage – a Wehrmacht officer
who was cool to his Jewish step-mother and to Michael. Peter

described how German troops poured petrol over Russians and set fire to them during the campaign on the eastern front. After the decree that Jews had to wear the Star of David, the boy endured insults in the street, only sometimes receiving surreptitious gifts of food and once a kind word from two Russian women prisoners who were working as slaves. The Wiecks put as many edible scraps into their dustbins as they could, to help the scavenging Russians forced to work as refuse collectors.

On the Sabbath, the Rabbi remembered those who had recently left on the transports. No one spoke of what happened in the camps, although there were suicides among some of those ordered to the assembly points. Michael Wieck and his school friends were even used as messengers by the Gestapo to summon the victims.

It was a time of isolation, of solitary bicycle trips (when he still wore the partly covered star) – to swim in the city ponds or to suburban woodland or riding along the Pregel, past the warehouses and the slow-moving barges. Michael had a job at a cabinet-makers' where the work was arduous, much of it making coffins; the owner warned against some ardent Nazis in the workforce and passed over extra food, but another apprentice was a bully. Aged fourteen, Michael was moved, possibly as a result of a denunciation, to the chemical factory where his mother worked – a foul place thick with the steam from cauldrons of boiling liquid for soap, detergents and cleaning fluids. Gradually those wearing the Star of David became fewer and fewer as the deportations gathered pace, among them the girl that Michael Wieck thought of as his sweetheart – and the campaign against the Jews intensified at the first signs of imminent defeat. Michael questioned the idea of a merciful God that could permit such wretchedness.

On 26 August 1944, after he and Klaus, the child of their neighbour who was in the Hitler Youth, had said goodnight in Morse code by blinking lamps, the huge RAF raids began; three nights later the inferno reached its limit when napalm set the city on fire and no one could go into the charred centre. For Wieck, the August raids were the real end of Königsberg as a German place, their terrifying power destroying the old dream that the city could outlive any of its citizens as it had survived the previous Russian and Tatar invasions, the Thirty Years War and Napoleon. In the clear-up, the remaining Jews and the Russian and French prisoners were given some of the hardest work. Soon a new sound began – that of distant artillery. One of the few surviving Jews told Michael that he should rejoice for the Russians would be their liberators.

Some Germans became friendly as the Red Army came closer: to Gumbinnen, then to Insterburg. Refugees began to arrive in Königsberg with stories of Soviet atrocities; Russian planes flew low over the city, firing at whatever moved; people dreaded clear skies, that blue East Prussian brightness later to be remembered with such nostalgia. In January 1945 the suburb of Metgethen fell, only five and a half miles from where the Wiecks lived – then was recaptured a month later. Lasch, the commandant, and Goebbels's propaganda machine made the most of what was found in the retaken Metgethen – the destruction, the hanged and raped German women.

The siege had now lasted almost four months but General Lasch, under Hitler's orders, held out. Michael Wieck saw the bodies of young soldiers hanging from gallows by the North Station, with signs round their necks, 'I had to die because I am a coward.' Rumours began that all the Jews were to be taken away before the Red Army entered the city. On 8 April the street fighting moved away – and from the cellar next to where his family was sheltering, the boy went out and saw a solitary Russian soldier on a bicycle: then a tank with its Russian crew eating breakfast on the open part at the back. At noon, the first Russian entered the cellar. He asked if there were any German soldiers and took Michael's father's watch, proudly showing what a collection of 'uri' he had. More soldiers arrived; one lost his temper when Michael's mother whistled what had become the family theme tune, from the second movement of the Beethoven quartet opus 59/1 – and fired off his pistol.

The conquerors' hatred became clear. They weren't interested in the Jewish Star as a sign of opposition to Hitler – and they searched relentlessly for women. Michael Wieck thinks that if Lasch had surrendered before the last great assault had begun, many civilian deaths and much destruction could have been prevented – because they were still at war, the Russians felt no restraint. The wild drinking, the looting and the rapes began, the legends of the Tatar invasion and the Thirty Years War becoming a horrific reality. The city filled up with the mangled, swollen bodies of the dead – troops and civilians – which came to seem enviable, at peace, beside the desperate living.

The Wiecks and most of the surviving Germans were marched out towards the Samland. There were signs of humanity among some of the Russian guards and a Red Army lieutenant who spoke German with a Yiddish accent raised their hopes – but, when told that the Wiecks were Jews, he said that they must have worked for the Nazis because Hitler had killed all the Jews. One evening the Russians sang folk songs – a beautiful contrast to their apparent heartlessness – and Michael's mother played on a violin some salon pieces by Kreisler and Wieniawski. The guards' expressions relaxed before the captives were marched back through devastation to the city where already some of the signs were in Cyrillic script. The transformation into Kaliningrad had started.

There followed months of shifting corpses and scavenging for food: naked women defiled and raped; old men and children shot stabbed or strangled; suicides either hanged or poisoned; people burned in the huge fires. Communication began with the Russians – just a few basic words – and the horrors of what had happened on the eastern front emerged, comprehensible enough. Dysentery and typhus took hold in the icy late winter. Separated from his parents, Michael Wieck found himself in the former Rothenstein barracks among prisoners bloody and bruised from interrogation.

At night he dreamed of the Curonian Spit, of the glorious air; how good it would be to live there as a fisherman. A Russian soldier beat him with a rifle. Just a teaspoon of sugar brought ecstasy – also the forsythia blooming again, as if God had spoken to him, as he had once spoken to Moses. Back in Königsberg, where he was marched from the barracks, the Russians seemed to soften. One brought him more food – and Michael Wieck wondered if they saw their prisoners as humans at last although the rapes went on.

His mother, with phenomenal energy, went out every day to beg or barter for food and to haul water from a mile and a half away. He saw the Russian signs of joy when the German surrender came – the firing of guns in the air, and the Red Army triumphant in the rubble. More and more the task of the breadwinner fell on Michael as his mother became exhausted and his father, helpless with age and despair, took refuge in studying Chinese. You worked for the Russians or you starved.

Michael found a job repairing a wharf – a twelve-hour day with an hour off at midday. He received food and also stole from houses that were still standing – goods that his mother bartered for more food. He worked as a carpenter in a bakery yet it was harder to steal food from there and a new threat emerged – gangs of orphaned Russian and Polish children who had followed the Red Army and were now feral, sometimes carrying knives, even pistols.

The new Kaliningrad had music issuing from loudspeakers at street corners – often deep, nostalgic military choruses. As if to reflect this, the Red Army soldiers could be sentimental, kind to children, but mostly the Germans still experienced hatred from those they had been taught to despise. Michael and his parents were evicted six times to make way for Russians who had been settled in the city. He was taken on as a carpenter in a new plant for smoked fish, scavenging the occasional fish head or tail or leftovers before being transferred to a construction site. His mother became adept at the black market. At last his father worked, as a security guard, and Michael's new job as a bricklayer's assistant brought in more money.

Danger was always lurking; his mother was robbed and knocked down by a Russian, he himself was attacked by another Russian with an axe – and lice, typhus, reputed cannibalism and malaria from the lakes and the ponds that were polluted by decaying corpses and rubbish threatened the survivors. In December 1945 Michael ran a high fever and was near to death, treated by German doctors while his mother brought food. Rations became even more meagre; the Soviets seemed to want to rid East Prussia of Germans through starvation – just as the Nazis had wanted to rid it of Jews.

The Wiecks both aged terribly and suffered from lice; urine was the only disinfectant easily available. Michael found work as an electrician, even though he knew little about it. He stole lamps or sockets and sold them again on the black market, before being caught and released by an unexpectedly kind police officer. Relying on the theft of wood and the use of the electrics at work and at home to keep warm during the icy winter of 1946/7, he heard Soviet propaganda booming out from the loudspeakers set up on the streets, interspersed with beautiful music – Bach played by David Oistrakh. The family's salvation was a brick oven, built by Michael, in which they baked a sweet biscuit beloved by the Russians. The boy exchanged bread and roubles for a violin owned by a German prisoner of war. He started to play at dances in the newly founded German Club.

He even began to like the Russians as the hatred faded a little. One with connections in the Riga Conservatory offered him a scholarship to study there if he became a Soviet citizen, but he refused to leave his increasingly helpless parents or to choose absorption into the life of a totalitarian state. In the New Year, he went with a small band to play at the coastal resort of Rauschen in temperatures of 30 degrees below to drunken Soviet soldiers. At last, near the end of the winter of 1948, the trains started to leave for Germany.

20: 'Do you see in the east
the brightening dawn?'

Michael Wieck was partly why I went to Yantarny, a little seaside place about twenty miles from Kaliningrad. There was also Johannes Jänicke, the Protestant clergyman who was at Palmnicken (Yantarny's German name) from 1935; and Martin Bergau, once in the Hitler Youth, who's written about what he saw in the village in January 1945.

Johannes Jänicke thought later that the scene at Palmnicken rectory in the winter of 1945 might have come from Dostoevsky – the hammering at the door, a foreign soldier glimpsed through the window, the dark anticipation, the shout of 'Frau komm . . . Woman come!' Dostoevsky – his idea that demons lurk within us all – is easily linked with darkness and Stalin reached for him when excusing the brutality of his troops to the Yugoslav communist Milovan Djilas.

In Palmnicken rectory, that winter day took another Dostoevskian turn, from darkness to redemption. Unlike many from Palmnicken, the Jänickes had stayed on in 1945 rather than escape west and Johannes shouted that the woman would not come. The Red Army soldier broke the glass, cutting himself and bleeding 'like a pig'. The clergyman, who had a first-aid kit, opened the door and bound up the man's wound. The soldier, suddenly pathetic and very young, said, 'Du gut! Frau nicht gut! Russe schlecht!' to which the clergyman answered, no, all were good – and the Russian left, watched by the two Jänickes.

Martin Bergau's father was the Palmnicken sexton. As a boy,

Martin went to church, ignoring Johannes Jänicke's pronouncements from the pulpit against National Socialism because he'd found adventure in the Hitler Youth, and it's Martin – an old sharp-eyed man, rather small – that Michael Wieck takes me to hear in Stuttgart. The meeting is in the Haus der Heimat where the lost German east is kept alive through exhibitions, meetings and concerts. Some of those who cherish that mythical place won't like what Martin has to say. There's redemption, however, not only in his honesty but in the questions afterwards and the evening ends with Michael Wieck playing two melancholy violin pieces by Bloch. Johannes Jänicke might be surprised to see how far his land has come since that battering on his door in 1945.

The two men from Palmnicken – Martin Bergau and Johannes Jänicke – parted after the war. Jänicke chose communist East Germany, becoming Bishop of Saxony before his death in 1979; Bergau came to Ulm, in the west, to find work as an engineer. But what happened in the village in 1945 took them both into a Dostoevskian night.

Born in 1900, Johannes Jänicke grew up in Berlin where his father was a missionary in the city's poorest parts, among the unemployed, many of whom had come there from East Prussia. One of three brothers – who knew hunger during the First World War – he found comfort and inspiration, like Peter Kollwitz, wandering through the country outside the capital – a protest, Jänicke thought later, against bourgeois life. On these trips, he felt an intense romanticism deepened by his love of music – a feeling that, combined with nostalgia, was, he felt, brilliantly manipulated by the Nazis. Johannes became a minister in the evangelical church. He married a girl from a family of prosperous lawyers – conservative and Prussian – who were not enthusiastic about their daughter's love for a poor, radical priest. His first duties were in an industrial parish south-west of the city; from 1929 until 1935 he was in Halle, another industrial town where the poverty turned him further towards socialism.

The Nazis horrified the Jänickes. Listening to the Day of Potsdam, Hitler's display of patriotic and military nostalgia, on the radio in March 1933, Johannes's wife wept as the choir sang a beautiful chorale that seemed suddenly a hideous insult perpetrated by this new, godless regime. He became the representative of the new anti-Nazi Confessional Church in Halle and was held for three days in the cells with other clergymen – over seven hundred were pulled in on 16 March 1935. He wasn't treated badly, his congregation stood by him and he refused to sign a concocted statement.

The Jänickes left Halle for Palmnicken in East Prussia at Whitsun of that year, into what must have looked like exile. Bible study had become a fundamental of the Confessional Church – a way, it was thought, of fighting Hitler's assault on religion – and Johannes's small Bible-study group came to the station to see him off, singing as the train pulled out 'Bless and protect us through your grace.' Jänicke later denied that he'd been forced to go. But it seemed odd that a young Berliner should leave voluntarily for East Prussia which was, as he himself said, somewhere on the way to Russia, practically 'in China', out of 'the storm of life'. He claimed, however, that he had wanted to leave Halle because his wife needed a sea climate for her asthma. The years in Palmnicken were, he concluded later, the best and the most demanding, if the most terrifying, of his life.

In 1935 there were about 2,400 inhabitants of this small coastal village, clustered round a main street near the Baltic. The total number of people in Jänicke's parish, which included several other small settlements, was 4,000. Fishing was still a local occupation, but the main employer was the large amber works where they mined 'the gold of Samland'. Until recently this had had a Jewish owner, Moritz Becker, who had also built the evangelical church with the aim of improving the morals of his workforce. When the Jänickes arrived the company was part of the conglomerate Preussag, Becker having been forced out.

Attendance was good at the small ugly church, built in

1893, the numbers swelled in summer by holidaymakers staying in rented rooms or hotels – sometimes visitors who, the East Prussians said, had come from 'the Reich', thereby stressing their own isolation since the Polish Corridor had been established. Johannes Jänicke considered his parishioners generally conservative and quite dour, although they sang hymns loudly. Many of the locals didn't come to church although they weren't against it. His only serious opponents were some Nazi functionaries – not many in this remote place, although their tentacles reached out from Königsberg.

In old age, moved by memories of the place's wild beauty and his terrible last ordeal, Johannes Jänicke tried not to romanticize Palmnicken. The new order, the religion of Hitlerism, *had* been strong there. Guests at the rectory had included Dietrich Bonhoeffer and others from the new Confessional Church – and the Church authorities hadn't liked this. In Königsberg, Jänicke was interviewed by a disapproving National Socialist colleague who later, overwhelmed by shame, killed himself.

The church is still there in what was Palmnicken and is now Yantarny (the name means amber in Russian) – a small stone building with a pale-purple corrugated-iron roof and a short steeple that has a cross on top. Now the priest is Russian Orthodox instead of German Protestant but beside the main door are two tablets that record the laying of its foundation stone under Emperor William I in 1887 and its completion in 1892, during the reign of the last Emperor, William II. Another notice says that in 1991 the place was consecrated an Orthodox church by the Bishop of Kaliningrad and Smolensk – which makes the interior, with its bright colours and icons, very different to the austere Lutheranism of Johannes Jänicke's day. Nearby are Prussian redbrick buildings, one of which might have been the rectory – now used in summer as a children's camp.

Not far along the street is a museum, partly a display of carved amber, partly also 'heritage' items from the German time, some in bad condition. The place is supervised by a custodian who, while saying she knows absolutely nothing at all about the collection, radiates anger and contempt. After looking round, it's easy to excuse her irritation; there's really nothing extraordinary about an accordion splayed open on a cracked wooden chair, some scattered old bricks and stones, a sewing machine with foot controls (emblem of lost East Prussian domesticity), many plates, often chipped or painted (some with romantic views of German cities), a rusty iron bed frame and a case of china drinking steins, one bearing the initials of the Hofbräuhaus in Munich. The apparent regional obsession with empty bottles is evident – lots and lots of them, some thicker than others, slightly green in colour or cloudy with age, arranged in rows, sharply glinting in the sporadic sunlight as if about to explode. Here, at least, are remnants of some good times.

Outside, scaffolding and boards are up on several of the buildings, one of which is a café advertising German beer. Some have the toy-town air of much of the new Kaliningrad construction – close to pastiche, like the new development of offices, shops and apartments by the river in the city: neither Soviet nor Russian nor German, yet slightly reminiscent of a Königsberg revival – but as if in caricature. Stalls sell amber or trinkets and further along, at what could be a symbolic crossroads, you meet Yantarny's two pasts: the Soviet war memorial – its most obvious feature a statue of a bare-headed young soldier, a cloak cascading off his shoulders, one outsize arm raised as if to halt an entire invasion – and, to its left, lined by a double avenue of lime trees, a street of white German villas that leads to the sea.

They are improving the infrastructure of the beach, putting in a complex of thatched beach umbrellas and what will be a café or a bar. Back from the sand and the rough Baltic, a heavy concrete sea wall looks as if it keeps all Samland in check. Below the wall, in a partly cleared space, is a small pile of stones, held together with thick patches of mortar, against which rests a wreath of plastic flowers and manufactured foliage beside an engraved black marble stone. On the stone, engraved in Hebrew and in Russian, is an inscription declaring that seven thousand Jews were driven into the sea and killed here in January 1945.

During his talk in the Stuttgart Haus der Heimat, Martin Bergau recalls the old Palmnicken, a seaside paradise engulfed by the new spirit. At the time of Kristallnacht, the shop run by the Jewish Friedlander sisters was attacked and the young Bergau was taught in school that the Jews were parasites. He saw the removal of Jewish names from the town's war memorial and the swastika flag hung outside his house even though his parents scoffed at the Nazis. There was in Palmnicken a renewed pride in being on the edge, in the north-east bastion of the Reich, combined with a deep sense of the consequent danger.

Bergau couldn't wait to join the Hitler Youth. He revelled in the summer camps and the mock battles, in travelling with other schoolchildren by horse-drawn wagon to join the joyful crowds at Polennen that greeted Hitler. Martin's father had fought in the last war, at Tannenberg, at Verdun and in the Carpathians. The sexton thought that defeat had come because of the arrival of the American hordes and the betrayal of the troops by politicians – but people in Palmnicken were worried in 1939 when soldiers and artillery came to the town. By 1940, however, after the great battles in the west, East Prussia was calm, enveloped by a trust in the victorious Führer. When Poland was overrun and France fell, the Palmnicken mine band played 'Do you see in the east the brightening dawn?' – and Polish prisoners came to help on the farms. This time no enemy seemed to threaten from across the eastern frontier.

In that summer of German triumph, Martin Bergau went to a Hitler Youth Camp on the Kurische Nehrung. After days of orienteering and hiking, they marched through the woods on the mainland, on the historic route from Berlin to Petersburg – three hundred young men in the light rain singing 'Today Germany belongs to us, tomorrow the whole world', watched by two apparently oblivious elk. Christmas 1940 was even colder than usual but full of hope as the little swastika flags on a map in the village school advanced across western Europe. In February 1941, more soldiers, weapons and armour started to arrive at Palmnicken station, the locals fascinated to see these legendary victors. At Easter, Martin Bergau went with friends from the Hitler Youth on a bicycle trip to Memel, the town that Hitler had retaken in 1939, and they slept on straw in farmsteads, finding it all a glorious adventure.

Later Johannes Jänicke felt overwhelmed by guilt that he hadn't done more to fight the Nazis. In August 1939, he left Palmnicken to be chaplain to an artillery unit in Poland where he saw lines of terrified Jews who had been brutally expelled. This inhumanity, he told a comrade, will engulf us all and in East Prussia we won't fight it enough because of traditional Prussian obedience. It seemed a dreadful intimation of man's helplessness before hypnotic ideology and technological power. In 1940 Jänicke returned to Palmnicken, not leaving it again until 1943, when the village was still quiet, to work on a hospital train near Tapiau. Another clergyman was sent to the village by the diocese, ostensibly to bring order to the parish – but the parish didn't accept him so he left. There were no further attempts at change.

The invasion of Russia was, Martin Bergau remembers, a surprise, even in Palmnicken where the build-up of forces had started months before. The early successes reminded older people of Tannenberg; 'It is all going to plan,' some of them said. That winter of 1941, however, the flags on the map stayed still, after the astonishing advances of the summer and autumn, and the wounded who ended up in hospitals in Königsberg told bleak stories which reached the outlying villages. The sense of crisis was added to by appeals to civilians for warm clothes for the front. Soldiers stationed nearby said that their comrades in the east reported worsening conditions.

For the thirteen-year-old Martin there was a new thrill – that of gliding, again fostered by the Hitler Youth, and that summer, in May, he'd gone for instruction in Masuria. Back in Palmnicken, he played football on the restored town pitch, ran along the small paths to the beach to bathe naked and back through the woods and took a late-summer job helping with the harvest. Finally the horror of war came when one of the Polish prisoners refused to work; the overseer called the police, the Pole panicked and ran and a policeman shot him dead. What shocked Bergau was that it was all so close; the policeman was a neighbour. He wondered if there might be a protest from the church – but none came.

Technically minded, and obsessed with gliding, he hoped to do war service attached to the navy – but in January 1944 he was sent to Königsberg to serve in an anti-aircraft battery and then to Tilsit for pilot training. To glide over the eastern frontier district, to see Memel and the crystal lakes, the Baltic and the Reich's borders gave him a surge of patriotism, a sense of his land's beauty. On his return to Palmnicken, a friend told him that the war was lost and he should join a committee for free Germany. To Martin Bergau, this was treachery and nonsense. Still only fifteen, he returned to the battery in the summer of 1944, to have a terrifying affirmation of what his friend had said. The warning signs began: the invasion of Normandy in June, rumours about the assassination attempt on Hitler in July and, in August, the most obvious – the giant British raids on Königsberg. The burned corpses of women and children among the ruins enraged him.

He was given the choice of staying with the battery or of going on a flying course further west, at Allenstein. Opting for the flying course, he wept when saying goodbye to his comrades, yet was soon happily gliding over Masuria, as if above an endless tranquillity and beauty. Even here, still supposedly miles from the front, the wounded were flooding into the town's military hospital. From the air, Martin Bergau could see the refugees, at first only single wagons interrupting his idyll, then much longer lines.

*

In August 1940, the widow of Elard von Oldenburg-Januschau died in the Insterburg hospital, looked after by her grandson Hans von Lehndorff, who was an assistant surgeon there. Her husband had gone three years before; the death of the old man, in 1937, had been marked by an obituary in the London *Times,* hailing Januschau as the best sort of Junker: an unashamed nationalist, 'reckless and hard-hitting in political controversy, but endowed with a fund of mother wit, a genial personality, and a warm heart which gained him the respect and often the affection of his opponents'. Ten of his eighteen grandchildren were at the burial in the park at Januschau.

By the end of 1941, several members of Hans von Lehndorff's family had been killed in the war. His notebook told his true feelings, at this time of German victories: 'It is not for our Germany that our brothers have fallen.' Lehndorff felt that even if the war was won, there would be nothing left of the world into which he had been born. His Christian faith had grown, as if to challenge godless National Socialism. He joined a Bible-study group of forty or fifty people: mostly older men, led by a teacher who had been ordained in the anti-Nazi Confessional Church. Lehndorff felt as if he was one of the persecuted early Christians in the catacombs of Rome.

Johannes Jänicke was also part of the group which met sometimes in the church, sometimes in private houses. Koch, the Nazi Gauleiter, let the teacher continue with his ministry; Lehndorff recalled later – when the Gauleiter was put on trial – how grateful the congregation had once been to him. During the winter of 1943, as the war began to turn against the Germans on the eastern front, they discussed the Ten Commandments, analysing, with the help of soldiers on leave, the fifth, 'Thou shalt not kill.' This dilemma – of active resistance or acquiescence – confronted Lehndorff when he was ordered to take up military duties. His superior at the hospital declared him to be indispensable so he stayed. Lehndorff saw the hand of God in this escape either from death at the front or from disobedience that carried the death sentence.

In June 1944, he went to Berlin during his leave – partly to visit a friend who was in the Moabit prison under sentence of death for having conspired against the regime. Shocked by the bomb-damaged city, Lehndorff saw other friends who hinted that something would happen soon. He called at the Goebbels family house, to try to intercede for his friend; the family was not there and Lehndorff met two guests – an old woman and her beautiful granddaughter, both calm supporters of the regime, apparently still with complete faith in the Führer.

Back in East Prussia, Lehndorff saw signs of disintegration amid the old brutality. In Königsberg, his mother had been arrested, ostensibly because of her friendship with a clergyman who was politically 'unreliable'. At Insterburg, his cousin Heinrich, the owner of Steinort, came to see him to say that the denouement of the plot against Hitler was imminent. Hans felt that there was a Christian basis to the assassination but believed that with the violence should come forgiveness. Soon the Bible class had grown to more than a hundred, many of them young men about to go to the front; and when a local leader of the Hitler Youth asked if he and his colleagues could join, Lehndorff wept.

On 25 and 26 July, Russian bombers attacked Insterburg, damaging the church although it remained standing. At Rastenburg, on 20 July, another bomb had exploded, the culmination of what Lehndorff had heard in Berlin. His involvement, small beside his cousin Heinrich's who paid for it with his life, troubled his strengthening belief in non-violence. He felt that the failure of the conspirators had been for the best. Untested by what would have been demanded of them if they had succeeded, their ideals had stayed pure, martyrdom transforming them into a beautiful myth.

21: 'The highest pleasure on earth'

In Berlin, on 30 January 1933, Alexander Dohna saw the triumphalist National Socialist demonstrations. In March, before the ceremony at the Garrison Church in Potsdam, he wrote to President Paul von Hindenburg, who had appointed Hitler chancellor, to wish him luck. Over a year later, Dohna attended Hindenburg's funeral at Tannenberg – a magnificent spectacle, he thought, with the First World War generals in their imperial uniforms and the evident pride of the old soldiers.

There was much, he claimed later, that he and his friends disapproved of in the Nazis: their boycott of Jewish businesses, the propaganda against the churches. But many joined the party, to influence it or from real enthusiasm – and stability of a kind returned to their lives. Income from farming and timber sales went up; by 1936 the Dohna finances were in much better shape. Alexander Dohna could afford to restore the lead figures on Schlobitten's façade. He could install central heating in the east wing and buy electric cookers for the kitchen.

In the summer of 1933, Hitler came to East Prussia, with Reinhard Heydrich and Himmler and Alexander Dohna's old school friend Karl Wolff, then Himmler's adjutant. Invited to meet them at a cousin's house, Dohna thought Hitler crude; as a vegetarian and teetotaller, the new Chancellor seemed ill-suited to the table habits of the East Prussian gentry. Heydrich flew into a rage during the after-dinner game of bridge. Himmler was quieter, more reflective, it seemed to Dohna, as the Nazi poked around at an archaeological site in the woods at Prökelwitz, on the Dohna estates, searching for evidence of early Aryan (or German) life before the arrival of the Orders.

It was Göring, the war hero and the son of a former governor of German South-West Africa, with whom the old families felt most at ease partly because he was the nearest to them in his tastes and manner. Dohna invited Göring to shoot, giving his guest the same rooms as the Emperor William II had used thirty years before. A list of approved food and drink was sent beforehand by the Prime Minister of Prussia's adjutant – beer, Sekt, different types of Schnapps, asparagus, mushrooms, morels, light meats, new potatoes, fruit and crab or crayfish and caviar. Dohna met Göring at Marienburg airport, to find the fat Marshal in Luftwaffe uniform, wearing the Pour le Mérite and accompanied by six huge suitcases. The joviality was switched on, manifesting itself particularly to the children of the house. Göring was as unlike Hitler in his tastes and appetites as it was possible to be; he ate like a horse, wore clothes of blinding brightness and listened to all the complaints about the regime, instructing his adjutant to make notes. Dohna showed him the Schlobitten art collection in the hope of proving that such places were worthy of special treatment. Göring shot three roebuck before flying back to Berlin.

Koch, the Gauleiter, perhaps seeing the Junkers as a challenge to his authority, not only ignored their special pleading but inspired criticism of them in the East Prussian press. In December 1934, Dohna went to Berlin, to speak to Göring about this; the Prime Minister of Prussia was distant, but in the autumn of 1935 Koch was suspended. The Gauleiter, however, appealed to Hitler and was reinstated.

To the Junkers, the suspension of Koch showed that Göring was almost a gentleman; his love of hunting was another reason that they felt drawn to him. They knew, after all, about his extraordinary efforts to improve his vast domain that lay south from Königsberg, near the new Polish border. This was Rominten, the former hunting preserve of the Prussian kings – some sixty thousand acres of woodland and open country that had been cherished by the Hohenzollerns since the Grand Duke Albrecht in the sixteenth century.

*

For William II, the last German Emperor, Rominten was an isolated feudal world, far from the new industrial Germany and socialist Berlin. The village, now the Russian Krasnolesye in the Kaliningrad district, has an air of dishevelment, with old grey German houses along a main street that includes the school where the schoolmaster worked for a year without pay. But you can go freely into the forest now, quite different to the German time when much of it was out-of-bounds to the public.

Ponds and a larger lake, its banks overgrown, and glades and meadows interrupt the dense, dark trees, bringing light to the journey before the old life appears – the last Emperor's bridge over the Rominte stream, long stripped of the carved stone stags that once decorated its balustrades. Memorials, obvious or symbolic, are scattered through the forest: a tall stone dedicated to Prince Friedrich Carl von Preussen, who hunted there before his death in 1884; another marking the hundredth stag shot at Rominten by the last Emperor; and one with the name Gertrud Frevert, and the year of her death, 1940, when she shot herself.

Gertrud's husband, Walter Frevert, a forester and huntsman, wrote about the lost Rominten. He had known the forest in all its guises: its solitude, its appeal to sportsmen and its power – almost tangible in the white winter nights, the sudden spring and the stifling summers when the place rang with birdsong. Frevert had seen all the types of wild creature that lived in it. He had killed, or helped to kill, many of them: the deer, the elk, the boar, the wolves, the lynx and the hares.

Near the end of one of his books, there's a photograph of Walter Frevert returning from stalking, dressed in his hunting kit of high leather boots, breeches and a dark-green Loden coat.

Binoculars are strung round his neck, he wears a brimmed hat with a frothy plume and a bright silver badge and has a rifle slung over one shoulder. A roundish face looks at the camera, not smiling but clearly at ease in his kingdom, a place that, he believed, should impose a certain morality through its magnificence. Walter Frevert's *Rominten – The East Prussian Hunting Paradise* – a bestseller on its publication in 1957 and still in print – is not only an account of the forest but a portrait of the man for whom Frevert worked: Hermann Göring.

A romantic, moved not only by nature but by ceremony and by music, Walter Frevert was born in 1897, the son of a dentist who owned property near Hamm in North-Rhine-Westphalia. A keen hunter from early on, encouraged by his father, the boy declared what he wanted to be: 'A hunter, a soldier, a father' – all of which he fulfilled in a life of success and tragedy. During the First World War, he joined the army, a volunteer aged only seventeen (like Peter Kollwitz), and, after winning the Iron Cross on the western front, found the final surrender unbearable; his country and his Emperor, the ideals of his life, for which he would gladly have died, had been destroyed. How could he and his comrades return to humdrum civilian lives when they could never forget the dead of Cambrai or of Verdun? It would be better to go on fighting in some distant place, to win, he said, the laurels of victory or to die.

Frevert did fight with the Freikorps against the Poles in Upper Silesia. But he also stuck to his studies and qualified as a forester. He had been briefly in East Prussia during the war, finding it 'an Eldorado', but it was not until 1936, after years working in the woods at Battenberg, that he was called east, to a post at Nassawen on the north-east edge of the Rominten Heath. After the Emperor's abdication, the Prussian state had the use of the huge property although it was still owned by the exiled monarch; the Social Democratic Chief Minister of Prussia went there with his guests and other ministers. When the Nazis came to power in

An East Prussian forest.

1933, the new Prussian Prime Minister was Hermann Göring –
a passionate hunter, who made himself chief huntsman of the
Reich (Reichsjägermeister) and took Rominten seriously in hand,
buying it from the Emperor for the new Germany.

The forest's hunting lodge – with its chapel nearby dedicated
to St Hubert – had been built by William II in the style of the
Norwegian wooden houses that he had seen during his northern
summer cruises. By the time Frevert arrived, more buildings had
already been finished or were under construction, planned by the
forest's new master – a complex of high-ceilinged halls, sitting
rooms with cavernous stone fireplaces, areas for the storage of
guns and equipment, further guest accommodation and long
sheds for the treatment of what had been killed. Inside, the walls
were covered with hunting trophies – deer antlers, skins, pelts,
snarling wild boar with curving white tusks, glum-looking elk.

Walter Frevert was nervous when he first met Göring. Introduced by a colleague as the best dog-handler in Germany, Frevert felt Göring's impatience as the Reichsjägermeister declared that he never needed dogs to find a wounded deer as he always shot the animal dead. An officer in the party advised that one should be completely straight in any dealings with this formidable man. Soon Frevert, as careful in the handling of people as he was with his beloved bloodhounds, had the Reichsjägermeister's trust.

Göring introduced new game laws, many of which still stand in Germany today, setting up a national Deutsche Jägerschaft, of which Walter Frevert was a member, to enforce them. Rare animals and birds were protected, the cruellest traps were forbidden and taxes were levied on hunters to pay for work on the forests and nature reserves. The new officials had to be National Socialists – Frevert joined the party in May 1933 – and Göring's role as a conservationist went alongside the delight he took in the hunt and the kill. When Poland was divided between Germany and the Soviet Union in the Ribbentrop–Molotov Pact in 1939, he pushed successfully for the enormous virgin forests of Białystok in the east of the country to be treated as German, ostensibly for the value of their timber. This brought into Göring's hands a unique natural world, undisturbed since pre-history – and the origin of the devilish pact entered into by Walter Frevert.

At Rominten, in an eastern dawn that came an hour earlier than in Berlin, Frevert, Göring and his guests pursued stags whose nicknames reflected their size and splendour: the Lieutenant, the Matador, the Chandelier, the Robber Chief, the Prince, the Recruit, Theoderich, the Schoolmaster. The greatest were reserved for the Reichsjägermeister or for his more important visitors: the British Ambassador, Sir Nevile Henderson; King Boris of Bulgaria; Miklós Horthy, Regent of Hungary; Count József Lipski, the Polish ambassador: Franz von Papen (one of Hitler's predecessors as Chancellor), Konstantin von Neurath (the former Foreign Minister) or Himmler. Göring liked to stalk his prey rather than wait for it on a high seat – a raised platform some twenty or thirty feet high – in a forest glade. He would set out before dawn, walking often with Frevert, perhaps for seven hours, to find a stag. Like the last Emperor, the Reichsjägermeister's longest visit each year was in late September and October: the time of the rut, when the woodland echoed to the beasts' roars. In January, he shot wild boar, in piercing cold with the creak of footsteps through deep snow breaking the forest's silence.

Nevile Henderson gives a vignette of Göring's Rominten during October 1937, a year after Hitler had occupied the Rhineland, openly breaking the Treaty of Versailles. Having arrived early in the morning, the British ambassador was sent out that afternoon to a high seat to wait for the large stag ('a fourteen pointer') that had been seen close by. Göring liked to tell the British that they had become soft, that the Germans were the only ones actively fighting Bolshevism – and this had been reinforced at Rominten with some sharp banter about Henderson's fellow countrymen being quite good with shot guns but useless rifle shots. Anxious to prove his host wrong, the Ambassador, seeing the stag some way off, left the high seat and approached the animal on his hands and knees before shooting it through the heart. Göring said afterwards how good it was to see a diplomat crawl.

The Englishman never forgot the display of the day's kill in a ritual that seemed to reach back to some elemental myth. In the evening, after the guests and their host had eaten, the dead stags were laid out on the grass in front of the lodge, the scene lit by a huge, crackling bonfire of pine branches. Behind the beasts stood the foresters in their dark-green uniforms, outlined against the flames and the light of a full moon. Walter Frevert announced the number of stags that had been shot and who had killed them, Göring answered with some words of thanks; and the foresters sounded a fanfare – the *Halali* to mark the death of the stag – through long thin horns that were looped across their chests. As the notes faded, Henderson – 'the so cool Englishman' much moved at last – seized Frevert's hand and said, 'That was the most beautiful day's hunting of my life.'

At Rominten, Frevert claimed, the new, brutal Germany vanished, to be replaced by the forest and its natural world. Göring's ideas on conservation, the massively increased spending on the place, his decision to cut the number of deer killed each year to let the stock grow – these were what delighted Frevert. The forester claimed to have been repelled by Göring's sycophants but always, after 1945, spoke admiringly of him, declaring that only those who foresaw what National Socialism would become were entitled to throw stones. The revival of order and confidence, the surge in prosperity and the power handed to Frevert at Rominten made him reluctant to seek out distant truths. So his devotion to this man, whom he called 'cunning like a fox', grew.

The grand guests came: foreigners like Henderson, the Hungarian Prime Minister Gömbös, the Finnish Marshal Mannerheim, the German Field Marshal von Brauchitsch and the crude greedy Foreign Minister von Ribbentrop. The Gauleiter of East Prussia, Eric Koch, was despised, one senior officer calling Koch, who had once worked on the railways, 'the ticketpuncher'. What moved Frevert most were the wartime fighter pilots who had won the Knight's Cross and been rewarded by Göring with a stag at Rominten. Months or weeks after they had left, he often heard of their deaths in battle.

There was order at Rominten. When a foreign ambassador or statesman coincided with a German guest, the stag shot by the foreigner should be the better of the two. The best heads were kept for Göring; everyone quaked at the prospect of the furious, pumpkin-like face of the Reichsjägermeister if, by mistake, a guest shot a reserved animal. Like many of the Nazis, he was fascinated by the planned breeding of species, particularly if there was a link to an ancient Germany. He encouraged the revival of the extinct aurochs, a massive beast that it was thought could transform cattle farming, letting these loose at Rominten, and he had Trakehner horses pull some of the wagons. Dogs he disliked, although Frevert, characteristically, persuaded the Reichsjägermeister to love one of his bloodhounds; and he was terrified of snakes. He ordered three hundred hedgehogs to be let loose on another of his properties, having heard that these were lethal to adders.

Göring thought most creatures tame beside his real favourite – 'there are animals,' he told Frevert, 'and there are lions.' In 1937 the foresters at Rominten waited to greet their master with a fanfare on their horns. As the cavalcade approached, an officer ran ahead, shouting, 'Don't blow – the lion will go mad.' Special trains were put at these creatures' disposal although in the hunting lodge they were confined to the bathroom when not wanted by the Reichsjägermeister.

For Oberforstmeister (Senior Forest Master) Frevert, these were rich years. To him, a life without style or plenty – 'luxury' – was worthless and he lived at Nassawen 'like a little Prince', with four horses, a smallholding with cattle and pigs and vegetables, a car, two drivers, a housekeeper and two maids. Each year, at the start of the Rominten winter, after Göring's longest annual visit, Frevert was allowed to invite some friends of his own. After the stalking came the ritualized relaxation: the drinking from a beaker of horn and silver, engraved with the words, 'To hunt is the highest pleasure on earth.'

One event Walter Frevert considered the high point of this time, perhaps of his life: the great Berlin international hunting exhibition in November 1937. It was not only the pride that he felt in the heads and trophies from Rominten, a spectacular part of the display, but the sense also that the improved forest and his achievements there had become part of Germany's rise from humiliation. In Berlin, Frevert could also indulge his love of music, nurtured during visits to the festivals at Bayreuth and Salzburg. Later he recalled particularly a special performance at the Berlin Staatsoper of Weber's *Der Freischütz* attended by leaders and huntsmen from all over the world. Göring posed with some of the guests – the Reichsjägermeister in his uniform with the foresters and gamekeepers also formally dressed, clustered around him.

Frevert claimed later never to have been an enthusiastic supporter of National Socialism, despite photographs of him in SA uniform in Battenberg before he came to Rominten. He admired Göring's revival of hunting and forest management and, like so many of his 'hardened generation', welcomed the new national feeling brought by the Third Reich: 'our proud Great German empire . . . from the Lithuanian frontier to Luxembourg, from Schleswig to Karawanken.' But when Prague was seized by Hitler in March 1939, it became obvious that such coups must end in conflict. Frevert wrote later about the second great war of his lifetime, publicly condemning its 'criminal nonsense'. He thought that the German conquests showed the folly of trying to impose a different culture on people. But he qualified this with the claim that the victor's influence could do good if his culture was of a higher kind than that of the defeated. No doubt Frevert was thinking here of the vast, undeveloped lands of eastern Europe.

Called back to the army in 1939, Walter Frevert fought in Poland and won a bar to his Iron Cross. In December, he was allowed to take up his civilian duties again at Nassawen and during this winter his personal life changed. Frevert had married Gertrud Habich, the daughter of a pastor, but they had no children – an affront to Frevert's belief that a man's life without children was a life condemned to 'purposelessness' although the couple adopted a boy. The forest community respected Walter and liked Gertrud but disliked Frevert's occasional public humiliations of his wife, such as when he made Gertrud bend over a dead stag while he whacked her playfully with a bunch of twigs. The others who were present laughed at first but quickly became embarrassed, and then shocked. The whacking, apparently, quite spoilt 'the good atmosphere'.

In the winter of 1939–40, Frevert combined the management of his own part of the forest with that of a colleague, Dr Paul Barckhausen, who had been killed in Poland. Barckhausen left a twenty-four-year-old widow, Heinke, and, in spite of the extraordinarily deep snow and temperatures of 35 below freezing,

Göring inspecting the kill at Rominten.
Walter Frevert is behind him, to the left.

Frevert made the journey often to the Barckhausen house. Soon there were rumours, reinforced in September 1940 when, under the tutelage of Walter Frevert, Heinke shot a fine stag.

It was also during the first winter of the war, and for the next year, until he was called back to military duties in April 1941, that Frevert's subservience to Göring led him into the most controversial period of his life. In 1937 Göring had taken Frevert to Białowies, the immense virgin forest in eastern Poland. Invited there to shoot boar, wolf and lynx by Count Lipski, the Polish Ambassador to Germany, and Count Potocki, the owner of vast estates, Göring had never forgotten the place and, in 1940, the Reichsjägermeister wanted to enlarge the Rominten reserve south-east into the newly conquered Poland. This involved making a new hunting and forestry district, 'the Eagle's Field', which, under the thorough new regime, entailed deporting Poles from some ten villages, at very short notice, to distant makeshift settlements. This intimate experience of National Socialist methods shocked Frevert. But he obeyed.

The making of 'the Eagle's Field' coincided with personal tragedy. On 13 October, Frevert celebrated his birthday away from Nassawen, with Heinke Barckhausen. The next day he heard that Frau Frevert – Gertrud – had shot herself with one of his rifles, leaving a note to say that she wanted to leave the way free for Frau Barckhausen. Everyone in the small forest community knew the background to the tragedy but 'an iron silence' descended.

Gertrud Frevert was buried in the small cemetery near the forestry office at Nassawen, where the grave still stands. Those at the funeral said that Frevert's expression seemed to be set in stone; others reported a complete breakdown in private. For the next three months he was away from Nassawen, on duties in Poland or other parts of East Prussia. In his memoirs Walter Frevert makes no mention of this tragedy. Soon afterwards he married Heinke, who wrote that they were 'a very happy pair'. Frevert's wish for children came true; they had five sons and he became stepfather to Heinke's two daughters from her previous marriage – and the husband of a woman some twenty years younger than he was. Heinke survived him by thirty-five years.

On 1 May 1941, Frevert went back to the front, to serve as a battery commander in the huge army that invaded the Soviet Union a month later. His part in the invasion lasted only a week before another call from Göring – this time ordering him back to work on turning the virgin forest of Białowies, in what had been eastern Poland, into a new national park, for hunting and for the preservation of its unique world.

In Białowies, Frevert found a romance even greater than at Rominten. A thousand years seemed a brief span in this prehistoric place that showed man's smallness in nature beside the bison, deer, bears, wolves and other wild creatures which, nonetheless, he had the power to destroy. As in 1940, with the Eagle's Field, the evacuation of the local people was brutal; Frevert and his troops surrounded the villages and gave the inhabitants half an hour to pack up before they were taken east on wagons for resettlement and the abandoned wooden buildings burned. It's been estimated that, during the last part of July 1941, some thirty-five villages were destroyed; Jewish men were shot by death squads and others deported. Wehrmacht commanders warned that such tactics would encourage support for partisans who were fighting the Germans. When this happened, Frevert's group took the hardest measures; up to the summer of 1942, some nine hundred people were killed. It was Frevert who decided which suspects should hang and which should live, if there were any living suspects left.

Walter Frevert remarked often upon his luck. In the autumn of 1941, during this devastation, he was taken ill and went to Berlin for an operation, not recovering until the end of March 1942. His defence of what happened was that he was obeying Göring's orders. Later he wrote that the virgin forest resembled man in the hardness and brutality of its struggle to survive. This brutality threatened him when the war turned. By October 1944, he was back in Rominten – with his own world (and the new schemes for Białowies) on the edge of collapse.

22: *Storm in January*

In July 1933, Karl Wolff arranged for Alexander Dohna to join the SS. Himmler thought of him as a friend and in 1934 sent a Christmas gift to Schlobitten of a ceramic 'un-Christian' Yule candlestick. With this intimacy came the need to accept certain limits; Dohna was told not to write to the former Emperor, then in exile in Holland, and to abandon his former half-Jewish lawyer. His children joined the Nazi youth organizations and it was while bicycling to a party meeting to celebrate the Führer's birthday in April 1939 that the eldest boy, Richard, fell, hit his head and died.

The Hitler Youth wanted to cover the coffin with a swastika flag but Dohna insisted on a bright blue standard embellished with a silver cross and the family's arms. This tragedy, and the feudal manner of the boy's funeral, showed that the estates were, as Dohna wrote later, like a family. After their marriage, 'Titi' (still in her twenties) was approached by a woman who had worked at Schlobitten for forty years who said, 'You are like our mother and we are your children.' The atmosphere, Dohna says, was apolitical; of the five hundred estate workers, few belonged to a political party.

But you couldn't isolate yourself, even behind such strong walls. It was undeniable that times were improving for farming, with the National Socialist policy of self-sufficiency and the decision to build up the eastern territories. Those days when Dohna had waited with a gun to fight off communist gangs seemed distant in the new ordered land. In 1935, with rearmament under way, former soldiers were given the chance of doing four- to five-week refresher courses. Alexander Dohna attended these each

year at Allenstein until April 1939. By 1937 he was a lieutenant
in the reserve, another way, he thought, of influencing Koch.
When in 1935 and 1936 fortifications went up near the eastern
frontiers, against Poland, the Soviet Union, Lithuania and Latvia,
Dohna felt sure that war must come again.

His war was mostly on the eastern fronts – in Poland, in the
Balkans and in the Soviet Union. Reading his diary years later,
Dohna tried to reach behind the flat description of the welcome
that the invading troops received in the Ukraine and his pride in
liberating the land from Bolshevism; there were no entries about
the German atrocities. On 14 October 1941, his unit reached the
harbour of Mariopol and he saw the Black Sea. In November at
Rostov, when the German army was pushed back and winter
began, Dohna realized that they could not win the war. In 1942,
a bear was seen near Schlobitten, for the first time since 1732; a
year later, another bear was sighted, as if invaders from the east
were testing his defences

By September 1942, Dohna was outside Stalingrad. Even in
bitter December weather, German morale was high but the terrible fighting, and the gradual encirclement of General Paulus's
army, changed everything. On 16 January 1943, Dohna was told
to take a message to army headquarters, on one of the last flights
out; his general had, he thought, selected him to be saved because
of his young children. After months of near-starvation, his health
collapsed and he was given a year's home leave. Not until January 1944 was he ordered to join a corps in Italy, in Abetone, in
the foothills of the Apennines. In March there was an atrocity
near Abetone; American prisoners were shot. When Dohna
protested, he was sent home, regarded as reliable only for local
duties in East Prussia.

In the summer of 1943, he had told his wife and some of the
estate staff that they would soon have to leave Schlobitten.
'Titi' went with their children, first to her old home in Saxony,
then further west to relations in Thuringia. Dohna knew of
the plot against Hitler – but not the timing. In July, the day after

the bomb, he was at Rastenburg station, having an appointment with his cousin who had been one of the conspirators. No one was there to meet him so he went back. The purpose may have been, he thought, to offer him a role in the new post-Hitler East Prussia; after all, many of the conspirators had, like Dohna, once supported the regime. As news came of the arrests and the suicides – many of the victims were his friends or relations – it became clear that if Dohna had been found on his way to see the cousin he too would have been under suspicion. The Gestapo called on him to ask if he was hiding Heinrich von Lehndorff.

Schlobitten was now clearly at risk. In the late autumn of 1944, Dohna included more of his workers in the plans for flight, even though Hitler had forbidden civilians to leave. He plotted the escape on old army maps – through Pomerania, by Stettin across the Oder, then a route north that avoided Berlin. He spoke to Marion Dönhoff, who was managing the nearby estate of Quittainen; neither of them bought fertilizer that year, saving the money for the forthcoming trek. Dohna had sent some furniture, silver, works of art and archives out to a cousin in Hesse, to his brother-in-law in Saxony and to the relations in Thuringia. But in the subsequent chaos only a small proportion survived of an inventory of the contents of Schlobitten that he had made after Stalingrad: almost none of the fifty-five thousand volumes from the library and a mere fraction of the family papers. By the end of 1944, Alexander Dohna was living in three rooms of the icy palace.

*

In the middle of October 1944 all men between the ages of sixteen and sixty were ordered to join the Volkssturm, the German equivalent of the British Home Guard. Martin Bergau, back in Palmnicken after his pilot training, and his father reported for duty – to the local commander: Hans Feyerabend, a former First World War officer who ran the estates owned by the amber mine.

The distribution of arms to the new conscripts showed the

extent of previous German conquests: French and Italian carbines, a Norwegian rifle. The terror came closer when Eydtkuhnen on the edge of East Prussia, earlier taken by the Russians, was recaptured and those who had been trapped there told horrific stories of the Red Army's brutality. The proximity of danger, however, could be exciting for some; Martin Bergau felt a thrill when, while bicycling eastwards towards the enemy with a friend, they found a chicken and killed and cooked it. They saw loose horses and abandoned Russian weapons, then blood in the beds of a deserted house.

The reality of invasion seemed to come in January 1945 when the boy was woken at three in the morning by shots from outside in the snow. Bergau's first thought was of the Russians – so, disobeying his father's call to stay inside, he ran out with a pistol and spotted some shadowy shapes. A woman seemed to be trying to come in through the garden gate; seeing the boy, she turned to go out again, there were more shots and she fell. Still sleepy, Bergau could make out a long column of raggedly dressed figures, stumbling forward to the sound of more gunfire, some breaking from the column before being shot like the first woman, others vanishing into the night.

The truth was more complex than the obvious enemy threat. What the boy saw was the last throes of the Holocaust. There were several concentration camps east of Danzig, a city that had been retaken by the Germans in 1939. At Soldau, ten thousand people were murdered, including the mentally ill or physically handicapped; at Stutthof several sub-camps started in the summer of 1944 to take Jews evacuated from Baltic cities like Riga and Kaunas; a camp was set up in Königsberg in August 1944, on the site of a rail-coach factory formerly run by a Jew. It was the fate of the prisoners evacuated earlier from Stutthof and from Königsberg that Martin Bergau witnessed in January 1945.

The Red Army offensive into eastern Germany began on 12 January 1945. The plight of the East Prussians has often been described: the slaughter, the mutilation and the rapes; the desperate rush west across a frozen landscape; the evacuations from the coast – on a much greater scale than Dunkirk – and the tragedies like the sinking of the *Wilhelm Gustloff*, with the loss of more than 9,400 lives, by a Soviet submarine off Gotenhafen (now Gdynia). Johannes Jänicke accompanied some of his parishioners from Palmnicken to the port of Pillau and felt bitter when saying farewell to them as they boarded the liner *Steuben*. His and his wife's real home wasn't in East Prussia: much more in Berlin or Halle. Why was he staying, Jänicke wondered, in a rare moment of consideration for himself? What lay ahead was either a Russian prison camp or death. In fact his decision saved his life for the *Steuben* was torpedoed; all those whom Johannes Jänicke had seen off were drowned.

The Germans began to evacuate the camps before the Red Army reached them. Many roads to the west were blocked but it was still possible to go east to Königsberg so the winter marches began. Weaker inmates were left dead by the roads, many of them shot. By the middle of January there were probably some seven thousand Jewish prisoners collected in Königsberg – some at the old carriage works, others in a twine factory and a military barracks. The authorities then decided on a final evacuation. On 26 January the Jews who had been brought to the city began the walk to the Samland and to Palmnicken, through the snow and ice, shod in makeshift clogs and wearing only thin blankets and rags. As on the earlier marches, anyone who weakened or fell out was shot or beaten to death with rifle butts.

The column left in the early morning. It moved slowly – and the sky was already darkening, on a bitter, grey afternoon, when a fourteen-year-old girl standing in the street saw SS guards forcing it forward, shooting those who fell out while other guards threw the corpses on to an accompanying lorry. Her description evokes a deadly mime show: an SS man raising his arm, pointing a pistol at the person who then fell, the shots muffled by distance and the stifling fog. The guards were a mixture: three SS officers (of whom the commanders were Fritz Weber and Otto Knott), twenty-two SS soldiers and between a hundred and twenty and a hundred and fifty members of Organisation Todt, slave labourers from the conquered territories – Frenchmen, Ukrainians, Lithuanians, Belgians and Dutchmen in earth-brown uniforms. The army commander of Königsberg, General Lasch, wanted the prisoners out of the city – but the person who had ordered the march was probably the Gestapo district commander, a man named Gormig. The destination – the amber mine at Palmnicken – seems to have been suggested by Gerhard Paul Rasch, the head of the amber works who was based in Königsberg, as an appropriate place for the final executions. It was assumed, rightly, that the Mayor of Palmnicken, Kurt Friedrichs, would cooperate. Later Gormig killed himself.

The march lasted for about thirty miles, through the icy night, past villages with those distinctive East Prussian names: Metgethen, Drugehnen, Kumehnen, Polennen, Kirpehnen, then Palmnicken. About two thousand of the prisoners were killed or died en route and many locals saw the column: among them, a boy solder at the anti-aircraft battery, several children and a subordinate of Hans Feyerabend who was returning from Pillau by horse-drawn sledge after taking some children to the port for evacuation. Two German soldiers, separated from their unit at the front, were making their way west, when they saw the first corpses – obviously Jewish, mostly women and children – then the column. The soldiers asked one of the SS men what was happening, only to find that he didn't speak German; another said that his colleague was a Flemish volunteer and, when challenged about the killing and cruelty, simply said, 'I wish I wasn't here.' At least one of the SS troops was so horrified by it all that he deserted. Two to three hundred corpses were found on the road between Palmnicken and Sorgenau, villages that were not much more than a mile apart.

A few of the prisoners escaped. One, Maria Blitz, watched her sister collapse, saying she wanted to be left by the road – so that she could go to her mother who had been murdered in Auschwitz;

the SS shot her. Maria broke away, in the village of Kirpehnen, and by luck stumbled into the house of the Hoppe family where, after a debate, the old grandmother said they must help the young woman. A doctor came and removed the Auschwitz number tattooed on her arm; she slept in clean sheets ('I believed myself in heaven'), had a bath and was given good food. The neighbours joined in the lie that she was a Pole. Many wanted her to be with them when the Russians came so that they could be seen to have helped a Jew; there were also, she thought later, a few good people among them. German soldiers in retreat streamed through the village, one asking her to marry him, again for protection against the invader – but she was already married. Later, after the Russians came, Maria Blitz went to the new Soviet Königsberg, worked in a bakery and served Germans who pathetically asked for bread.

Johannes Jänicke was away on medical duty, so his wife Eva was alone at the Palmnicken rectory when, after opening the window, she saw footsteps in the snow. The woman who worked in the rectory garden told her that a Jew had knocked at their door but she hadn't dared to help. Another Palmnicken resident, then a child, remembered fifty years later the terrified eyes of a snow-covered Jewish fugitive. Others recalled corpses that lay for days, partly covered by snow, sniffed at by foxes and dogs, encircled by crows.

The director of the amber mine refused to open the mine shaft designated by the authorities in Königsberg for the mass execution. Instead he let the prisoners and their guards into the mine's workshop, out of the intense cold. Hans Feyerabend, the local Volkssturm commander, came later that morning – and the SS commander, Weber, found himself eclipsed. A survivor from an older Germany, reminiscent – with his neat moustache, clipped hair and air of authority – of Elard von Oldenburg-Januschau's pre-1914 world, Feyerabend is remembered among descendants of those who knew him as a fine officer and an estate director who was kind to all his workers – Germans and Poles. Surveying the horrific scene, he declared that not a single Jew would be killed here; there was no question of another Katyń and the prisoners must be properly looked after. Straw was brought in for bedding, and bread and peas for food, cattle were killed to provide beef and the staff of the kitchen in the works canteen were ordered into action. In vain the mayor of the town, Kurt Friedrichs, protested to Feyerabend that there was no point in looking after these people because they were all to die.

'You have,' Feyerabend told the SS commander, 'besmirched the German flag' – and betrayed German military honour by making war on innocent civilians. Asking if he could speak 'man to man', Weber, apparently in tears, protested that he hadn't given orders to shoot, and the murders on the march had been committed by the Lithuanian and Estonian guards. Feyerabend shook Weber's hand as a fellow officer. In that case, he said, the matter was closed; henceforth the prisoners should be well cared for. But the army, or this branch of it, now had a different code. Weber seems to have contacted Königsberg. On Tuesday 30 January Feyerabend was ordered to take a hundred Volkssturm members to the front at Kumehnen. Finding that the commander there had no role for them, overcome by shame as he realized that this had been a ploy to get rid of him – and that Weber's honour did not exist – Hans Feyerabend shot himself. There have been claims that he was murdered, possibly on Weber's orders.

That evening, Mayor Friedrichs summoned a dozen members of the Hitler Youth, including Martin Bergau, to his office. Here he distributed large amounts of alcohol and sent them, with three SS men, to a disused mine shaft near the shore. At the mine, Bergau saw forty or fifty women and girls – Jewish prisoners, shadowy, frail figures who had been herded into one of the crumbling buildings. The SS men ordered these to form up in twos, the commands hard to understand because, Bergau thought, they were in one of the languages of the multi-national victims and guards: Hungarians, Dutch, French and Balts. Two prisoners at a time were led to a hidden side of the building where SS guards were waiting. The Hitler Youth heard the pistol shots. Bergau stood at the end of the line, beside those who had to wait the longest to die; across from him was a classmate, holding a cocked rifle. One woman asked if she might move forward to be with her daughter, so that they could walk 'this last way' together and Bergau granted the request. Those killed that evening were only a small proportion of the prisoners.

The next day, Wednesday 31 January, Hans Feyerabend's body – like 'a fallen oak' – arrived back in Palmnicken on a horse-drawn sleigh, to be taken to the neighbouring village of Dorbnicken, where he had lived. Feyerabend was buried four days later under some trees near his house. There were many mourners, the Volkssturm providing a guard of honour for a burial thought to be appropriate for a German officer and a sportsman: the corpse in uniform, a sword placed beside it in the coffin, his hunting dog shot and laid on the grave which was surmounted by an oak cross crowned with a steel helmet. His widow was told he had been killed in action, not by his own hand. Feyerabend was a conservative nationalist, an officer in the First World War who believed in duty and order, perhaps (as Eva Jänicke thought) initially sympathetic to the Nazis, like Stauffenberg and many of the July conspirators – then shocked by their brutality before becoming another of their victims. It's strange now to read of his funeral – the dead dog, the attempt at a ceremony that reflected military honour – but he was brave during those January days.

That evening, the rest of the prisoners were herded out of the mining company's buildings, having been told that they were to be taken to Pillau to be put on a ship for Hamburg. Crossing some fields, out of sight of most of the village, they were escorted by armed SS guards to the beach, which had been lit by flares. On the sands, the guards chased the victims into the frozen sea, firing at them – not killing all in the darkness, leaving many to die of wounds or in the Baltic, trapped between the ice or pushed under by the guards' rifle butts. Of the seven thousand prisoners who had left Königsberg, probably only fifteen survived. After some days, when the ice and snow had partly melted, bodies appeared on the route of the march or on the beach, many still in the striped clothes of the camps, their number increasing as the sea washed up more.

Three Jewish girls struggled up from the beach the next morning, after the SS men had left. They reached the next village of Sorgenau and sought refuge in a house owned by a farmer called Voss. At first, Voss hid them in the attic but then announced that, with food in short supply, he wouldn't shelter Jews; it would cost him his life if they were found here and he believed in a German victory. The girls asked him to shoot them. He refused, saying others must do it – so they fled, sheltering in a nearby coal store. Voss fetched the police and a dog but the girls were hidden by a neighbour, Albert Harder, first in an empty room in his house, then in a deserted chicken coop and finally in the Harders' house where the couple ran them a bath and gave them new clothes. Voss remained a threat – but the girls survived, claiming to be Poles. They became inconspicuous among the crowds of passing refugees from Memel and the eastern districts already overrun by the Red Army, until the Russians took (or, as one of the Jewish fugitives said, 'liberated') the village ten weeks later. One of them later looked after the widowed Frau Harder in a displaced-persons' camp in Germany. Herr Harder's last words, as he lay dying in a Russian prison, were 'Have you heard anything about the girls?'

It was 15 April when the Red Army reached Palmnicken. Rumours spread that the Jewish corpses washed up on the shore were the result of Soviet atrocities further up the coast, perhaps in Latvia: that the Russians were going to kill five Palmnicken civilians for every murdered Jew. The survivors – who spoke of how some locals had helped them – were surprised to find themselves treated as liberated 'Soviet civilians': a strange liberation for it was followed by desperate conditions that bred typhus and starvation. Most of the guilty – Friedrichs the mayor, Weber the

SS commander – had fled, but some members of the Hitler Youth were sent off to prison where many died. Contrary to expectations – which had been dark given how much German propaganda had trumpeted the Red Army's brutality – retribution didn't take the form of mass slaughter. Instead the Russians forced the women of the village to dig up some two hundred and sixty corpses from makeshift graves with their bare hands. The bodies were then laid out, witnesses were made to tell what had happened and the women faced two machine guns, to show – as a Jewish Red Army major told them in German – how easy it would be to do to them what had been done to the Jews.

Like everyone in Palmnicken, Martin Bergau had dreaded the arrival of the Russians. In fact, before Palmnicken fell, he was called to defend what was left of the Reich. He joined a ship at Pillau, not imagining that this would mean a separation of some five years from his family or that he would never see his younger brother or grandparents again. Captured in April in Mecklenburg, he was taken with thousands of other prisoners east again, first on foot and then by train, the slits in the walls of the cattle trucks revealing the route – the Vistula, Insterburg, Gumbinnen, Eydtkuhnen, then out of East Prussia, through Kaunas, Vilnius and Minsk. The train stopped sometimes for the dead to be taken off. It turned south-east towards Kiev, then north again, past destroyed tanks and transport and lines of wooden crosses crowned with helmets to Smolensk, Wolchow and further north – some of the names familiar to Bergau from the map on which he had stuck flags during the German advance of 1941. At Segesha, the journey ended. They had reached Karelia, a land of forests and lakes and the midnight sun, and were put into blockhouses, on an island with a large paper factory, powered by German machines.

An old lady in the town was kind to Martin Bergau, even though she had lost two sons in the war. She gave him food to supplement the meagre camp rations that scarcely gave sustenance after hard work in the factory or on a collective farm.

Bergau also stole oats, risking his life. Sometimes he was treated brutally but mostly he was favoured because of his youth, even getting more clothing to survive the winter. Deaths from hunger were common, he caught bad fever and was put into the camp hospital, though rumours of a visit by the International Red Cross meant that the food briefly improved. The winter of 1947 passed; there was silence from Palmnicken until 1948 when his uncle wrote that Martin's parents had left for Germany. Bergau realized that what was now a Russian village could never be his home again. He clasped a small piece of amber given to him by another East Prussian prisoner and cried.

The only sweetness was a love affair, with Maruschja, a Russian prisoner, that stifled envy of those who were being sent back to Germany. When he was discharged, Martin Bergau wept again, this time at leaving the girl. On 25 June 1948, he arrived in the new West Germany. Discovering that his parents had settled in Finsterwalde in the communist east, Bergau decided to stay in the west, eventually finding a job that suited his technical skills, with an industrial firm in Ulm. Every March he went to reunions in Cologne of people from the old Palmnicken – not political occasions but overlaid with a sense that those attending had suffered an expulsion from paradise.

The mayor, Kurt Friedrichs, fled west on 15 April 1945, over the Frische Nehrung. Imprisoned by the British until October 1947, he was given a West German pension and lived in comfortable retirement until called to give evidence at Ludwigsburg in 1961 when the contradictions in his self-justificatory statements were exposed. The SS commander, Weber, was also brought before a court, but not until January 1965, in Kiel. Here, on the night of 20 and 21 January, while awaiting trial twenty years after the death march, he killed himself in his cell.

Martin Bergau, a spotless innocent compared to Friedrichs and Weber, also had to live with what he had been involved in during those last icy January days in Palmnicken. He came to think that the organizations of expelled East Prussians set up in the new Germany – together with refugees from other lost provinces, a potent lobby group – had either forgotten or wished to forget this outrage in their portrayal of their pre-1945 home as a lost paradise. In 1991, however, everything changed in his old home; the Soviet Union crumbled, Kaliningrad opened up to the world and Bergau came back to Palmnicken, returning henceforth each year to find that the interpretation of memory on the Russian side had been different. Holocaust victims throughout the conquered territories were buried as victims of fascist brutality, regardless of their religion. Sand took over the graves dug at Palmnicken. When, in the 1960s, corpses surfaced as a result of digging by people looking for amber, they were thought to be Russian soldiers slaughtered by Germans. A memorial stone went up to these Soviet 'heroes' who were remembered each year with a laying of wreaths and a parade.

Martin Bergau persuaded the authorities of the Kaliningrad Oblast that these corpses were Jews. In 1999, the site was restored by young German and Russian volunteers, aided by the German and Russian governments. Supported by Kaliningrad's small Jewish community, Bergau spoke at the launch of the campaign to raise money for the memorial, mentioning Feyerabend and the desecration of his grave in April 1945 by the Red Army. On 31 January 2000, the fifty-fifth anniversary of the massacre, a memorial stone was consecrated on the shore for the victims, with an inscription in Russian and Hebrew.

Martin Bergau's description of the massacre in his autobiography – *The Boy from the Amber Coast* – had been published in Germany in 1994, breaking through the idea of East Prussians as pathetic victims. Faced with what had happened, some refugee organizations sought to blame the Palmnicken deaths on General Vlasov's Russian volunteers who had fought on the German side; only Lorenz Grimoni's former Königsbergers carried an impartial investigation of it in their bulletin, the *Königsberger Burgerbrief*. The massacre showed how long the Holocaust had lasted, how it could even reach a remote village far from any camp or German invasion route, how during the Red Army's hate-filled shattering of the neat German world, another barbarism had remained.

*

The prospect of annihilation was hard to grasp, in spite of all the propaganda about Russian brutality. Arno Surminski's short story, 'Storm in January', starts with a young Königsberg school teacher in January 1945 thinking about summer holidays during the power cuts that herald the arrival of the Red Army. She's sent on war duty to a school near the Lithuanian border – and, after a train journey through frost-covered ruins, she finds a village where the locals still apparently live in a wonderland of sugared apples, hot blueberry soup, huge St Bernard dogs, sleighs on the streets, peppermint tea, bergamot marmalade, warming rum, innocent fresh-faced pupils and fresh milk: the appurtenances of a secure world.

But there's the distant murmur of violence. She learns that the school was burnt by the Russians in August 1914, that a teacher was killed then by the Cossacks; already the deep winter silence is broken by artillery fire, flames flicker through the woods in the darkness and a widow shows her a school photograph of some years before, reciting a litany: 'He is dead, he is dead, he is dead.' No one doubts, however, that, as in 1914, the enemy will be repulsed.

The Jänickes, in Palmnicken, were not so hopeful. Johannes had done medical duty on the eastern front so he knew what was happening. In his absence, Eva had been in charge of the parish and coped with the refugees. By January 1945 over three hundred people were crowded into the rectory and the little church, against a background of what seemed to be an endless sound of rolling wheels in the streets as carts and tractors and lorries passed through on the way west. To her the flight was like the Thirty Years War, with moments of enlightenment, as when a small group who had sought refuge in the rectory made music there one evening. It was at that time that Eva opened the window to see signs of the death march. Some days later she helped to bury some of the victims.

Johannes came back in April 1945, leaving his medical duties to return to his parish. One of the few pastors who did not flee west, he was taken ill himself, spending some days in the small hospital near the church with eczema and furunculosis. The village was dark with fear of what its people could expect, fed by the stories from towns further east that had been captured by the Red Army, a manifestation of the belief in East Prussia as the last bastion of western civilization. The January massacre of the Jews on the beach had been of those whom they had been taught to think of as sub-humans – certainly not civilized.

Refugees were already dying in Palmnicken, from disease and weakness. By 15 April, Johannes Jänicke was well enough to take a service in the church, choosing as his text for the sermon the lines from the Gospel of St John: 'Let not your heart be troubled: ye believe in God, believe also in me. In my father's house are many mansions.' Shortly after the service, earlier than people had thought, after much fighting further east and with Soviet planes swooping over the town to fire on the houses while people sheltered in the cellars, the Russians arrived.

A Red Army sergeant, searching for German troops, entered the rectory, finding instead the pastor in his black Lutheran robes. Jänicke said he had been a hospital orderly and was a priest. The soldier accepted this before searching all the rooms except the bedroom, where Jänicke's field-grey uniform from his time at the front lay on a chair; if that had been found the pastor would have been taken prisoner or, more likely, shot. Later Jänicke wondered if an angel had been standing at the bedroom door.

Others were not so lucky. The rumours turned out to be true; Germans were evicted from their houses, forced to live in cattle stalls or in barns, the men sent off to camps or murdered, the village wrecked. The Jänickes left the church and rectory in May, taking refuge in the abandoned house of the manager of the brick works. On what she thought would be her last day in her home,

13 May 1945, Eva looked at the garden in spring – the apple blossom, the trees in bloom, a sickle moon in the sky – and remembered the many sunlit hours and the laughter of friends. She thought that their life could never be so beautiful again.

23: *The Fall*

In the autumn of 1944, Hans von Lehndorff watched that unfailing event in the East Prussian year: the storks leaving for the south. November gales stripped the trees and snow came before the last Christmas. Extraordinarily, the remnants of the Junker society arranged shooting parties, even celebrations of the New Year.

Lehndorff had moved from Insterburg to work in a hospital in Königsberg. As the Red Army closed in, order and hope began to break down. The parents of his closest colleague and soul mate – a woman doctor whom he calls 'the Doktora' in his diary – killed themselves. News came that the Red Army had reached far into the west, to Elbing and to the Vistula. Königsberg was surrounded; its commander General Lasch had been forbidden to surrender for it had been designated one of Hitler's 'fortress' cities – islands against the enemy, supposed to tie down Russian troops and to await German successes in the west or Germany's much-touted wonder weapon or a Soviet collapse. Wouldn't the capitalists and the imperialists, the Americans and the British, soon fall out with Stalin's Soviet Union, allowing Germany to escape again? By the standards of one of the great gamblers of history, this last throw of the dice doesn't seem too harebrained. A route to the port of Pillau remained open. Lehndorff recalled the Bible's words, 'Pray ye that your flight be not in winter.'

Looting began, in the snow and the frozen ruins. Lehndorff felt that his work was completely of the hour, that the great test had come – 'the Last Judgement' that moved him to sing a hymn in tears of joy. Many still thought that Hitler had lured the Red

Army deep into the Reich to bring about its annihilation. Nazi propaganda insisted that everyone fleeing East Prussia would be back in time for the spring sowing.

In March the thaw came, swans flew over the city and a red deer was seen near the cemetery. People were already learning Russian forms of greeting and one hospital mess had a photograph of Churchill, in preparation for the surrender. Sometimes Hans von Lehndorff amputated ten legs in succession. He and his fellow hospital workers were living, he knew, an ardent life – and he dreamed of a thatched cottage by a wooded snow-covered slope, with Russians moving through dark trees holding torches that flickered below their wild, strange faces. Rumours came that surrender was imminent. Late one night the firing stopped.

On 9 April Hans von Lehndorff saw his first Russians: two soldiers rummaging in a trunk, having dashed a nurse to the ground and broken her jaw. To him, they seemed a lesser species as they took his fountain pen, spurning his shoes – alien short-legged creatures with hands dropped so low that they were almost on all fours like apes, a mob of them squabbling over tinned food in the hospital stores, one weeping because he couldn't find a watch. Their strange growling speech, the way these maddened adolescents threw themselves on women: these were, to Lehndorff, nothing to do with Russia but what happened when mankind abandoned God. This was the old East Prussian fear of barbarism coming from across the border, transformed into horrific reality. Later Johannes Jänicke took issue with Lehndorff's contempt.

*

Alexander Dohna never met the conquerors. In November 1944, he had Christmas at Schlobitten and joined his family in Thuringia for the New Year before returning to East Prussia, surprised by the ease of travel.

The last weeks at Schlobitten were eerily calm. Often alone, Dohna watched others work as if there was no threat and found it almost macabre to ride through the woods and over the fields. Would they never again harvest the crops here or plan the woodland planting or cut the timber? He knew that the house would be a mass of rubble. In January 1945 the place filled up with refugees – strangers, friends and relations on carts, wagons or sledges. A German army officer responsible for art on the northern part of the eastern front – who in 1943, outside Leningrad, had supervised the German dismantling of the Amber Room in Tsarskoe Seloe in order to 'rescue' it – arrived to save the Dohna treasures, but could only take a small number. They failed to find room on one of the lorries for the part of the 'silver' library of Duke Albrecht which had been moved from Königsberg to a house near Schlobitten.

Dohna sent some mementoes of their East Prussian life to his family with the last post – a piece of amber, an old ring, a seal – but these never arrived. He left Schlobitten at 3.00 in the morning of 21 January, travelling by wagon beneath clear star-filled skies to Prökelwitz, his family's other property, across frost-hardened land that was white with powdered snow. Rifles and a telescope lay next to him, the lights were dead in the villages, but all seemed calm, apparently oblivious to the coming destruction. Dohna removed his best hunting trophies and shot his dogs, letting loose the other animals – cows, foals, pigs, sheep – thinking that it would be better for them to die free rather than to starve in captivity. Then briefly he faltered. Should he stay and try to claim neutrality through his family's Swiss relations, putting the Swiss flag above the house? Now the idea that the Red Army would have respected this island of Swissdom seems absurd. Dohna quickly abandoned it.

Elaborate plans had been made for the columns of estate people to meet, from Schlobitten and from Prökelwitz – and the westward journey began, fraught with searches for bridges that had not been destroyed, for places to stay, and with the constant need to jettison baggage. Dohna was proud of the discipline that kept together a party of more than three hundred people. Old people and sick children fell away, babies were born and died on the trek. Historic names – Kleist, Bülow, Thadden, Arnim – sheltered or joined them. Further west, he imagined that they must soon be safe, little knowing that the Red Army would cross the Vistula, then the Oder and the Elbe, and they passed scenes of misery, a breakdown of order – although the freemasonry of aristocrats ensured that they were welcomed in castles or big houses on the route. Nine children died on the journey, all under a year old. The trek consisted of three hundred and thirty people, a hundred and forty horses and thirty-eight wagons and lasted nine weeks, a journey of nine hundred miles. Dohna claims it was the largest group to come out of the east. What made him proud was to have got so many out – a sign, he thought, that even in a terrible crisis the care for what he thought of as his people had held.

Perhaps the most celebrated aristocratic refugee of that winter is Marion Dönhoff, a lone rider – on her foxhunter Alaric, with an old Spanish cross in her saddle bag: a scene that still resonates because of her position in post-war Germany and her bestselling memoirs. Her workers, at the Dönhoff property of Quittainen, not far from Schlobitten, had started out with her before the trek stalled in deep snow; she wrote later that her companions urged her to go on without them. She, the landowner (they said), was the one whom the Russians would kill whereas they, the workers, would be needed to milk the cows, to work the fields and to keep everything going.

In Dönhoff's account, the way westwards becomes crowded with symbols. She saw three wounded German soldiers hobbling across the bridge over the Nogat at Marienburg, near the castle of the Teutonic Knights – and thought this symbolized a passing civilization: the defeated men and herself, a woman whose ancestors had come into what was then an eastern wilderness six hundred years before. When Marion Dönhoff reached Varzin, the Bismarck estates in Pomerania, she found that the widow of the Iron Chancellor's son (who'd been Governor of East Prussia before the First World War) had already had her grave dug in the garden and was supervising the loading of the Bismarck archives on to farm carts for the journey west. Dönhoff stayed at Varzin for two days, fascinated by the reminiscences and the character of this survivor from imperial times as the refugees trailed by outside and an ancient butler served bottles of vintage wine. When her young visitor rode off, the old lady waved a small handkerchief, before turning back into the house to wait for the Red Army and for the death its troops must bring.

Two years later, in 1947, Marion Dönhoff heard in a letter from Friedrichstein what had happened to those who had thought that they would be needed by the conquerors. Many had been shot, others sent to camps in the Urals where most died; those who did stay to work for the Russians became victims of disease or starvation. For Alexander Dohna, however, the old links stayed stronger. At the reunions, held every two years, of those who had come out with him on the trek, it seemed possible to recover, briefly, the old spirit of the place; photographs show large numbers, swelled increasingly by children and grandchildren. On 23 January, only a few days after the trek had left, Soviet tanks reached Schlobitten station – and the big house and the smaller Dohna property at Prökelwitz were both destroyed.

Further east, another landmark fell. Some of the contents of Rominten – the grandiose paintings of stags, the best trophy heads, a few of the statues of deer from the grounds of the lodge – were taken west. Walter Frevert and the foresters decided not to destroy the high seats; with these, he wrote later, there was to be no scorched-earth policy for the enemy should enjoy them. With one of his bloodhounds, Frevert raised the Lieutenant, a fine stag that Göring had hunted only a few days before, and killed it with three shots. It was, he thought, an appropriate farewell to the old Rominten, a determined assertion of the place's identity – with Red Army parachutists rumoured to be landing nearby.

Having sent his family west, Walter Frevert prepared to defend Rominten with his 'fighting group'. Already room had been found for his favourite bloodhound on the special train that

Göring had organized for the lodge's contents – and his luck came again; a knee injury was serious enough to lead to his evacuation to hospital in Berlin, sparing him the final battle when his colleagues were killed or taken into brutal captivity. Frevert's last experience of war was as commander of German forces in The Hague where, the night before surrendering, he dined with a Dutch baron in his 'very tastefully furnished house', staying up late to talk about 'God and the world', consigning these 'to the Devil'. The next morning he waited, 'like a great war lord' with his staff officers opposite the Hôtel des Indes to hand the city over to the Canadian divisional commander.

Released from a prisoner-of-war camp in Holland in early 1947, Frevert established his family near Hanover. He earned money as a night watchman, sold fox skins on the black market, picked up forestry work on some private estates and, by October, was chief of the forestry district of Murgthal in the Black Forest. An investigation began into what Frevert had done in Białowies and seemed to run out of steam; he was classified a Nazi 'fellow-traveller' but could show that some officials had thought him politically unreliable because of his apparent detachment from the movement, although he had been a party member since 1933. What seemed a release from all this came in 1953: the 'dream' position of Oberforstmeister of Kaltenbronn in Gernsbach in Baden-Württemberg in the northern part of the Black Forest.

For Frevert, the east remained unforgettable. Pieces of it had survived: some of the contents of the lodge at Rominten, the trophies, including the head and antlers of the Lieutenant which hang today in the German Hunting Museum in Munich, and the memories of a world that had been built up over centuries. Rominten might have become the Russian Krasnolesye – but, as if to show that at least the name could survive with him, Frevert called his house in Gernsbach, 'Rominten'. Already, soon after his release from prison, he had begun to write about the forest: a description partly of its natural world but also of the people – the grandees, Göring and, more in the shadows, himself. It took a long time; Frevert was determined to be accurate and contacted old colleagues and experts. Post-war letters took ages or didn't arrive and many of the old Rominten team were dead or in Soviet prisons. But he had his old photographs and records. It was, his wife recalled years later, very emotional, a cathartic task.

The end of the book seems to reach furthest into its author's feelings. What he had tried to do, Frevert wrote, was to convey the idealism and achievement of those days in a place that had been German for seven hundred years, shaped by German ingenuity and effort. He wanted to bring back the stags, the elk and the Trakehner horses ('the best horses in Europe'). But this was also an evocation of a lost province: of the wild life in the Memel delta, of the tall pines, of the cattle and the well-worked farms, of the amber, of the university of Königsberg that had nurtured one of the most famous men in the world, Immanuel Kant. Seven hundred years of history had gone after one lost war, he wrote. Frevert's purpose was to prompt memory and also to sustain the belief that this former German land would return to its former people and be rebuilt.

Walter Frevert's old life started to come back. His skill as a dog-handler made him much in demand as a judge of competitions and an adviser to breeders and owners. At the International Hunting Exhibition in Düsseldorf in 1954, the biggest in Germany since the Berlin extravaganza of 1937, he organized a display of old Rominten heads. Frevert wrote of hunting and dog training in magazines and books. But it was the publication of *Rominten* in 1957 that brought him fame. The photographs – of the landscape, the lodge and the trophies, of the pictures by Richard Friese of stags in the wild, of the memorial to the first husband of Frevert's wife (Paul Barckhausen, killed in September 1939 outside Warsaw), of the uniformed foresters, of pine logs burning at night beside dead stags – made the evocation even more sharply nostalgic alongside the clear, occasionally humorous, quietly impassioned writing. To some, the bestseller was a work of fine evocation; to others, it seemed menacing and grim.

In an introduction, a former Freikorps member, National Socialist and hunting official under Göring, Ulrich Scherping set the
tone. The story of the German Rominten, Scherping declared,
was not at an end, though the wrenching change of identity still
brought pain. The loss shown by Frevert must affect even those
who had never known the forest.

*

Rominten, however, was a work of nostalgia, describing a world
very different to what Hans von Lehndorff saw in April 1945
when the Red Army stormed through Königsberg. Lehndorff had
expected a savage horde seeking justifiable revenge before a quick
adjustment to a new world – but the ordeal was much, much
worse. What remained of the German population crept about
like the walking dead, already searching for food. His companion, the Doktora, was assaulted; Lehndorff thought that she had
met the Devil.

Hans von Lehndorff's profession as a doctor saved him at first
for he treated some of the Russians. He and other Germans were
marched in a long column out of the city. Near Palmnicken, he
managed to run away from the column but was recaptured,
ending up with several thousand others back in Königsberg, in the
Rothenstein barracks. Here there was little water, no latrines and
rampant dysentery and venereal disease. Lehndorff joined a small
medical team, wondering what use he was as the Russians seemed
to want all the Germans to die. Some Germans tried to ingratiate
themselves with the Russians as informers, picking out Nazi Party
members. For Lehndorff, his God was the great comfort, even
though it might seem that he had been abandoned – this and the
invaders' strange unhappiness, as if such destruction was morally
doomed.

Lehndorff let his contempt go; the Russians were like children. They were insensitive to noise, yearning for the brightest
possible light or, at their worst, inhuman so that, for him,
everything was permitted to ensure survival: an exciting but, he

thought, a dangerous state for a Christian. With the Doktora, he read the daily watchwords from the Bible. They saw many deaths from starvation – no revolt, just sudden collapse after what seemed like a sense of calm – and other terrible injuries: blocked bowels through eating unripe fruit, extreme gangrene when part of the face falls away, swollen legs from under-nourishment and thirst, huge neck carbuncles infested with maggots, mad patients screaming. Water at first came from the castle pond, now crammed with floating corpses, until a local pump began to work. Abandoned gardens supplemented rations kept to a very low level to starve the Germans to death. Old Königsberg still appeared through the rubble; books were scattered among the rooms of the ruined houses and, in the hospital, a professor read a volume of Bismarck's recollections.

The Doktora had terrible lice. The itching made her desperate, unable to sleep, so she took sleeping pills and died: not, Lehndorff was sure, from suicide. He found a notebook in her Bible and read the words, 'Russia – and there was a time when I wanted to go there. Now it has overthrown me.' Through them, he thought of another text, 'These are they which came out of great tribulation and have washed their robes and made them white in the blood of the Lamb.' By the end of July Lehndorff too was weakening; amid the suffering he recalled the German brutality towards Russian prisoners – 'we imagined that only Asiatics were capable of such a thing.' By October he had recovered enough to leave Königsberg, fearful of rumours of his imminent arrest. He and a sick woman got a lift on a horse-drawn lorry, heading out on the Lowenhagen road, the route to Friedrichstein.

Lehndorff wanted to reach the country districts in what was now the Polish part of East Prussia where he thought conditions might be better and where some of his own family lived. They continued on foot; the woman collapsed and urged him to go on his own across a deserted land, past unharvested corn, mutilated trees, burned-out tanks and vehicles – partly walking, partly getting lifts on more lorries. Eventually he reached what he thought was the new border and ran for it, striking out across muddy forest paths, sheltering in abandoned houses and given food by people who had more than there was in Königsberg. Lehndorff found the railway – he'd been here just after Christmas 1944 – then the line to Mohrungen and felt suddenly brave on a brilliant October day.

An inner voice urged him to go on to find his sister and brother-in-law's house which was still standing. An old man told him that the owners had ridden off when the Russians were almost at the village. Further on, Lehndorff found his aunt in a gardener's cottage on another family property. The aunt told him that earlier she had gone to Januschau in search of Hans von Lehndorff's mother. In Januschau, she had found Russians who had tried to keep her there – but she escaped, took a train back, was attacked in it by a Russian and again escaped to reach the cottage with a sprained foot. The villagers hadn't welcomed her because they'd worked out a way of living with the Russians and the Poles. She said she couldn't complain of the way the Poles had treated her. They had beaten her once yet this was better than what she had experienced with the Gestapo while under interrogation at Allenstein as a suspected enemy of the Reich.

Lehndorff stayed in the house, recovering slowly. He started to practise again as a doctor under the Poles, also organizing services in an empty church. Did he ever have a Polish name, a Polish woman doctor asked? He said that in the Thirty Years War the name Mgowski had been linked to the Lehndorffs – and she got him a certificate that said he was called Jan Mgowski. Over the next sixteen months, he worked in Masuria, travelling on foot or on one of the few trains or by lorry, threatened by Russians and Poles or German informers and locked up briefly before escaping. Being a doctor protected Lehndorff – but increasingly his spiritual survival seemed to depend upon the familiar, strong and immutable landscape and what remained of the historic towns – Allenstein or Osterode, with the Tannenberg monument now a mere temporary phenomenon, crumbling 'like a bad dream'.

24: Hope Deferred

In Palmnicken, under Russian rule, Johannes Jänicke went about his business as freely as he had under the Nazis. He was hit only once by Red Army soldiers – when he tried to stop them from taking his wedding ring. People of all faiths came to his services in the old brick works, including communists. Jänicke walked for miles to other villages, including the seaside resort of Cranz where he preached in a devastated hotel from the text, 'If God is for us, who can be against us?' from the Book of Romans. The service was interrupted by a drunken Russian with a knife. The small congregation responded by singing as loudly as it could until the intruder left.

The hunger became worse, the deaths multiplied, burials took place most days – yet the two sides, German and Russian, grew closer. At the 1946 May Day celebrations, Russians danced with German girls and got drunk, now with less violence. Eva Jänicke recalled how fantasies slightly soothed the suffering – that the Americans had reached Königsberg, that the English paratroopers would come. In the autumn of 1946, the congregation moved back into the church but it was too cold in the winter so the services were transferred to a bakery.

Johannes Jänicke, the only evangelical pastor for miles, enjoyed his long solitary walks to other churches, accompanied at first by a sheep dog which he saw as his protector until he sold it to a Russian to pay for a sack of flour. In the winter, by candle light, he could at least read, once at Easter 1946 declaiming from Goethe's *Faust* in the company of some doctors who had also stayed behind. Jänicke's poverty was complete – with no ration card and daily survival dependent upon scavenging or the help of others; the challenge was to obey the commandment 'Thou shalt not steal'. At times a hopeless lethargy crept over him. Christmas in 1946 felt even more desperate than usual – still with the threat of drunken Russians and those dreaded words, 'Frau komm!' Eventually some verses found on a page torn from a book raised him up: Harlequin singing to the unhappy Ariadne, from the libretto written by Hugo von Hofmannsthal for Richard Strauss's opera *Ariadne auf Naxos*:

> Love and hate and every pleasure,
> Hope deferred and every pain,
> Human heart can bear in measure,
> Once and many a time again.
>
> But bereft of sense to languish,
> Painless, joyless, numb and cold,
> Who can bear such cruel anguish,
> Worse than death a hundredfold.
>
> Rest you from such gloom and sorrow,
> Wake, if but to fiercer pain;
> Live, for joy may come tomorrow,
> Live, and wake to love again.

Eva Jänicke's diary for April 1947 recorded that twenty people had been buried in one week, fifteen the week before – constant deaths from hunger and typhus: quite quick deaths, often soon after the person had come back from work. Whole families had gone. What food there was came from a world before trade or transport – fish from the sea, turnips from the fields, what a garden could produce, trapped animals and birds. But to find and prepare all this needed energy and will; and Eva Jänicke saw how hunger changed people into sullen, base shadows. Reports came of cannibalism in Cranz and Königsberg: men killing a young girl, grandmothers and mothers eating dead children – for starvation destroyed even the mother instinct. Letters came and went, not always reliably, but news did arrive. That was one lifeline.

Towards the end of June, goods wagons came to take the Germans out of what was now Soviet territory – the two hundred and seventy people in Palmnicken who were still alive out of the fifteen hundred who had been overrun on 15 April 1945. The train was to leave very early in the morning. That night, unable to sleep, the Jänickes went to the beach, so taken up with thoughts of what the place had meant to them that – Eva later regretted – they didn't think of the Jews who had been murdered there two and a half years before. Clouds shaded part of the moon and stars glinted over the Baltic for this last glimpse of what she had come to think of as their land, apparently inseparable through the darkness from the gentle waves.

On the slow train, their possessions were turned over by Russian and Polish officials – but this didn't matter. Johannes Jänicke thought of a passage from the Book of Psalms: 'They wandered in the wilderness in a solitary way; they found no city to dwell in. Hungry and thirsty, their soul fainted in them. Then they cried unto the Lord in their trouble, and he delivered them out of their distresses . . . ' As they crossed the Oder at Frankfurt, he sang 'Now thank we all our God', the words taken up by others, echoing through the wagon and out over the river as the East Prussians reached their new home.

Because of their socialist principles, Johannes and Eva Jänicke went to live in their country's Russian zone. He became Provost of Halle and, in 1955, Bishop of Saxony: a central figure in the sometimes fraught relationship between the communist authorities and the Church. Retiring in 1968, three years after Eva's death, he died eleven years later aged seventy-eight in an old people's home in Halle. His memoirs, published posthumously, challenge the account of the last days of German East Prussia written by Hans von Lehndorff. To Jänicke, Lehndorff's *East Prussian Diary*, a bestseller, was too anti-Russian, not grasping the extent of the hatred built up by a war of unsurpassed brutality and racist contempt. Surely it *was* Dostoevsky who had understood the souls of those who had invaded East Prussia. Johannes Jänicke saw them as not only Russian but terrifyingly human in their mixture of demon and angel.

*

Where were you when the Russians came, I ask?

Klaus Lunau, then a young boy, had left in time. He and his mother were on the last train out of Cranz in January 1945, reaching Gotenhafen in a large fishing boat where they boarded the liner *Deutschland* with ten thousand other people, (including four thousand wounded soldiers) bound for Rügen, further down the Baltic coast, and then by train to Denmark. No German town would take them. Klaus's older brother, a soldier, was shot on the Frisches Haff.

So Klaus missed what happened when German troops withdrew from Cranz at the start of February – but he knows the details. For three days the stillness was like that last Christmas before the January offensive – people walking in the cold streets, looking out across the frozen sea (as if in hope of a last-minute rescue ship), trying to find food, knowing that they were no longer protected. Some three thousand had stayed. The 4th of February was colder – 30 degrees below, one of the coldest days – when the 'Ivans' arrived, some on foot, others in tanks or jeeps. Many of the men of Cranz were shot in the streets; the other inhabitants were ordered out of their houses before being marched off to the south-east, five or six miles a day, during which many died. They were left near the old German border. Most tried to make their way back to Cranz, where the women were raped, some many times.

Gerda Preuss was in Königsberg. She came out of a cellar to hear that the Red Army was in the city – and as she walked near the ruined castle, passing some horse-drawn carts, she saw Soviet soldiers coming up the hill towards her, in the silence after the surrender. That evening troops came to the clinic where Gerda worked and ordered the staff out into the street before forcing them, as in Cranz, to march to the edge of the city where they were left without food or drink, forced to take water from puddles or ponds. A week later they were allowed back in to Königsberg. For Gerda, Germany faded quickly. She fell in love with Maria, a Russian woman, and stayed in the new Kaliningrad, with her partner. After 1946, Gerda Preuss, who'd learned Russian before the war, scarcely spoke German again. Before her death in 2008, she probably deserved most to be called the last German in Kaliningrad.

*

The graves remained – and at least those who came afterwards could honour the silence of the dead. To reach the Polish village of Drwęck (until 1945, the German Dröbnitz) you take a back road south-west from Olstynek (Hohenstein) through scrubby land, past a large pond, once a good breeding ground for trout. Probably there are no more than a hundred people in Drwęck – no post office or church, just a small shop and a school. After the war, the population changed; Poles moved in from the east, from what had been Wilna in post-1918 Poland (since 1945, Lithuanian Vilnius) or from the newly Sovietized Ukraine. By the end of the 1990s, the last old Masurian – a survivor from the pre-1945 period – had gone; this seventy-five-year-old woman had moved to Olsztynek. The other East Prussians had left soon after the war.

The German red brick houses remain, as does what is left of two cemeteries: an evangelical one for the civilian dead, the other some soldiers' graves from the First World War. Of the civilian cemetery, only a tree near the centre of the village has survived; but, because of the work of Borussia – a cultural organization that seeks reconciliation through an understanding of the past – the war cemetery is now recognizable as a tribute to the dead of what Poles might see as the former enemy. Volunteer groups – often Germans and Poles working together – have done much of this work since the end of the Soviet empire. It's a contrast to the

1980s when a school teacher was called to Olsztynek by the local Communist Party committee for 'instructive conversations' after he had expressed regret for the dereliction of the old German graves.

In post-Second World War Poland, with its newly changed borders, those coming to the former parts of East Prussia had, theoretically, simply to move into the empty houses of the Germans who had left. The new settlers seem to have formed two groups – those who had followed the Red Army from central Poland in search of a better life and others from the eastern parts that had been taken over by Stalin. Poland had shifted westwards – losing land to the Soviets in the east but, in the west, gaining cities like Breslau (now Wrocław) and Posen (Poznań), previously centres of German history and culture. Little help was given to the new settlers. Many were stranded on slow-moving trains or left at the mercy of a few bureaucrats in what became often little better than a land grab.

In a light-filled modern block at the Warmian-Masurian University in Olsztyn (Allenstein), a professor in the German department takes me into his room where I notice, on the desk, a small bust of Lenin, now no longer an object of threat. We speak of north-east Poland (what had been the old East Prussia) and I say what I've heard – that it's still a poor region. There had been the wrenching change after 1945 – a new identity yet still linked to the past, not like the Soviets' fresh planned utopia in Kaliningrad. After all, Poles had lived here for centuries, as part of Prussia or Germany or the Polish–Lithuanian Empire. The trinkets and plastic armour and imitation battle axes on sale by the Grunwald battlefield told of many more years of engagement than the Russian statues in Kaliningrad of Peter the Great and the Empress Elizabeth or the memorials to the Red Army dead. In Polish East Prussia, the sense of shared history meant that even the old enemy could be assimilated, as in the restored castles of the Teutonic Knights. Since 1989, after communism, a new idea has come – of a Baltic Atlantis, a once submerged and now redis-

The ruins of Königsberg cathedral.

covered city of an all-embracing past: ancient Prussia, Prussia, Polish Prussia, Germany, the Soviet empire, the new Poland of the European Union.

The Professor's pale eyes are humorous behind rimless glasses, most unlike Lenin's cold gaze. There are, he thinks, still some ten thousand people in the Polish part of what was East Prussia who have German origins. After the war there'd been perhaps half a million; then most Germans were expelled and the Polish-Germans (whom the last Kaiser had called 'our Poles') stayed; the decisions were made by communist officials. The expelled people were sent out on trains from 1946 to 1949, often in squalid and brutal circumstances.

This left some hundred and twenty thousand former East Prussians in their old homes, in the new Poland. At first the

German government wanted the Germans to stay; the new frontiers had not been confirmed by treaty and might change again. There was a preponderance of women and old people and children; many others were either dead or in camps in the Soviet Union. German language and culture were forbidden in communist Poland but secret schools and church instruction went on and the ban was unenforceable in private homes. For many, German remained the second language.

In 1972, the Federal German government agreed to fund the costs of Germans who wished to settle in Germany – recognition, perhaps, that the eastern territories had gone. German bastions that remain are the Marion Dönhoff private school in Mikołajki, German classes in state schools, a German House in Olsztyn and publications financed from Germany. Most skilled and educated Germans left. It's hard for the Professor to say this but some of the Poles who came in from the east after the war, in the 1940s, were primitive people.

After 1918, many cemeteries were established in East Prussia, the only part of Germany to have been invaded during the First World War – some large, others with only two or three graves. The modest stones at Drwęck are very different to the huge Tannenberg Memorial that was only a few miles across the fields. In 1918, there was respect for a defeated enemy, with the Russians given similar burials to the Germans; at the cemetery at Olsztyn (then Allenstein) an inscription reads:

Here rest Russian soldiers
Who following the command of their leaders
In battle against the liberators of East Prussia
Met death and
Lie far from their homeland.

But at the end of the 1920s, many of these cemeteries began to be embellished with tall crosses or monuments representing national pride, similar in atmosphere to what the Krügers did at

Hohenstein. To a later generation, this old work was seen as arrogant and a dark memory. In the late 1990s, a German student involved in the restoration of the cemetery in Drwęck asked in his diary: why not let nature take over? 'I ask myself about my connection to the First World War and believe there is none. I feel no aggression against a country or any people as a result of this war . . . Why am I in this little Polish village cleaning up a cemetery?' Wouldn't it be better to be doing something linked to the future? The old lady – the last Masurian in Drwęck, who had moved to Olstynek – expressed herself more trenchantly. 'The Poles must renovate the soldiers' cemetery. That is the rule. After all, the Poles destroyed it.'

Two weeks later, the German felt differently. It *had* been strange to have Germans, Poles and representatives of the expelled East Prussians working together. The descendants of former East Prussians knew much more about the region's history and still showed signs of resentment at the loss. But out of this had come a sense of the land's past, of colours coalescing. To work among the dead, shifting what had been a shared earth, had reconciled the past of these Germans and Poles.

But the old lady, Drwęck's last Masurian, had lived through a time that the students could only imagine. In her German childhood – when Drwęck was Dröbnitz – people had spoken Polish (or Masurisch), talking easily to the Polish prisoners of war who had come as forced labourers, and ethnic divisions were fluid, in spite of Hitler. In November 1945, most of the inhabitants had been told to leave, taking only what they could carry in their carts. Very few of the men had survived the war. The old lady's husband had been shot by the Red Army and the new settlers – from the former Polish east – threw stones at her windows, hoping to drive her out. But she had stayed, with her two daughters, and had been able to work part of a field and get a job at the post office. She'd been worried for her girls, both of whom became teachers, one going to Germany, the other finding a place in a Polish school. The old lady now had no hope of

Polish–German understanding. She couldn't think what these young people were doing in Drwęck.

Her world had gone long ago. Is the new one any better, she asks? Tourists who come to Drwęck would probably think so. The cemetery has become an attraction, not as colourful as the mock ancient battles with people dressed in lightweight armour or the medieval feasts laid on in some of the castles – but useful enough. Often flowers are left on the graves; not long ago there was even talk of rebuilding the Tannenberg Memorial to draw in more visitors and help the region's economy. Not all of the Krügers' stone had gone in the destruction; some was in the rebuilt Olsztyn and Warsaw, even, ironically, in the Olsztyn memorial built ostensibly from gratitude to the Red Army. Today part of this unloved symbol is a car park.

A street in the Polish town of Lidzbark Warmiński – formerly the German Heilsberg and still dominated by a castle of the Teutonic Knights – has had several names. Until the late 1930s, it was Bartenstein Street (to show that it led to nearby Bartenstein), then Adolf Hitler Street, then Lenin Street and now the Polish Bartoszycka Street – a hopeful circle perhaps, for it's now again called after a place rather than a dictator. In March 1946 the last Germans were evicted and the new settlers arrived. The lucky ones came on goods trains with their cows and pigs, others having struggled there on foot or in carts, from the east that Stalin had taken over – now Lithuania or Belarus or Ukraine. They were astonished to find running water in the farm buildings and the solid brick houses, even if some of these had been burned.

In 1945, there was little sympathy for the expelled Germans, after the recent brutal German occupation when some six million Poles had been killed. The evictions had the support of all Polish post-war politicians, communist or non-communist – and by August that year much of the forced change had taken place. The Poles were even more relentless in their persecution of the Germans than the Red Army had been and in some places the Russian soldiers were seen as protectors. By the end of 1945, tens of thousands of Polish settlers from the east had come to the old East Prussia – to towns like Drwęck and Lidzbark Warmiński, often after terrible journeys. The winter of 1946/7, when the changes continued, was as cold as that of 1945/6 and many Germans herded into the railway carriages died on the journey west. Some Masurians managed to stay, like the old lady at Drwęck, because of their Polishness. It was part of the realization of a homogeneous population, mentioned to me several times: without Jews or Germans or Ukrainians – a dream of Poland for the Poles.

Many of the new arrivals thought that they would not be there long because the Germans would come back. Within the new Federal Republic, organizations of former German inhabitants of the eastern lands called for their return and opposed official recognition of the new borders. After 1945, the new Germany absorbed some twelve million refugees from the old east, nine million of these in the Federal Republic or West Germany – ethnic Germans from Hungary, Rumania and Yugoslavia and former German territories like East Prussia. Konrad Adenauer, who became chancellor in 1949, wanted to anchor a peaceful country among its new European allies. But to the expelled Germans, or to their spokesmen, the war was not over; what had happened to them, many thought, was the temporary triumph of the Asiatic hordes. To join NATO, as the Federal Republic did in 1955, was fine – but there should be no recognition of the eastern frontiers or closer links to the communist east. They called for *Heimatrecht*, or the right to one's homeland. Some of the younger expelled people also said that they should not be held responsible for what may have been done by their parents' generation.

One determination was to hold on to memories; to forget would be the ultimate surrender. This could anaesthetize the present through dreams of a fabulous past. In 1983 the poet Gertrud Papendick recalled the Königsberg of her youth, before it had disappeared behind frontiers and closed military zones, so that 'we could find it again, not lost and not damaged, and all as it once was . . .' – an idea made more powerful by its impossibility. Another poet, Agnes Miegel, wondered why God had turned against the land's blameless victims and vowed to keep her old home alive in her work. Hans von Lehndorff acknowledged German guilt. In his new home in the Rhineland in the 1970s, he reflected that Steinort (now the Polish Sztynort) would have been his as a result of the deaths of brothers and cousins, including Heinrich who'd been murdered by the Nazis. If the Germans hadn't been expelled, these tragedies would have made him heir to the park with its four-hundred-year-old oaks, the lakes, the manor house, 'the great wilderness'. All this had been – and (in Lehndorff's heart) still was – his home. Partly because his Christian principles rebelled against the ownership of so much, he didn't want it back – but it remained shining within him.

The German travel magazine *Merian* had an issue on East Prussia in 1953 – when northern Poland and Kaliningrad were both closed to Germans. By then, a salvo of new names had hit the region. Under the Russians, Königsberg became Kaliningrad, Insterburg dissolved into Chernyahovsk, Gumbinnen into Gusev, Tilsit into Sovetsk. The Lithuanians changed Memel to Klaipėda; the Poles turned Allenstein into Olsztyn, Heilsberg into Lidzbark Warmiński and (in a particularly well-targeted assault) Rastenburg, once the town nearest to Hitler's eastern headquarters, into Kętrzyn, after Wojciech Kętrzyński, the Polish nationalist who'd been born with the German name of Adalbert von Winkler. Further west, near the old Danzig (transformed into the Polish Gdańsk), Marienburg, the fortress of the Teutonic Knights, perhaps the greatest symbol of German conquest, became Malbork.

Merian, however, stuck to the old names, as if there'd been no change. The issue was filled with pre-war photographs of Königsberg, Marienburg and other towns – and of the landscape of the lakes, the coast and the Spit. The Tannenberg Memorial, complete against a darkening sky, was on the cover. The first article said that the eastern cities were entirely German in origin; before them there'd been nothing but a barren place. These had, through the ages, often been destroyed. The scarred, vanished world, it was implied, could again be rebuilt.

One *Merian* contributor reached back to a pre-nineteenth-century Königsberg, before industry and new building had defiled it, returning to his own memories of what seemed a dream through the dust and ashes. Another, Agnes Miegel, wrote about her beautiful childhood, on the Kneiphof, the island on the Pregel and site of the cathedral and Königsberg's oldest part. A fortune-teller had once said, while holding Miegel's 'young sun-burnt hand', 'By flowing water, not between flowing waters, were you born. Don't allow yourself to go away from flowing waters.' But there couldn't be any advice in *Merian* on how to get to the places described for the whole of old East Prussia was out of bounds to Germans, completely closed.

Faced by these Cold War barriers, the only reconstruction could be through memory. The flash of brass instruments in the sun during fanfares from the Königsberg castle tower; the trips to the coast; the cosy but hard-working farm life; the lakes, the horses and the forests – much of this was resurrected in publications by the firm of Gräfe and Unzer, once based in Königsberg (where it had run the largest bookshop in Germany) before setting up after 1945 in Munich. So from Munich, books of photographs, calendars, recipes, dialect dictionaries and memories kept the old East Prussia, or a version of it, alive.

*

The Königsberg Museum in Duisburg whose director is Lorenz Grimoni began because Duisburg was Königsberg's godfather city. One way of keeping the old place alive had been to get cards to all the traceable former inhabitants, asking them for their old Königsberg address and where they lived now. The museum still has over three hundred thousand of these cards – once useful, now forgotten. Revival of a kind came with the 1955 celebrations in Duisburg of Königsberg's seven-hundredth anniversary although by then most knew that they would never return. Look,

Lorenz says, pointing at a photograph of people sitting in the tiers of a temporary grandstand – that's the poet Agnes Miegel, a homely-looking woman in a small dark hat known as the Mother of East Prussia.

The Germans weren't the only destroyers and in the museum there are photographs that show the ruins left by the British bombs. Because of this – and the devastation of other German cities – Lorenz's father had objected to the award at Aachen in May 1956 of the Charlemagne Prize to Winston Churchill. Never, Herr Grimoni told his son, would he understand the decision to give this to the destroyer of so much of European culture. Lorenz isn't angry but he wants to penetrate Britain's self-satisfaction about its past. Then he stops. The silence, I sense, holds a new freedom – to speak of matters that wouldn't have been raised even ten years ago. He goes on to say that the expelled Germans had hoped just after the war that they might return. They'd even sent a request to the victorious Allies for the restoration to them of their ancient homeland but, of course, Germany was then the hated nation.

Germany was seen as a monster after the war, because, Lorenz Grimoni says, of the terrible murder of the Jews; this has eclipsed everything else about it. A quarter of old German land and hundreds of thousands of people were lost in the east. But mourning for this loss is restricted to a small group, even within Germany itself – and this distorts what should be a part of the German identity. Terrible things happen to countries – yet most of them can be proud of much of their past; here such pride skulks in secret, as if within a forbidden sect.

When Lorenz went to Kaliningrad in 1991 he wasn't shocked by the desolation as he'd previously visited an aunt in the old DDR, the communist East Germany. The Russians were kind, but Lorenz saw the two memorials in a park near the old castle – both of them in honour of the commander of the Soviet submarine that had sunk the German liner *Wilhelm Gustloff* in 1945, with the loss of thousands of civilian lives. Should such a tragedy be publicly celebrated? There shouldn't be memorials to those, like the submarine commander or to Air Chief Marshal Sir Arthur Harris, the British chief of Bomber Command, who killed civilians, Lorenz thinks. In Kaliningrad in 1991, Lorenz and others had built a Lutheran church – or a good enough temporary one, on an old German graveyard – in three weeks. It had opened with a concert by a choir from Frankfurt. I wonder if he may be hinting at what might have been done if the Germans had had the chance to rebuild Königsberg – as they'd rebuilt their ruined west after 1945 and then (after reunification in 1990) the old communist east, or Mitteldeutschland as my old German teacher had called it.

Think of the vast shadows over East Prussia between the wars, Lorenz says – Bolshevik Russia to the east, a new nationalistic Poland to the south and west. Memel, previously the most eastern town in Germany, went in the Treaty of Versailles – one of the oldest frontier towns in Europe. That was why there was the colossal East Prussian vote for the Nazis. Against this, in the war of memory, he cites the Königsberg liberal tradition. Wasn't it also the city of Kant?

Less popular among the *Vertriebene* (the expelled people) than the obvious magnificence of Kant were sceptical contemporary writers like Siegfried Lenz and Arno Surminski whose not so golden nostalgia darkened the roseate glow. To the poet Johannes Bobrowski, for instance, the dislocation from the beautiful past had come earlier than 1945. Settling after the war in communist East Berlin, where he worked first in children's and then in evangelical publishing, Bobrowski started by writing with conventional nostalgia about his old homeland before creating a mythical landscape in poems of austere beauty that went much further back – to the lost world of Sarmatia, before any western German intrusion, before the Teutonic Knights. For Bobrowski it was the massacre of Jews and prisoners, and the destruction of so much history, which he saw as a soldier on the eastern front that marked the real break with the old East Prussia where different peoples had once lived together – not the defeat of 1945.

Like other West German politicians, Adenauer appeared to court the expelled Germans, giving generous subsidies and saying that the 1937 borders should be restored; privately, however, he doubted the chances of this. What Adenauer wanted was to embed the Federal Republic in the west. A Roman Catholic Rhinelander (not a Prussian), he saw, not entirely regretfully, the eastern territories as lost. But the stridency of the expelled Germans was useful in negotiations with the western allies; listen to these people, see what an explosion of nationalism there might be, Adenauer said, if West Germany is not given more of what it needs or wants. Stridency also made it easier to dismiss the expelled Germans' claims, even if, at election time, all parties courted them. When Michael Wieck, a survivor of the Holocaust, went back in 1992 to Kaliningrad, he heard someone in his tour group say that there was only one person who could change this mess: Hitler. And it's still easy to get some of those who feel they have a claim on Germany's old eastern territories to come out with this sort of thing as they contemplate their loss. Not surprisingly, memories of violence and horror can flare up again across the new frontiers. In September 2003, during a debate about a proposed Berlin memorial to the expelled Germans, Erika Steinbach, one of their leaders, was shown in a cartoon in a Polish paper dressed as an SS dominatrix riding on the back of the pathetic-looking German Chancellor Gerhard Schröder, over the caption 'The German Trojan Horse'.

When the southern part of East Prussia came within their new frontiers, the Poles could think that they were absorbing land linked to Poland for centuries. But the Soviet occupation of Königsberg and the north was different. The renaming of the city – in July 1946 – symbolized more than Russification. Mikhail Kalinin was a grim Bolshevik – one of Stalin's creatures. Kaliningrad meant the transformation of what the new rulers saw as a Prussian militaristic bastion into a Soviet utopia.

At the war's end, after General Lasch's surrender, some hundred and thirty-seven thousand Germans were still in Königsberg, survivors of horrific destruction. Red Army commanders took over the smartest German villas; Gauleiter Koch's residence became an officers' club. That first summer of Soviet possession, the place was in chaos – unharvested crops, no public transport, terror for women, ravaging hunger (with the occupiers suffering almost as much as their new subjects) and rumours of wolves roaming the city. At first the Russians wanted at least some Germans to stay, to teach them how to run the place. German newspapers came out and German clubs were set up, with dances where Germans met Russians. But in October 1947, Stalin ordered the deportation of the German former citizens of Königsberg; by November 1948 the Red Army General in charge was reporting that the exodus was over. A total of 102,125 Germans had left, leaving only a few hundred useful experts who stayed until 1951.

Soviet citizens were encouraged to settle in the new zone, with a free journey, the promise of a home and a period free of tax. Many who came were widows with children, having lost their husbands in the war; often they were horrified by their first glimpse of the ruins – and wanted to leave without getting out of the train. In 1946, some within the new Russian authority believed that the comprehensive destruction made rebuilding impossible, that the ruins should be left as a memorial to the dead of the Great Patriotic War – and stones and bricks were carted off to be used in the repair of other Soviet cities. Then a new symbolism took root, that of a heroic place; Kaliningrad was the final victory; it was also a new fortress, against capitalism and the west. The city must become a revolutionary utopia, representing the defeat of the Prussian military past.

The blasts of propaganda began. *Kaliningradskaya Pravda* declared in 1946 that in the devastated country many districts had seen a harvest 'of which the Germans had never dreamed'. The city centre – the castle, cathedral and university district – was what the Soviets changed most, hollowing out the old Königsberg while leaving whole suburbs untouched. Slowly the settlers, from all over the Soviet Union (including some ethnic Germans), began to arrive.

Stalin had wanted the city as an obvious reward for the Soviet people's terrible sacrifices and also because of its ice-free port on the Baltic. Kaliningrad became the headquarters of the Baltic Fleet, closed to foreigners and as hard to reach as the Arctic wastes. Slowly the soulless avenues and concrete of Soviet planning began to fill the centre, alongside the reproachful ruins. During the 1960s, architects and intellectuals called for the castle to be restored, emphasizing its historic links with Russia through visits by Peter the Great and Marshal Suvorov and the trial there of German Social Democrats who'd helped Russian revolutionaries. Old Riga had been rebuilt by the Soviets, as had the tsars' palaces in Leningrad – and the Polish communist government had rebuilt Warsaw, Marienburg (now Malbork) and Gdańsk; why couldn't something similar happen in Kaliningrad, to show the uniqueness of its past? The castle ruins even featured in tourist posters that encouraged people from within the Soviet Union to come to the Baltic – 'door to the gothic, to jazz, street cafés, the door to Europe . . . ' But the Kremlin of the grey, stifling Brezhnev era ordered the city government to blow up the castle.

To the writer Alexander Solzhenitsyn, however, German East Prussia couldn't be so easily rubbed out. His time there at the end of the war had fascinated him all through his post-war years in the Gulag, not only through its glimpse of a previously unknown west but because he thought that one of the crucial moments of twentieth-century history had happened in Ostpreussen – one of the 'nodal points' in European destiny. To Solzhenitsyn, the August 1914 campaign and the Russian defeat at Tannenberg presaged not only the eventual collapse of the Germans but also the revolution of 1917. In 1945, through the smoke and flames of destruction, he'd seen the arrogance of 'the towers of Hohenstein' – the Tannenberg Memorial to that German triumph. 'Untouched I'll leave you,' he wrote of East Prussia later, in a poem composed in a Soviet prison camp,

'I'll be off
Like Pilate when he washed his hands.
Between us there is Samsonov,
Between us many a cross there stands
Of whitened Russian bones. For strange
Feelings rule my soul tonight.
I've known you now for all these years . . .
Long since a premonition rose,
Ostpreussen! That our paths would cross.'

So it was to Kaliningrad that he went in the summer of 1967, in search of atmosphere for a series of novels about the First World War and the revolution, of which the first volume was to be *August 1914*. This research had an additional fascination as Solzhenitsyn's father had fought under the Russian General Samsonov in that fatal campaign. There was also nostalgia: he wished to revisit where his artillery battery had been in 1944 and 1945. On the way north, they camped out – the Solzhenitsyns and another couple, their friends the Etkinds – the author reciting to them from memory by the camp fire the whole of his poem about the 1944 and 1945 invasion, *Prussian Nights*. It wasn't possible to see all Samsonov's 1914 route through the old Germany – much of it now being over the border in the new Poland. But the woods and marshes and the once-diligently drained fields and towns and villages near Kaliningrad hadn't lost that solid feel that Solzhenitsyn recalled from twenty years before; nor, in spite of its gutted centre, had the city itself where, in the tomb of Kant and the old German houses that remained, the novelist sensed centuries of proud history and bourgeois care.

To Solzhenitsyn, the Prussian past may have been discernible, even dominant; to the first post-war German visitors it seemed virtually dead and some of them, like Lorenz Grimoni and Marion Dönhoff (with her statue of Kant), tried to bring about a tactful resurrection. Two almost simultaneous processes began: a rediscovery of Prussiandom and the further imprinting of a Russian identity. In the Soviet era, it had been thought that the

Soviet triumphalism: the Monster goes up.

ruined cathedral, site of the tombs of early Prussian kings, might become a mass grave for the twenty thousand Red Army troops killed in the storming of Königsberg. Eventually, however, the gothic brick building was restored, partly with German money, to resemble a concert hall more than a place of worship; it was saved partly by Kant's grave. In 1971 the construction of the giant headquarters of the local Communist Party started; frozen in 1981, the building is still unfinished inside, has never been used and is generally known as 'the Monster'. It is inconceivable that it will ever be demolished, not only for sentimental reasons but because of the risk of disturbing its massive concentration of lethal asbestos.

The Monster, however, can be seen from all over the city, dominating the sky line, rivalled in height and presence only by the golden domes and gleaming white towers of the new Ortho-dox cathedral. Both are symbols of Russification, like the statue of Mother Russia, on a triangle between two busy streets off Lenin Square, with one finger pointing at the ground as if to assert possession. More decorous is what remains of the other past that really makes this place unique – Schiller elegant outside the neo-classical theatre, the small plaque to Agnes Miegel on what was once the poet's house, the Käthe Kollwitz relief of her grandfather Rupp near the solemn pillars of Kant's tomb.

25: The Living Museum

Käthe Kollwitz missed the final destruction, dying in 1945, just before the war's end, in a house in Saxony on the estate of a prince who had given her refuge from the bombing of Berlin. A last tragedy had been that of her grandson Peter in 1942, killed, like her son, at the front. Her work – with its emotional call for change and peace and an end to the exploitation of women, its sometimes sweet yet often searing portrayal of motherhood – appealed to many: to the left, to feminists and to the Nazis (whom she loathed). In post-1945 Germany, she was taken up by the communist east, by the Federal Republic and by the reunified state that emerged after 1992; her version of the *Pietà* is at the centre of Schinkel's pavilion – the Neue Wache, on the Unter den Linden in Berlin, which is now a memorial to the war dead and to the victims of Fascism. Her face – serene, only slightly disgruntled – is on the stamps. Käthe Kollwitz is definitely a good German.

Major General Sir Alfred Knox lost his parliamentary seat to Labour in the British general election of 1945. He retired to a pleasant house in Berkshire where he remained uncharacteristically silent, writing nothing more than the occasional explosive letter to the newspapers, until his death in 1964.

Alexander Dohna met up with his wife and children in the west in 1945 and was forced into the Volkssturm before surrendering to the British. He was then arrested for suspected complicity in war crimes in Italy; General Dostler, for whom he had worked, was hanged but Dohna was in jail for only a week. Dohna found it hard in the new Germany and in 1948 went to

Bern, where, because of his family connections, he was given a Swiss passport. From 1950 until 1960 he worked for the drug company Hoffmann-La Roche at Grenzach. These were, he said, the worst years of his life apart from the war. He became involved in attempts to get compensation for loss of property in the old German east, receiving some money for Schlobitten and Prökelwitz but only a tiny fraction of their value. In 1959, he bought a property in Germany, at Lörrach near the Swiss border, and started an express dry-cleaning business helped by his wife and children. From 1961 they lived in Basel where he died in 1997.

Walter Frevert's book about the old Rominten was a success. In 1959 he won the German Hunting Protection Society's literary prize, also becoming a radio and television personality with considerable theatrical talent, if sometimes on the brink of self-caricature. He had already, in 1951, presented a two-hour programme on a Baden-Baden radio station about hunting and its culture to coincide with Hubertustag, the day of St Hubert, the sport's patron saint – and *Rominten* greatly helped this new career. Frevert's reputation prompted the firm Puma to ask him to design a new hunting knife. He took to wearing a monocle and dignitaries came to his home in Kaltenbronn, including the Federal Chancellor Adenauer.

Frevert was apt to adopt a mystical tone when speaking of the forest, of hunting, of the great wild places, of his horror of animals in captivity. He claimed to have found on shooting trips to Africa that utopia where, if he had been younger, he would have lived. As his fame grew so did his propensity to philosophize – to hold forth in an orotund and self-satisfied manner on how hunting revealed man's origins. His confidence and his vanity could be offensive; to invite the former German Chancellor and servant of Hitler Franz von Papen, who'd been tried for war crimes, to shoot at Gernsbach was foolish and incurred open criticism.

Frevert had, he said, four gods – Bacchus (wine), Apollo (music), Venus (love) and Diana (hunting). Certainly great gusts of pleasure seemed to have blown through his life – not only in the liking for luxury but in youthful memories of what had moved him in the old Germany: to have heard Wilhelm Kempff playing Beethoven's *Appassionata* on a moonlit night in a castle with a view of 'the eternal mountains'; or *Parsifal* at Bayreuth, or Shakespeare in the Prince Regent Theatre in Munich; or to have experienced the primitive, never failing, delight of an open fire – 'what luck it is, to be of mankind.' People who knew about his past sometimes couldn't resist taking some of the air out of him. One old Rominten colleague mocked the highly coloured description of the shooting in October 1944 of Frevert's last Rominten stag, the Lieutenant, remarking on how this account neglected to say that the animal had already been wounded some days before by Göring: 'not so much pedal, Herr Oberforstmeister.'

It was Białowies that darkened all this. In 1958, the war-crimes investigator Simon Wiesenthal, who had been involved in bringing Adolf Eichmann to justice, came several times to the forestry offices in Kaltenbronn in 1958 to conduct long interviews with Frevert. The Oberforstmeister had not been mentioned in similar investigations taking place under the Polish and German governments. Further moves were made during the summer of 1962 to reopen inquiries in Poland into what Frevert had done in Białowies. This was a shadowy threat, or background darkness; it's certain, also, that Frevert, with his worship of energy and strength, had a horror of physical failing and had started to feel depressed. His ability to control his beloved dogs seemed to be weakening. A quick death was what he wanted, he said. There may have been shame too: over the suicide of his first wife and what had happened in eastern Poland, a hidden fragility beneath the bombast.

At the end of July 1962, Frevert set out one evening from a hunting lodge in Kaltenbronn with his rifle and favourite blood-hound, Blanka, for a high seat. The next day, when no one had seen him, a search began – and his body was found, the dog sitting beside him, Frevert still clutching its lead. A fatal wound was found, in his left breast, penetrating the heart.

It seemed an obvious suicide although the public, or 'official', line spoke of a hunting accident, perhaps caused by a stumble involving the dog. The funeral took place on 2 August 1962, in Gernsbach on a day of brilliant sunshine. The oak coffin had Frevert's forester's hat on its lid and a covering of leaves and was escorted by forestry officials; the President of the Bundestag, Eugen Gerstenmaier, gave a eulogy. Later, a small pine branch from Rominten was put on the grave and in1964, the forestry directorate put up a commemorative stone to Frevert a hundred yards from where he had been found dead. His widow Heinke survived him until 1997, in old age remembering particularly the Hanoverian bloodhound trials where this legendary figure had been an inspiration. 'How long is it since we had such delightful hunting days together?' she asked a friend near the end.

Hans von Lehndorff resumed his work as a surgeon after the war, settling in Bad Godesberg, marrying Margarethe Countess Finck von Finckenstein, from another Prussian aristocratic family, and having two children. He became a Protestant deacon, declaring that the most decisive event in his life had been his meeting with Jesus Christ through the Lutheran Confessional Church in 1941 and 1942. In 1961, he published his diaries of the last days of East Prussia, which became a bestseller in the new Germany, and gave the profits to religious charities. In an effort to retrieve some of the spirit of what he had known, Lehndorff would take his two sons on holiday to Finland where the landscape reminded him of the old East Prussia. After 1945, because of the deaths of cousins and brothers, he became the notional heir to Steinort, as we have seen. The place was still locked up in the communist system when Lehndorff died in 1987 and is now the property of the company that operates the marina on the lake below the partly ruined house. Germans (but not the Lehndorff family) have tried to reclaim through the courts land that they once owned in the old East Prussia – a process watched with anxiety by the Poles. Some German businessmen had the tentative idea, through lease or purchase, of setting up Steinort as a museum of the old

German presence in the east, envisaging a calm long view (rather than a celebration) of history.

In 1975, the French writer Michel Tournier, whose Goncourt Prize-winning novel – *The Erl-King* – is set in wartime East Prussia, went with Lehndorff to his old homeland. Tournier had never been to the place he'd written about. Expecting a grim landscape, he found, in what were now Polish lands, a bright place of lakes and forests, full of young people on holiday, walking or in canoes or camping – a sign, at least superficially, of a secure new identity. With Tournier and Lehndorff was the proprietor of one of Bonn's grandest delicatessens who clearly looked on Lehndorff as a saint, attending to his needs, sometimes carrying this frail figure whose health had been lastingly affected by his ordeals. The Mercedes in which they travelled was filled with examples of the shop's finest wares, which were given to the people in Steinort (now Sztynort) and others languishing under the grim diet imposed by communist Poland. This was Lehndorff's first visit since the war and Michel Tournier watched with immense sympathy his friend's confusion among the ruined houses and unrecognizable gardens of his childhood, the vanished trees and paths and the overgrown graves.

Soon Allenstein, Rauschen and the Kurische Nehrung, even Königsberg, will be strange names on sepia photographs hung up for the tourists in Polish or Russian hotels or needing explanatory footnotes in history books; soon that wordless sense of what they meant to those who lived there – how they really looked or felt – will be gone, after the deaths of the last people who knew them. The plans for the museum at Sztynort (or Steinort) have, as yet, come to nothing; the Königsberg and East Prussian museums in Duisburg and in Lüneburg go on, but with few visitors. Meanwhile in the Russian Zelenogradsk, or the old German Cranz, some twenty miles from Kaliningrad, Klaus Lunau is the last exhibit in what one might call the region's living museum, now that Gerda Preuss is dead. Having left Cranz as a boy in January 1945, just before the arrival of the Red Army, he now lives there

Hans von Lehndorff in old age.

for at least six months of the year with his Russian wife Valentina, after a career in the West German police, mostly in Bonn.

During the post-war years, Klaus and his fellow East Prussians held annual reunions in the Federal Republic, often thousands gathering to keep the old world alive. In 1995, some fifty years after Klaus's schooldays there, the old pupils of the Cranz village school decided to return to where they had grown up; and the Russian post-Soviet authorities, keen on tourism, encouraged this. Eighteen elderly but skittish Germans came and Valentina (who was one of the interpreters) remembers how quickly they reverted to behaving like children, reincarnations of their 1945 selves. A year later Klaus returned, to have the same interpreter; when his German wife died, Valentina came to see him in his West German home at Langenhagen and they married. Her Russian citizenship allows them to have property in what is now Zelenogradsk (although he has kept a flat in Langenhagen). They both seem very happy in the small yellow-painted wooden house, the neatest residence in the street (someone in Kaliningrad told me, 'You can't miss the German house').

A vigorous man of over eighty, Klaus prefers the climate here to Langenhagen, where he spends less and less time. He finds the East Prussian air cleaner, the skies brighter and, of course, he can smell and see the sea, as in his childhood, although the old pre-war wooden barriers on the beach have been let go and the Soviet times brought some hideous building. He still works very hard, as a contact for those interested in the German past, sometimes staying up all night answering emails, running his own website and editing a journal called *Our Beautiful Samland* that has memories from the diminishing group of former inhabitants and news of what is happening in the region now.

Klaus likes the Russians very much. As a German, he has never had any trouble in Zelenogradsk and has set up a system of life saving here so that tourists in summer are watched from the beach when they swim. He is still stunned by the changes that have taken place since the Soviet Union ended – better shops, better hotels, lively cafés, a sense of joining the world; now Arabs and oligarchs from Moscow buy property in the village. But, strangest of all, he was asked to give a talk about his wartime memories, what Cranz had endured when the Russians came. At the end, several people wept, telling him that they felt ashamed of the Red Army.

Most summer days Klaus swims, still very energetic in his eighties. The Baltic is difficult and dangerous, he knows, with quick currents and undertows – but, after years of practice, he has mastered them. You need to learn, he says, when to let yourself be carried along rather than struggle against the relentless grey water: also when precisely to kick free, when to strike out or to make for home.

Notes

Introduction

i For Arno Surminski on East Prussian mixed blood, see his *Polninken oder Eine deutsche Liebe* (Hamburg 1984), pp. 21–2.

1: The Whispering Past

17 What remains of the German Königsberg is described in Baldur Köster, *Königsberg: Architectur aus Deutscher Zeit* (Husum 2000); Yuri Ivanov, *Königsberg und Umgebung* (Dülmen 1994); and Veniamin Eremeev, *Monuments of Defensive Architecture* (Kaliningrad 2006). For a guide to Kaliningrad today, see Neil Taylor et al., *Baltic Capitals* (Chalfont St Peter 2001).

19 Otto Lasch published a self-justifying account of the siege in *So fiel Königsberg* (Munich 1959).

24 For the House of Commons debate, see Hansard HC vol. 406, 15 December 1944, cols 1477–1578. Also Matthew Frank, *Expelling the Germans* (Oxford 2007), p. 75.

25 'this enormous crime': George Orwell, *Collected Essays*, vol. 3 (London 1968), p. 327.

26 Kant's end features in Manfred Kuehn, *Kant* (Cambridge 2001), pp. 413–22. Also Zinovy Zinik, 'Letter from Kaliningrad', *Times Literary Supplement*, 26 April 2002.

26–27 Alexander Solzhenitsyn, *Prussian Nights*, trans. Robert Conquest (New York 1977). See also Michael Scammell, *Solzhenitsyn* (London 1985) pp. 137–48 for the writer's East Prussian war experiences.

29 See Michael Wieck, *A Childhood under Hitler and Stalin* (Madison 2003).

2: A Frontier Land

34 For Knox on India, see his speeches in the House of Commons: Hansard HC vol. 252, 13 May 1931, cols,1281–2.

34 'A bold raid into East Prussia': The National Archives, FO 371/1218 f.387.

39 See Knox's report. FO 371/1218 f 392-411.

40 'Eastern Germany lies outside the range': Baedeker, *Northern Germany* (London 1913), p. xvii.

44 Typescript of Eulenburg's memoir *Drei Freunde*, in the possession of his descendants at Schloss Hertefeld. I am very grateful to Professor John Röhl for letting me see this.

45 For the photograph of Alexander von Dohna and Mr Konarzewski, see Alexander Fürst zu Dohna-Schlobitten, *Erinnerungen eines alten Ostpreußen* (Berlin 1989), p. 327.

47 The Duke Albrecht manuscript was lot 25, Sotheby's London Manuscript sale 7 July 2009.

49 Diesch's obituary: Walter Pause in 'Nachruf auf Carl Diesch' in *Tübinger Frankenzeitung*, no. 95, July 1957, p. 16.

52 'common error': see 'Prussians aren't Slavs', letter from Professor Charles E. Townsend, *New York Times*, 7 September 1991.

52 '*Kultur*': Fritz Gause, *Die Geschichte der Stadt Königsberg* (Cologne 1968–72), vol 1, p. 5.

56 'meritorious': ibid., vol. 2, pp. 311–13.

56 'Jewish merchants': ibid.

57 For Knox's dispatch, see The National Archives, WO 106/1039.

58 'wonderful' – the start of a 'great adventure': Alfred Knox, *With the Russian Army* (London 1921), 1, p. 40.

58 Gause on changing names: see Gause, *Die Geshichte der Stadt Königsberg*, vol. 3, p. 3.

59 Januschau, lieutenant and ten men: see Elard von

Oldenburg-Januschau, *Erinnerungen* (Leipzig 1936),
pp. 109–11.

61 For Lehndorff in 1945, see Lehndorff, *East Prussian Diary*
(London 1963), pp. 185–249.

3. 'Talent is a Duty'

66 'wept and wept and wept': Käthe Kollwitz, *Die Tagebücher*
(Munich 2007 edn), 1 August 1919, p. 433.

66 'I want to be wild': ibid., 18 August 1910, p. 80.

70 'Don't worry, Mother': Elizabeth Prelinger, *Käthe Kollwitz*
(Washington DC 1992) p. 155.

73 'kitsch': Kollwitz, *Die Tagebücher*, 19 August 1909, p. 44.

75 'weeping, weeping': ibid., 11 August 1914, p. 153.

76 'like Goethe, "I saw the world with eyes filled with love"':
ibid., 27 August 1914, p. 157.

76 'Russia remains': ibid., p. 157.

4: A Polished Helmet

78 'as so many Russians are': Knox, *With the Russian Army*,
vol. 1, p. 46.

79 'I sit like an old woman': Wolfram Pyta, *Hindenburg:
Herrschaft zwischen Hohenzollern und Hitler* (Munich
2007), p. 42.

79 'a polished helmet': ibid.

80 'Tannenberg! A word pregnant': Marshal [Paul] von
Hindenburg, *Out of my Life* (London 1920), p. 92.

80 'I believe your old man may become famous': Pyta,
Hindenburg, p. 55.

80 'We had an ally': Janusz Tycner, *Auf den Spuren von
Tannenberg 1914* (Warsaw 2008), p. 51.

82 For statistics of 1914 destruction, see Andreas Kossert,
Ostpreußen, Geschichte und Mythos (Munich 2007), p. 202,
and Kossert, *Masuren* (Munich 2001), p. 236.

83 Tilsit, 'educated' man and the Lesch story: Tycner, *Auf den
Spuren von Tannenberg 1914*, pp. 75–81.

85 'the position was very critical': Knox, *With the Russian Army*, vol. 1, p. 173.
88 'nodal points': Scammell, *Solzhenitsyn*, p. 730.

5: The Grieving Parents

96 'It is ugly here, very ugly': Hannelore Fischer (ed.), *Käthe Kollwitz: Die trauernden Eltern. Ein Mahnmal für den Frieden* (Cologne 1999), p. 72.
96 'All a fraud': ibid., pp. 72–3.
97 'the English fellow': ibid., pp. 72–3.

6: Ober-Ost

99 'unbearable demands': quoted in F. L. Carsten, *A History of the Prussian Junkers* (Aldershot 1989), pp. 124–5.
100–1 'the worst thing since Tannenberg': Knox, *With the Russian Army*, vol. 1, p. 241.
101 'If ever there has been a Government': ibid., p. 334.
103 'My boy, I am with you': Kollwitz, *Die Tagebücher*, 12 November 1914, p. 175.
103 'faithful': ibid, 26 December 1914, p. 180.
105 'hard, awkward, haggard': quoted in ibid., note to diary entry for 10 July 1917, p. 821.

7: 'Seed corn is not for harvesting'

107 'Russia is a big country': Knox, *With the Russian Army*, vol. 2, p. 569.
108 'a repulsive individual': ibid., pp. 712–13.
109 'This is a type of British officer': quoted in Peter Fleming, *The Fate of Admiral Kolchak* (London 1963), p. 129.
110 'Seed corn is not for harvesting': Kollwitz, *Die Tagebücher*, October 1918, p. 840n.
111 'good and calm': ibid., 6 November 1917, p. 339.
112 'Bravo Hindenburg': ibid., 11 November 1918, p. 381.

8: *East Prussia's Versailles*

115 In 2003, a critic: see Gerrit Walther, 'Rechnerdaten zum Rittergut', *Frankfurter Allgemeine Zeitung*, 20 October 2003, p. 38. The *Simplicissimus* caricature is shown in Dohna-Schlobitten, *Erinnerungen*, p. 21.

117 For the Schlobitten collection, see Dohna-Schlobitten, *Erinnerungen*, p. 21, and also Carl Grommelt and Christine von Mertens, *Das Dohnasche Schloss Schlobitten in Ostpreussen* (Stuttgart 1962), in which Alexander von Dohna wrote the chapter on coins.

118–19 For photographs of little boy and shopkeeper Fürst, see Dohna-Schlobittten, *Erinnerungen*, pp. 10 and 319.

121 'Proletarians of the World Unite': ibid., p. 84.

9: *'Names that are named no more'*

129 'Dodo' refused to give up her religion: for Marion Dönhoff's view, see Kilian Heck and Christian Thielmann (eds), *Friedrichstein: Das Schloss der Grafen von Dönhoff in Ostpreussen* (Munich 2006), p. 79.

130 Marion Dönhoff wrote about her 1989 visit to Kaliningrad in 'Reise ins verschlossene Land oder: eine Fahrt für und mit Kant', *Die Zeit*, no. 36, 1 September 1989.

132 'I didn't cry when I was born': Yuri Ivanov, *Von Kaliningrad nach Königsberg* (Leer 1991), p. 125.

136 August's letters are cited in Marion Dönhoff, *Preußen: Maß und Maßlosigkeit* (Berlin 1994), pp. 8–10.

137 'loved' the place: Klaus Harpprecht, *Die Gräfin: Marion Dönhoff* (Hamburg 2008), p. 91.

10. *A Lost Victory*

142 'Who rules in Januschau?': Oldenburg-Januschau, *Erinnerungen*, p. 208.

142 '"faithful ones . . . hasten to my aid!"': 'Hindenburg's Call to Arms', *The Times*, 18 February 1919, p. 7.

144 For Walter and Johannes Krüger and their design, see Jürgen Tietz, *Das Tannenberg-Nationaldenkmal* (Berlin 1999), particularly pp. 47–85.

11: Fallen Oak Leaves

151 'It is enough': Käthe Kollwitz, *Die Tagebücher*, notes on July 1925, p. 887n.
152 'soulless': ibid., 22 October 1929, p. 645.
154 'Yes, yes': ibid., 14 August 1932, p. 669.
154 'The war was not a pleasant affair': ibid., July 1932, p. 667.

12: The Need for Order

156 'The Russians were just too simple': quoted in review 'An Attaché with the Russian Army', *Times Literary Supplement*, 24 November 1921, p. 759.
157 For Knox's adoption meeting and Desborough speech, see *Bucks Free Press*, 17 October 1924. Other speeches about Bolshevism etc. are quoted in ibid., 24 July and 10 October 1924.
157 'completely uneducated': *Oxford Dictionary of National Biography*, entry for Woodhouse (née Bousher), Vera Florence Annie, Lady Terrington.

13: Kantgrad

165 'the world must make up its mind': 'Kant Bicentenary', *The Times*, 23 April 1924, p. 17.
167 For Duisburg lectures on Kant, see Lorenz Grimoni and Martina Will (eds), *Immanuel Kant: Erkenntnis, Freiheit, Frieden* (Husum 2004).
167 'To brag of one's country': quoted in Isaiah Berlin, *Three Critics of the Enlightenment* (London 2000), p. 181.
168 'I am not here to think': quoted in Isaiah Berlin, *The Crooked Timber of Humanity* (London 1990), p. 223.

14: 'May every discord break against this monument'

169 'The accusation that Germany was responsible': 'Germany and War Guilt', *The Times*, 19 September 1927, p. 12.

170 'who have their stronghold in eastern Prussia': 'The Tannenberg Speech', *The Times*, 20 September 1927, p. 14.

171 'quite attractive': quoted in Andreas Dorpalen, *Hindenburg and the Weimar Republic* (Princeton 1964), p. 432.

171–2 'the affairs of the notorious East Prussian landowner': Horace Rumbold to Sir John Simon in *Documents on British Foreign Policy 1919–1939, 2nd series*, vol. 4 (London 1960), p. 393.

172 'accomplished': 'A Tannenberg Parade', *The Times*, 28 August 1933, p. 9.

173 'When I pursue my memories': ibid.

174 'the last triumph of the old army': 'Hindenburg's funeral', *The Times*, 8 August 1934, p. 10.

177 'where President Hindenburg rests': Baedeker, *Germany* (London 1936), p. xiv.

177 'one of the noblest war memorials': Bernard Newman, *Baltic Roundabout* (London 1939), p. 229.

15: The Great Wilderness

182 'one of God's blessings': Michel Tournier, *The Wind Spirit* (London 1989), p. 109.

188 'like an animal': Hans Graf von Lehndorff, *Menschen, Pferde, weites Land* (Munich 2004 ed), p. 125.

188 'still in order': ibid., p. 153.

189 'sensational': Joseph Goebbels, *Die Tagebücher*, ed. Elke Fröhlich (Munich 2004–7), part I, vol. 2/II, p. 123.

189 'Tolerable': ibid., p. 162.

189 'bold': ibid., vol. 7, p. 289.

190 'Don't worry': Lehndorff, *Menschen, Pferde, weites Land*, p. 262.

190 For the Jewish dentist, see unpublished memoir 4084, Wiener Library.

16: Journey to Irkutsk

193 In the interrogations: *Spiegelbild einer Verschwörung. Die Kaltenbrunner-Berichte an Bormann und Hitler über das Attentat vom 20.Juli 1944* (Stuttgart 1961), pp. 257 and 450.

193 'an unbelievable rabble': Peter Hoffmann, *Stauffenberg* (London 2003 ed), p. 115.

194 'We will meet again': Dönhoff, *Um der Ehre willen* (Berlin 1994), p. 143.

194 Dönhoff, 'Reise ins verschlossene Land oder: eine Fahrt für und mit Kant', *Die Zeit*, no. 36, 1 September 1989.

195 For the September 1962 trip, see Marion Dönhoff, *Polen und Deutsche* (Frankfurt 1991), pp. 27–35.

197 Ivanov's memories of 1989 are in Ivanov, *Von Kaliningrad nach Königsberg*, p. 138.

199 Her writing was strewn: Haug von Kuenheim, *Marion Dönhoff* (Hamburg 1999), pp. 50–2.

17: 'The Terrible and Great Way'

204 'the great error': Anni Piorreck, *Agnes Miegel* (Munich 1990 edn), p. 187.

206 'terrible and great way': Agnes Miegel, *Spaziergänge einer Ostpreußin* (Würzburg 2007), p. 98.

209 A group of Miegel admirers: 'Gedanken an Agnes Miegel', *Königsberger Burgerbrief*, no. 66, Winter 2005, p. 30.

210 'immoral' trade agreement: Hansard HC vol. 197, 25 June 1926, cols 719–20.

210 'It is a system that supported': Hansard HC vol. 234, 5 February 1930, col. 1975.

211 'A communist state': Hansard HC vol. 252, 13 May 1931, col. 1281.

211 'Wake up, England': *Bucks Free Press*, 11 December 1936.

211 'A panegyric on National Socialism': Hansard HC vol. 325, 9 June 1937, col. 1737.

211 'A real contribution to the cause of peace': ibid.

214 'The motto there is': Hansard HC vol. 344, 8 March 1939, col. 2215.

214 'untidy minds': Arnold Wilson, *Walks and Talks Abroad* (London 1936), p. 130.

214 'races, nations': ibid., pp. 154–5.

215 'This is not to ignore': Philip Conwell-Evans, 'Impressions of Germany', *The Nineteenth Century and After*, January 1934, pp. 72–82.

18: *The Prussian Sahara*

218–19 Bobrowski's poetry has been translated into English by Ruth and Matthew Mead in *Selected Poems* (London 1971) and *Shadow Lands* (London 1984) and by Leila Vennewitz in *Darkness and a Little Light* (New York 1994).

219 The gathering was partly to celebrate: Ivanov, *Von Kaliningrad nach Konigsberg*, p. 205–7.

221 'shot to pieces': Newman, *Baltic Roundabout*, p. 206.

225 *Mein Sommerhaus* (1931) has been printed as a pamphlet by the Thomas Mann Museum at Nida.

227 *Königsberger Allgemeine Zeitung* interview, printed in *Wie auf einem Schiff*, ed. Haupt and Urbonienė (Vilnius 2007).

229 'the hounds in the basement': Bernd Erhard Fischer, *Thomas Mann in Nidden* (Berlin 2007), p. 5.

231 'the mish-mash of hysteria': Donald Prater, *Thomas Mann* (Oxford 1995), p. 195.

231 'mongrel of Indian': ibid., p. 196.

232 'after the vicious presumption': ibid., pp. 357–60.

19: *'My dear Jews'*

236 'the active and devoted work': see S. Schüler-Springorum, 'Assimilation and Community Reconsidered: The Jewish Community in Konigsberg, 1871–1914', *Jewish Social Studies*, vol. 5, no. 3, Spring/Summer 1999.

238 'In German one lies': Felix Grayeff, *Migrant Scholar* (Freiburg 1986), p. 8.

238–9 'an even more rigorous eradication': Wieck, *A Childhood under Hitler and Stalin*, pp. 38-9.

242   'I had to die': ibid., p. 123.

20: 'Do you see in the east the brightening dawn?'

246   'Frau komm': Johannes Jänicke, *Ich konnte dabeisein* (Berlin 1984), p. 5.

248   'in China': ibid., p. 86.

251   'Do you see in the east': Martin Bergau, *Der Junge von der Bernsteinküste* (Heidelberg 1994), pp. 20–2.

252   'It is all going to plan': ibid., p. 30.

254   'reckless and hard-hitting': 'Herr von Oldenburg-Januschau', *The Times*, 17 August 1937, p. 15.

254   'It is not for our Germany': Hans Graf von Lehndorff, *Die Insterburger Jahre* (Munich 1991), p. 6.

21: 'The highest pleasure on earth'

257   Göring at Marienburg airport: Dohna-Schlobitten, *Erinnerungen*, p. 176.

259   'A hunter': Andreas Gautschi, *Walter Frevert* (Melsungen 2005), p. 9.

259   'an Eldorado': ibid., p. 16.

262   'the so cool Englishman': Walter Frevert, *Rominten* (Munich 2008 edn), p. 217. There is an account by Nevile Henderson in his *Failure of a Mission* (London 1940), pp. 89–91.

263   'cunning like a fox': Frevert, Rominten, p. 211.

263   'the ticket puncher': ibid., p. 222.

264   'There are animals': ibid., pp. 214–15.

264   'like a little Prince': Gautschi, *Walter Frevert*, pp. 66–7.

265   'hardened generation': ibid., p. 17.

265   'our proud Great German empire': ibid., p. 72.

265   'criminal nonsense': ibid., p. 75.

265   'purposelessness': ibid., p. 68.

267   'an iron silence': ibid.

267   'a very happy pair': ibid., p. 69.

22: *Storm in January*

269 'You are like our mother': Dohna-Schlobitten, *Erinnerungen*, p. 180.

273 Why was he staying, Jänicke wondered: Jänicke, *Ich konnte dabeisein*, p. 114.

274 'I wish I wasn't here': Martin Bergau, *Todesmarsch zur Bernsteinküste* (Heidelberg 2006), p. 33. Other accounts of the massacre are in Shmuel Krakowski, 'Massacre of Jewish Prisoners on the Samland Peninsula', *Yad Vashem Studies* XXIV 1994; Reinhard Henkys, 'Endlösung am Bernsteinstrand'. *Die Zeit*, November 2000, p. 94; Andreas Kossert, 'Endlösung on the Amber Shore', *Leo Baeck Institute Year Book*, 2004; and Bergau, *Der Junge von der Bernsteinküste*, pp.109-14.

275 'I believed myself in heaven': Bergau, *Todesmarsch zur Bernsteinküste*, p. 39.

276 'You have besmirched the German flag': ibid., p. 80.

277 'this last way': ibid., p. 47.

277 'a fallen oak': ibid., p. 164. For a description of Feyerabend's funeral see ibid., p. 113.

278 'liberated': Kossert, 'Endlösung on the Amber Shore', *Leo Baeck Institute Year Book*, 2004, p. 16.

278 'Have you heard anything about the girls?': Bergau, *Todesmarsch zur Bernsteinküste*, p. 129.

282 Surminski's 'Storm in January' is in his collection *Gewitter im Januar* (Hamburg 1986).

283 'Let not your heart be troubled': Jänicke, *Ich konnte dabeisein*, p. 117.

23: *The Fall*

285 'Pray ye that your flight be not in winter': Lehndorff, *East Prussian Diary*, p. 13.

285 'the Last Judgement': ibid., p. 20.

289 'fighting group': Gautschi, *Walter Frevert*, p. 90.

290 'God and the world': ibid, p. 92.

290 'dream' position: ibid., pp. 103-4.

291 'the best horses in Europe': Frevert, *Rominten*, p. 225.

293 'Russia – and there was a time when I wanted to go there': Lehndorff, *East Prussian Diary*, p. 131.

293 'These are they which came out of great tribulation': ibid.

293 'we imagined that only Asiatics': ibid., p. 137.

294 'like a bad dream': ibid., p. 174.

24: Hope Deferred

295 'If God is for us': Jänicke, *Ich konnte dabeisein*, p. 122.

296 'Love and hate and every pleasure': ibid., p. 130. Alfred Ralisch translation (Berlin 1922).

297 'They wandered in the wilderness': ibid., p. 132.

300 'instructive conversations': see essay by Robert Traba, 'Kollektives Gedächtnis und kulturelle Landschaft', in E. Kobylińska and A. Lawaty (eds), *Erinnern, Vergessen, Verdrängen: polnische und deutsche Erfahrungen* (Wiesbaden 1998), pp. 223–35.

303 'I ask myself about my connection to the First World War': ibid.

305 'we could find it again': Martin Kakies (ed.), *Königsberg in 144 Bildern* (Leer 1955) p. 1.

307 'young sun-burnt hand': Miegel, 'Glückselige Kindheit', *Merian*, 6/3, 1953.

311 'of which the Germans had never dreamed': quoted in Elena Tsvetaeva et al., *ArtGuide, Koenigsberg/Kaliningrad Now* (Kaliningrad 2005), p. 38.

312 For Solzhenitsyn's 1967 trip, see Scammell, Solzhenitsyn, pp. 592–3.

312 'nodal points': ibid., p. 730.

25: The Living Museum

318 'the eternal mountains': Gautschi, *Walter Frevert*, p. 133.

318 'not so much pedal': ibid., p. 90.

319 'How long is it since': ibid., p. 155.

Bibliography

Baedeker, *Germany* (London 1936)

——, *Northern Germany* (London 1913)

Beckherrn, Eberhard and Dubatov, Alexei, *Die Königsberg-Papiere* (Munich 1994)

Beevor, Antony, *Berlin* (London 2002)

Beiser, Frederick C., *The Fate of Reason* (Cambridge, Mass. 1987)

Bergau, Martin, *Der Junge von der Bernsteinküste* (Heidelberg 1994)

——, *Todesmarsch zur Bernsteinküste* (Heidelberg 2006)

Berlin, Isaiah, *The Crooked Timber of Humanity* (London 1990)

——, *Three Critics of the Enlightenment* (London 2000)

——, *Vico and Herder* (London 1976)

Bobrowski, Johannes, *Darkness and a Little Light*, trans. Leila Vennewitz (New York 1994)

——, *Selected Poems*, trans. Ruth and Matthew Mead (London 1971)

——, *Shadow Lands*, trans. Ruth and Matthew Mead (London 1984)

Brodersen, Per, *Die Stadt im Westen – Wie Königsberg Kaliningrad wurde* (Göttingen 2008)

Burleigh, Michael, *Germany Turns Eastwards* (London 2001 edn)

——, *The Third Reich* (London 2000)

Carsten, F. L., *A History of the Prussian Junkers* (Aldershot 1989)

Christiansen, Eric, *The Northern Crusades* (London 1997 edn)

Clark, Christopher, *Iron Kingdom* (London 2006)

Davies, Norman, *Europe* (Oxford 1996)

——, *God's Playground: A History of Poland* (Oxford 2005)

Davies, Norman and Moorhouse, Roger, *Microcosm: Portrait of a Central European City* (London 2002)

Denny, Isabel, *The Fall of Hitler's Fortress City* (London 2007)

Dohna-Schlobitten, Alexander Fürst zu, *Erinnerungen eines alten
        Ostpreußen* (Berlin 1989)
Dönhoff, Marion, *Before the Storm* (New York 1990)
——, *Kindheit in Ostpreussen* (Berlin 1988)
——, *Namen die keiner mehr nennt* (Munich 1964 edn)
——, *Polen und Deutsche* (Frankfurt 1991)
——, *Preußen: Maß und Maßlosigkeit* (Berlin 1987)
——, *Um der Ehre willen* (Berlin 1994)
——, *Weit ist der Weg nach Osten* (Stuttgart 1988 edn)
Dorpalen, Andreas, *Hindenburg and the Weimar Republic* (Princeton
        1964)

Evans, Richard J., *The Third Reich at War* (London 2008)

Fischer, Bernd Erhard, *Thomas Mann in Nidden* (Berlin 2007)
Fischer, Hannelore (ed.), *Käthe Kollwitz: Die trauernden Eltern. Ein
        Mahnmal für den Frieden* (Cologne 1999)
Fleming, Peter, *The Fate of Admiral Kolchak* (London 1963)
Frank, Matthew, *Expelling the Germans* (Oxford 2007)
Frevert, Walter, *Rominten* (Munich 2008 edn)

Gardner, Sebastian, *Kant and the Critique of Pure Reason* (Abingdon
        1999)
Gause, Fritz, *Die Geschichte der Stadt Königsberg* (Cologne 1968–72)
Gautschi, Andreas, *Walter Frevert* (Melsungen 2005)
——, *Wilhelm II und das Waidwerk* (Hanstedt 2000)
Goebbels, Joseph, *Die Tagebücher*, ed. Elke Fröhlich (Munich 2004–7)
Grayeff, Felix, *Migrant Scholar* (Freiburg 1986)
Griffiths, Richard, *Fellow Travellers of the Right* (London 1980)
Grimoni, Lorenz and Will, Martina (eds), *Immanuel Kant: Erkenntnis,
        Freiheit, Frieden* (Husum 2004)
Grommelt, Carl and Mertens, Christine von, *Das Dohnasche Schloss
        Schlobitten in Ostpreussen* (Stuttgart 1962)

Harpprecht, Klaus, *Die Gräfin: Marion Dönhoff* (Hamburg 2008)
Haupt, Dirck Roland & Urbonien, Simona (eds), *Wie auf einem Schiff*
        (Vilnius 2007)

Heck, Kilian and Thielemann, Christian (eds), *Friedrichstein: Das Schloss der Grafen von Dönhoff in Ostpreussen* (Munich 2006)

Henderson, Nevile, *Failure of a Mission* (London 1940)

Hindenburg, Paul von, *Out of my Life* (London 1920)

Hoffmann, Peter, *The History of the German Resistance 1933–1945* (London 1996 edn)

——, *Stauffenberg* (London 2003 edn)

Hoppe, Bert, *Auf den Trümmern von Königsberg* (Munich 2000)

Irving, David, *Göring: A Biography* (London 1989)

Ivanov, Yuri, *Königsberg und Umgebung* (Dülmen 1994)

——, *Von Kaliningrad nach Königsberg* (Leer 1991)

Jackiewicz-Garniec, Małgorzata and Garniec, Mirosław, *Schlösser und Gutshäuser im ehemaligen Ostpreussen* (Olsztyn 2001)

Jänicke, Johannes, *Ich konnte dabeisein* (Berlin 1984)

Kakies, Martin (ed.), *Königsberg in 144 Bildern* (Leer 1955)

Knox, Alfred, *With the Russian Army* (London 1921)

Kobylińska, E. and Lawaty, A. (eds), *Erinnern, Vergessen, Verdrängen: polnische und deutsche Erfahrungen* (Wiesbaden 1998)

Kollwitz, Hans (ed.), *The Diary and Letters of Käthe Kollwitz* (Evanston 1988)

Kollwitz, Käthe, *Briefe an den Sohn 1904–1945* (Berlin 1992)

——, *Die Tagebücher* (Munich 2007 edn)

Kossert, Andreas, *Masuren* (Munich 2001)

——, *Ostpreussen, Geschichte und Mythos* (Munich 2007)

Köster, Baldur, *Königsberg: Architektur aus Deutscher Zeit* (Husum 2000)

Krickus, Richard J., *The Kaliningrad Question* (Lanham 2002)

Kuehn, Manfred, *Kant* (Cambridge 2001)

Kuenheim, Haug von, *Marion Dönhoff* (Hamburg 1999)

Kuenheim, Haug von and Kurtz, Hans Joachim, *Ostpreussen, Auf den Spuren von Marion Gräfin Dönhoff* (Hamburg 2007)

Lasch, Otto, *So fiel Königsberg* (Munich 1959)

Lehndorff, Hans Graf von, *East Prussian Diary* (London 1963)
——, *Die Insterburger Jahre* (Munich 1991)
——, *Menschen, Pferde, weites Land* (Munich 2004 edn)
Liulevicius, Vejas Gabriel, *War Land on the Eastern Front* (Cambridge 2000)

MacDonogh, Giles, *After the Reich* (London 2007)
Manthey, Jürgen, *Königsberg. Geschichte einer Weltbürgerrepublik* (Munich 2005)
Merridale, Catherine, *Ivan's War* (London 2005)
Miegel, Agnes, *Es war ein Land* (Würzburg 2002)
——, *Die Frauen von Nidden* (Würzburg 2002)
——, *Gedichte, Erzählungen, Erinnerungen* (Düsseldorf and Cologne 1965)
——, *Ostland* (Jena 1940)
——, *Spaziergänge einer Ostpreussin* (Würzburg 2007)
Mosse, George, *The Nationalization of the Masses* (New York 1975)

Newman, Bernard, *Baltic Roundabout* (London 1939)

Oldenburg-Januschau, Elard von, *Erinnerungen* (Leipzig 1936)
Orwell, George, *Collected Essays* vol. 3 (London 1968)

Palmer, Alan, *Northern Shores* (London 2005)
Piorreck, Anni, *Agnes Miegel* (Munich 1990 edn)
Prater, Donald, *Thomas Mann* (Oxford 1995)
Prelinger, Elizabeth, *Käthe Kollwitz* (Washington DC 1992)
Pyta, Wolfram, *Hindenburg: Herrschaft zwischen Hohenzollern und Hitler* (Munich 2007)

Reed, T.J., *Thomas Mann: The Uses of Tradition* (Oxford 1974)
Röhl, John C. G., *The Kaiser and his Court* (Cambridge 1994)
Roy, James Charles, *The Vanished Kingdom* (Boulder 1999)

Scammell, Michael, *Solzhenitsyn* (London 1985)
Schwarzer, Alice, *Marion Dönhoff* (Munich 1997 edn)
Scruton, Roger, *Kant* (Oxford 1982)

Showalter, Dennis, *Tannenberg: Clash of Empires* (Hamden, Conn.
      1991)
Smele, Jonathan D., *Civil War in Siberia* (Cambridge 1996)
Solzhenitsyn, Alexander, *Prussian Nights*, trans. Robert Conquest
      (New York 1977)
*Spiegelbild einer Verschwörung. Die Kaltenbrunner-Berichte an
      Bormann und Hitler über das Attentat vom 20.Juli 1944*
      (Stuttgart 1961)
Stone, Norman, *The Eastern Front 1914–1917* (London 1998 edn)
Strachan, Hew, *The First World War: To Arms* (Oxford 2001)
Surminski, Arno, *Gewitter im Januar* (Hamburg 1986)
——, *Polninken oder Eine deutsche Liebe* (Hamburg 1984)

Taylor, Neil et al., *Baltic Capitals* (Chalfont St Peter 2001)
Tietz, Jürgen, *Das Tannenberg-Nationaldenkmal* (Berlin 1999)
Tournier, Michel, *Petites Proses* (Paris 1986)
——, *The Wind Spirit* (London 1989)
Tsvetaeva, Elena et al., *Art-Guide. Koenigsberg/Kaliningrad Now*
      (Kaliningrad 2005)
Tycner, Janusz, *Auf den Spuren von Tannenberg 1914* (Warsaw 2008)

Wheeler-Bennett, J. W., *Hindenburg: The Wooden Titan* (London
      1936)
Wieck, Michael, *A Childhood under Hitler and Stalin* (Madison 2003)
——, *Zeugnis vom Untergang Königsbergs* (Munich 2005 edn)
Wilson, Arnold, *Walks and Talks Abroad* (London 1936)
Winter, Jay, *Sites of Memory, Sites of Mourning* (Cambridge 1995)
Wood, Allan W., *Kant* (Oxford 2005)
Wormell, Sebastian (ed.), *Poland* (London 1989)

ACKNOWLEDGEMENTS

This book has relied upon the help of many people, none of whom should be held at all responsible for what I have written.

I particularly thank Antony Beevor; Jan Bielecki; Gottfried von Bismarck; Karl Heinz Bohrer; Governor Georgy Boos; Tessa Capponi; Piet Chielens and Fernand Vanrobaeys of the In Flanders Fields Museum in Ypres; Jan Dalley; Olga Danilova; Norman Davies; Johann van der Decken; Stephen and Irina Dewar; Frank Dombrowski; the late Marion Dönhoff; Vladimir Gilmanov; Anthony Griffiths; Lorenz Grimoni; Christoph von Grote; Neiti Gowrie; Eleonore von Haeften; Max Hastings; Guido Herz; Alexei Ignatiev; Tadeusz Iwiński; Josef and Christine Joffe; Daniel Johnson; Peter and Elfi Johnson; Laurence Kelly; Eduard Kurilovic; Kornelia Kurowski and the staff of Borussia in Olsztyn; Karl von Lehndorff; Krystana Lewańska, the Mayor of Frombork; Irene Lipowicz; Klaus and Vladimira Lunau; Dr Tomasz Makowski, director of the National Library in Warsaw; Dr Władysław Maknut; Keith Middlemas; Stephen Nicholls; Paul Oestreicher; Michael Pakenham; Andrej Portnjagin; Tim Robb; John Röhl; Ernie and Carol Rothkopf; Helmut Schmidt; Angela Schock-Hurst; Xan Smiley; Eugeniusz Smolar; Alexander Songal; Carl Leopold and Margot von Spaeth; Hartmut Pogge von Strandman; Dr Mirosław Supruniuk, director of the library of the University of Toruń; Gina Thomas; Michel Tournier; Vygaudas Ušackas; Stefan Wagstyl; Michael and Miriam Wieck; Henning von Wistinghausen; Magnus von Wistinghausen; Kazimierz Wóycicki; Peter Wunsch; Adam Zamoyski; Rafal Zytyniec.

For much of my research, I have relied on the patient staffs of The British Library, The German Historical Institute in London, The London Library, The National Archives at Kew and The Wiener Library. My agent Gill Coleridge has been most supportive throughout, as have my two remarkable editors: Kate Harvey at Picador in London (who inherited this book but has adopted it with sensitivity and enthusiasm) and Jonathan Galassi at Farrar Straus and Giroux in New York. Peter James has, as usual, been an excellent, probing copy-editor. For loving calm and tolerance at home – and an apparent wish still, after many years, to hear about what I am writing – I owe my wife Caroline more than I can possibly express.

Index